INSTRUCTIONAL STRATEGIES FOR

MIDDLE AND HIGH SCHOOL

INSTRUCTIONAL STRATEGIES FOR

MIDDLE AND HIGH SCHOOL

BRUCE E. LARSON AND TIMOTHY A. KEIPER

Routledge
Taylor & Francis Group
New York   London

Routledge is an imprint of the
Taylor & Francis Group, an informa business

Routledge
Taylor & Francis Group
270 Madison Avenue
New York, NY 10016

Routledge
Taylor & Francis Group
2 Park Square
Milton Park, Abingdon
Oxon OX14 4RN

Printed in the United States of America on acid-free paper
10 9 8 7 6 5 4 3 2 1

International Standard Book Number-10: 0-415-95309-X (Softcover) 0-415-95308-1 (Hardcover)
International Standard Book Number-13: 978-0-415-95309-2 (Softcover) 978-0-415-95308-5 (Hardcover)

Library of Congress Cataloging-in-Publication Data

Larson, Bruce.
    Instructional strategies for middle and high school / Bruce Larson, Timothy Keiper.
        p. cm.
    Includes index.
    ISBN 0-415-95308-1 (hb) -- ISBN 0-415-95309-X (pb)
    1. Teaching--Handbooks, manuals, etc. 2. Lesson planning--Handbooks, manuals, etc. 3. Educational tests and measurements--Handbooks, manuals, etc. 4. Classroom management--Handbooks, manuals, etc. I. Keiper, Timothy. II. Title.

LB1025.3.L367 2007
373.1102--dc22
                                                                              2006022158

Visit the Taylor & Francis Web site at
http://www.taylorandfrancis.com

and the Routledge Web site at
http://www.routledge-ny.com

CONTENTS

v

SECTION 2

INSTRUCTIONAL STRATEGIES

CONTENTS   ix

ACKNOWLEDGMENTS

We acknowledge the important roles many have played in the formation and development of the ideas in this book. Our students and colleagues at Western Washington University, and the many middle school and high school teachers we have the pleasure to work with each year, provided many creative ideas, feedback, and suggestions. Our families have been a continual source of encouragement as we engaged in the writing process. Their encouragement and support provided us with a foundation to get in the proper frame of mind to write. Many reviewers provided feedback on each chapter that challenged us to express our ideas more clearly. The entire editorial team at Routledge has been an excellent source of encouragement and assistance. In particular, the editorial direction of Catherine Bernard shaped our ideas from the start. Angela Chnapko, who took over from Brook Cosby, provided clear feedback that helped focus our writing and revisions.

INTRODUCTION

Instructional Strategies for Middle and High School is designed to be the primary text for secondary education teacher methods courses. These courses typically examine curriculum development, instructional strategies, classroom management, and student assessment. This book prepares preservice teachers for effectively using seven powerful instructional strategies and provides very clear guidelines for writing unit plans and lesson plans. Since effective classroom management and valid assessment techniques are important parts of student learning, we integrate practical ways to manage the learning environment and assess student learning for each instructional strategy. In short, this book is written to help teachers be successful. We define successful teachers as those who help all students learn important facts, concepts, skills, and attitudes. Successful teachers also enjoy this process. We believe teaching is a wonderful and exciting profession, and we hope the pages of *Instructional Strategies for Middle and High School* help excite and empower the next generation of classroom teachers.

WHY THIS BOOK?

As we wrote this book we were mindful of our students: preservice middle school and high school teachers who are enrolled in instructional methods courses. We call these students *aspiring* teachers, because they aspire to become effective in helping their students learn. We frequently notice, however, that aspiring teachers struggle with selecting instructional strategies, and often the strategies they select do not line up with the curriculum. For example, a teacher will decide to lecture because it is efficient, and not because it is deemed the best strategy for helping students learn a set of key concepts; or a teacher will use a simulation or group project to "add some variety" to the day, and not because these approaches will promote student learning more effectively than others. Similarly, decisions about the assessment of student learning, classroom management, use of digital technology, and many other common areas of the classroom are difficult for aspiring teachers to make because each decision is modified based on the content being learned and the instructional activities planned for the class session. Aspiring teachers need guidance as they make decisions, and we believe a book that provides this will be a unique and important contribution to teacher education programs. As a result of these thoughts, we decided to write *Instructional Strategies for Middle and High School*.

LINKING INSTRUCTION, ASSESSMENT, AND MANAGEMENT

Over the course of the text we explore seven categories of instructional strategies. Our decision for including these strategies was informed by conversations with many middle school teachers, high school teachers, and principals. All agree that the seven strategies included herein are most commonly used by teachers, are effective for helping students learn, and are needed for all teachers to understand. By listing step-by-step procedures for using these instructional strategies, this text gives aspiring teachers a deep understanding of each strategy and the tools with which to determine how to best use each with a classroom of adolescents. Along with teaching, beginning teachers often report that they struggle with making valid and authentic assessments of their students' learning. This book provides a concise overview of assessment, and offers many concrete examples of assessments to use with *each* of the instructional strategies. For example, valid assessments of what students learned from a role-playing activity will be different from assessments following a classroom discussion. Appropriate assessments are integrated into each of the chapters for the instructional strategies, with contextualized examples given in order to provide tangible ideas for the reader. We provide examples of unit plans, lesson plans, and rubrics that we have gathered from the many teachers who provided input on this book. In addition to exploring assessments specific to each strategy, we also discuss classroom management within the context of each of the teaching strategies. A common worry for aspiring teachers is how to manage a classroom with thirty students and how to discipline students who are disruptive. We have observed that many student teachers will not try student-centered activities for fear of "losing control" of their students. This book addresses concerns such as these by providing specific classroom management ideas for each of the instructional strategies. Most methods texts we have reviewed do not apply management theory or valid assessments to specific strategies of instruction. *Instructional Strategies for Middle and High School* does, because it is impossible to use a strategy effectively without considering unique management concerns and assessments for each strategy.

All of the ideas presented in this book are theory based, and our practical suggestions are built on extensive examinations of current and long-standing research. In writing this text we have made great efforts to focus on the

day-to-day teaching and learning that need to occur in classrooms because
we want to provide future teachers with the tools to proactively manage their
classrooms and ensure that all students are able to learn. The following ideas
directed our development of the contents:

> Effective teaching promotes student learning of the course content;
> teachers matter!
>
> Students bring diverse abilities, interests, and needs to the classroom that
> the teacher must accommodate.
>
> Teachers need skill with a large and diverse set of instructional strategies
> to help their students learn.
>
> The content students will learn will help determine the instructional
> strategies selected by the teacher.
>
> Each instructional strategy has unique assessments, and teachers must
> closely match the assessment to the strategy if they are to accurately
> and validly know what their students have learned.
>
> Aspiring teachers need tools for developing effective classroom manage-
> ment skills and student discipline strategies. Teachers often forget that
> each instructional strategy presents unique classroom management
> considerations, so part of a teacher education program needs to apply
> management theories to each instructional strategy.
>
> Teaching requires constant decision making. As such, decisions about
> class activities, student discipline, classroom management, and student
> assessment will be better if the teacher engages in a thoughtful deci-
> sion-making process.

THE STRUCTURE OF THE BOOK

Instructional Strategies for Middle and High School is divided into two sections. Section 1 is titled "Contexts of Teaching and Learning," and section 2 is
titled "Instructional Strategies."

Teaching on a Solid Foundation

The four chapters of section 1 explore theories and research about learning
and adolescent development. This provides the foundation for the content of
the book. Teaching extends beyond pure methods and strategies, and includes
areas such as tone of voice, subtexts of curriculum, classroom environment,
and classroom management. This first section describes contextual factors that
all teachers need to consider when planning, teaching, assessing learning, and
reflecting on their teaching, including:

> motivating students to learn
> diverse characteristics and needs of students

differentiated instruction
the use of digital technology
guiding principles for classroom management and discipline
national, state, and local standards
determining classroom curriculum
domains of learning
assessing student learning

Additionally, section 1 presents reasons for course goals and objectives, the components of a lesson and unit plan, and ideas for appropriate sequencing of content.

Seven Instructional Strategies

The seven chapters in section 2 provide ideas for teaching effectively, and will help a teacher provide instruction that is engaging, varied, and most appropriate for the content being learned. In each chapter we provide guidance about the process of selecting classroom activities that are appropriate and based on current ideas from educational researchers and theorists. Each chapter is devoted to a specific type of instructional strategy to allow an in-depth examination and provide step-by-step procedures for implementing the strategy in the classroom. To accomplish this, we very purposefully explore eight areas for each strategy:

1. an overview of the strategy
2. a description of what research has revealed about the strategy
3. step-by-step procedures for planning and implementing the strategy
4. a realistic exploration of the logistical concerns related to each strategy, including benefits and obstacles when using the strategy
5. classroom management and student motivation issues unique to the strategy
6. appropriate assessment techniques to use with the strategy
7. guidelines for deciding if a strategy is appropriate for the content of a lesson
8. opportunities for the teacher to consider how to use the strategy with the content to be taught

We start with instructional strategies that are teacher centered and move to strategies that are increasingly student centered. As mentioned earlier, *Instructional Strategies for Middle and High School* highlights classroom management and assessment as subsections for *each* instructional strategy. This integrates and contextualizes the management, assessment, and learning theories developed in the first section of the book. To help aspiring teachers understand this further, the book contains many examples from a wide range of middle school and high school classrooms. We have also compiled, in appendix E, all seven of the instructional strategies described in the book. It serves as a quick point of reference to help you select appropriate strategies in your classroom.

PUTTING IT ALL TOGETHER

Effective middle school and high school teachers select an instructional strategy for a lesson because they think it will help their students meet the day's learning objectives. Consider this example: If students need to learn the history and context around the development and writing of the U.S. Constitution, why might a teacher use a simulation, as opposed to a class discussion, classroom lecture, or an inquiry-based research project? Might these other strategies be more effective? How will the teacher determine what the students have learned? These questions are not easy to answer, and are a continual part of the teaching process. The strategies that a teacher selects for engaging students require a complex series of decisions that include the learning preferences of the students, the content being learned, the setting of the classroom, assessment procedures, and a teacher's comfort level with a particular approach to leading the class. When a teacher selects an instructional strategy without concern for the content or for student learning, all sorts of problems abound. This text provides clear guidelines for helping aspiring teachers engage in this type of thoughtful and effective decision-making process.

Classrooms are comprised of diverse learners, so we want the reader—the future teacher—to consider how each strategy might allow for differentiated learning. Also, we consider ideas for appropriately integrating digital and computer technology into the lessons. Additionally, each chapter has at least one section titled "Making It Work in Your Content Area." In these sections the reader will be asked to determine how to apply to a future subject area the ideas presented within the chapter. This helps in the process of thinking about teaching a specific content area, and further contextualizes the chapter. We have also found this to be a helpful tool for encouraging student teachers to explore what is taught in middle school and high school, and note the differences and similarities with how subjects are taught on the university level. It is our hope that all teachers will establish classrooms that have a positive impact on all their future students' learning.

1

CONTEXTS OF TEACHING
AND LEARNING

1

LEARNING, TEACHING, AND MANAGEMENT

As a future teacher you will face many challenging tasks. Knowing your students is one important issue; classroom management is another. Understanding the perspectives and backgrounds of your students and community and knowing the content of the courses you will teach all provide opportunities and challenges. In addition, your students are wrestling with their roles in the world, and trying to understand their growing and developing bodies as they leave childhood and become young adults. The purpose of this chapter is for you, the future teacher of adolescents, to consider many issues that surround student learning. By understanding how adolescents develop and how they perceive the world, you will be able to more effectively help them learn academic content, intellectual thinking skills, and interactive social skills. Throughout this book we will return to many of the ideas introduced in this first chapter that pertain to learning, teaching, and classroom management. Our intention is for this chapter to provide a foundation for thinking about your future students that will allow you to develop an increasingly complex understanding of how to effectively promote your students' learning.

ADOLESCENT DEVELOPMENT AND INSTRUCTION IN THE SECONDARY SCHOOL

When you walk down the halls of any middle school you will be amazed at the vast physical differences of the students. Some sixth grade boys and girls look as though they are still in elementary school, and some eighth grade boys and girls would appear to be high school students. Even students who are the same age develop very differently. All adolescents' bodies are going through dramatic physical changes, but they are not necessarily experiencing them at the same time. Your students will differ greatly in their biological, psychological/cognitive, and sociocultural development. The exciting news about this is that opportunities abound when teaching adolescents because of their newly developing cognitive skills, social interactions, and awareness of the world. One fruitful approach for thinking about middle school and high school students is to consider three areas of human development:

1. biological
2. psychological and cognitive
3. sociological and cultural

Biological development considers the influence of the body's physical changes on the adolescent. This applies to learning and teaching because physical changes impact adolescent body size and shape, nutritional needs, mood swings, and the many other changes that are occurring in the body. In many cases your future students will be observers of their own bodies, wondering how changes will affect them. Girls and boys develop at different rates within their same sex, but they are also developing noticeably differently between the two sexes. In sixth grade, girls are often the tallest in the class, and this slowly changes as boys experience growth spurts around the 10th grade. Puberty—with all of the hormonal influences that acompany it—occurs for all students eventually. Mood swings are a huge aspect of hormonal secretion. Not only do moods change, they also are magnified to extremes (e.g., high highs and low lows). The fact that students develop at different rates means you will have some students who are much more physically mature than others. The challenge is to realize that physical development is not linked to social maturity, emotional stability, or cognitive ability. For example, a 15-year-old student may look like an adult, but still have the maturity of a child. Physical changes will affect girls differently than boys (a topic we will explore later in this chapter), and physical changes will affect social, emotional, and academic domains of an adolescent. These physical changes will influence the instructional strategies you choose, the ways you manage the learning environment, your relationships with students, and many other elements of teaching.

Psychological and cognitive development considers how the mind impacts the adolescent. As children grow physically they also increase their cognitive abilities. Thinking skills improve as they develop, and adolescents begin to have cognitive abilities that were only starting to emerge in the fourth and fifth grades. For example, students in middle and high school will become increasingly able to think about possibilities, hypotheses, and abstract concepts. Adolescents gain the exciting ability of introspection, or the abilities to analyze and evaluate themselves and others. Specific theories about how adolescents develop cognitively are examined later in this chapter. The important idea to think about is that your future students have very capable cognitive/thinking abilities. You will help your students enhance these abilities by providing opportunities through which to practice using them. At times this presents a paradox for adolescents and teachers alike. Beamon (2001) suggests several of these contradictions that may be resolved simply with practice in your classroom:

> Adolescents may be technologically "savvy," yet lack skills to organize, evaluate and synthesize data.
>
> Adolescents may be used to fast access of information, yet lack motivation to see a task to completion.
>
> Adolescents may be socially active, yet lack the skills for purposeful social interactions.
>
> Adolescents may be independent minded, yet be vulnerable to peer and societal lures.
>
> Adolescents may be intellectually capable, yet be unpracticed in higher cognitive thinking.

Your classroom becomes an ideal place for developing and refining these cognitive abilities.

Sociological and cultural development receive a tremendous amount of attention when thinking about teaching adolescents because they are closely linked to physical, psychological, and cognitive development. As adolescents struggle with their own identity, they experience a series of identity crises (Erikson, 1959; 1968). These crises are closely tied to self-concept, our ideas/thoughts about who we are. As we make decisions about our identity, we question how we love, with whom we have intimacy, whether we have autonomy and initiative, and the effectiveness of our work ethic. Our culture, ethnicity, economic level, social status, athletic ability, academic prowess, and self-esteem are a few of the many aspects that are part of our identity. They each have a role in shaping our sociological development.

Elkind (1998) suggests that the cognitive and physical development of adolescents puts them sociologically in a time of extreme egocentrism. Children demonstrate this as they deal with an "imaginary audience" and a "personal fable." These two phenomena are initiated in early adolescence, and while we learn to manage them they may never leave us completely. Imaginary audience "accounts for the teenager's extreme self-consciousness. Teenagers feel that they are always on stage and that everyone around them is as aware of, and concerned about their appearance and behavior as they are themselves" (Elkind, 1998, p. 40). The idea of a personal fable stems from their thinking that they are "special, different from other people … [it gives them] courage to participate in many necessary but frightening activities" (pp. 43–44). In addition to creating a sense of invulnerability ("I won't be in a car accident"), the personal fable helps convince adolescents that no one has ever loved so deeply, been so excited, or experienced such emotions as they have. As Elkind summarizes, bringing the fable "in line with reality is part of maturing … only in finding out how much we are like other people, paradoxically, can we really discover our true specialty and uniqueness" (p. 45). The impact of sociological and cultural influences on adolescents, and implications for teachers, will be expanded upon in the coming pages of this book.

Learning

Our adult memories of adolescence can be detailed and specific. However, an adult thinking about her adolescence is very different from the thinking we did when we were actually adolescents. Adult memories of overcoming an obstacle, confronting a peer, interacting with a teacher, or studying for an exam are influenced by the fact that we know how the situation ends. Adolescents are in the process of living out these scenarios without this perspective; they therefore may look at them differently than would adults. When teachers consider how to best help students learn in school, their own memories of school should serve as a guide but not the driving force behind decisions. Certainly, teachers have all been apprenticed by the teachers who taught them. In fact, teachers tend to teach in the manner they were taught (Lortie, 1975). So our memories are useful, but not as reliable as we may think.

It is important for you to think about learning, since that is what teachers help students do in school. Many different theories attempt to understand how people learn. One definition of learning that we find helpful for teachers is provided by Ormrod (2006), who posits that learning is a "relatively permanent change, due to experience, either in behavior or in mental representations or associations" (p. 184). Teachers, then, work with their students to help bring about this change. For example, some suggest that memorizing is not "learning" because it is usually not permanent; it takes rehearsal, and memorized information usually fades over time. Others suggest that memorization is one form of learning because the process has brought about change. More important for you, however, is the realization that your opinion about this will impact the type of instructional strategies you select. If a sixth grade science teacher wants her students to learn the habitats of grizzly bears, she will choose classroom activities that are based on her belief about learning.

Behaviorism is a long-established approach for thinking about learning. According to behaviorists, learning occurs when the overt behavior changes. Over 100 years ago the famous behaviorist experiment by Ivan Pavlov involved a person ringing a bell and feeding a dog. After repeating the stimulus of ringing and feeding, the person rang the bell only. The dog had learned to associate the bell with food, and began to lick its lips in anticipation of food. This idea that behavior (salivating) could be influenced by a particular stimulus (the bell) ushered in the notion of behaviorism. B. F. Skinner believed that an organism's interactions with the world (or the environment) conditions behaviors. In other words, people are continually coming into contact with stimuli. At times these stimuli encourage us (e.g., praise when doing a good job), and at times they discourage us (e.g., punishment). Skinner has suggested that these stimuli shape who we are and what we learn.

The idea that behavior indicates learning is unsatisfying for cognitive approaches to learning. Cognitive approaches attempt to address what is happening inside our brains when we are learning. Jean Piaget, Lev Vygotsky, and other cognitive psychologists investigated how our brains functioned, and not just our behaviors. For example, Piaget believed that the brain becomes increasingly able to learn complex and abstract information as we grow. Adolescence begins in the final years of Piaget's "Concrete Operations Stage." During this stage children organize their thoughts logically and sequentially. Piaget suggests that near age twelve, children engage in "formal operations," where their thought becomes more abstract. They are able to generate abstract propositions, multiple hypotheses, and possible outcomes. Thinking becomes less tied to concrete reality. Vygotsky theorized about a "zone of proximal development" that exists between our current level of understanding something and the next level. To arrive at this next level, we need help. Tutoring, modeling, and guiding all provide examples of how to expand on our current levels of understanding. Current thinking about ideas tied to Vygotsky's initial theory have led to such terms as *scaffolding*, *constructivism*, and *hands-on learning*. These all imply that learning occurs when some additional source provides a support network to promote learning (e.g., in the same way that a scaffold provides support for a building).

The main goal of learning is to promote student achievement. In *How People Learn*, Bransford, Brown, and Cocking (2000) suggest that three findings consistently emerge from "research on learners learning and teachers teaching" (p. 14) to promote student achievement. Below we list these three, and follow each with a brief explanation.

> Students come to the classroom with preconceptions about how the world works. If their initial understanding is not engaged, they may fail to grasp the new concepts and information that are taught, or they may learn them for purpose of a test but revert to their preconceptions outside the classroom. (p. 14)

Students come to classes with a wide range of experiences and prior knowledge. If this knowledge is accurate, then teachers have the opportunity to tap into a wealth of knowledge that comes from these students. (Imagine how a unit on Japanese culture could be enhanced if one of your students had lived in Japan.) Conversely, misconceptions need to be "unlearned" so that students can relearn proper information. (Middle school and high school science students often have a misconception of the moon's orbit in relation to the Earth and the Sun.)

> To develop competence in an area of inquiry, students must: (a) have a deep foundation of factual knowledge, (b) understand facts and ideas in the context of a conceptual framework, and (c) organize knowledge in ways that facilitate retrieval and application. (p. 16)

Researchers have examined the performances and learning of experts and novices in several subject areas. An expert understanding of key concepts facilitates understanding of new knowledge. This allows experts to identify patterns, and note similarities or differences in a manner that novices cannot. Therefore, teachers should be able to teach key concepts and/or facts in depth. These "defining concepts" are important if students are to learn additional ideas and information, and they are important for helping students learn content on their own.

> A metacognitive approach to instruction can help students learn to take control of their own learning by defining learning goals and monitoring their progress in achieving them. (p. 18)

Metacognition, or "thinking about one's thinking," frequently takes the form of an internal conversation. Adolescents can be taught effective internal dialogues that will promote learning. For example, predicting outcomes, explaining an idea to yourself to improve understanding, noting when you do not understand, referring to background knowledge, and using strategies for studying are all elements of learning to be metacognitive. These are not used by all students, and should be taught by the teacher through modeling and other explicit ways of bringing out the hidden/internal voice for the students to observe (p. 21).

Learning Style Preferences

Litzinger and Osif describe learning styles as "the different ways in which children and adults think and learn" (1992, p. 73). Often teachers engage students in a wide range of learning activities in order to provide a variety of learning opportunities. Given our earlier definition of learning, *learning preferences* does not mean that students will learn material differently; it means that students may prefer one type of instruction over another. For example, some students will prefer to work on inquiry or research tasks, others will prefer to listen to a lecture, and still others may prefer to see examples as they hear new information. If you believe that all students have different learning preferences, then you will quickly realize that you have preferred styles, too. The challenge is to teach with a variety of styles, and not solely using the style you most prefer.

Multiple Intelligences

The idea of more than one form of intelligence was developed at Harvard University by Gardner, whose *multiple intelligence theory* suggests that long-standing ideas about intelligence such as the intelligence quotient, or IQ, are limited. Gardner notes that our society tends to value linguistic skills (speaking, reading, and writing) and logical-mathematical skills (number sense and reasoning). People who are "well-spoken," "logical," and "calculated" are highly esteemed. This value might overlook students who have intellectual capabilities in nonlanguage or mathematical areas. Actors, designers, musicians, dancers, counselors, and naturalists may not be valued by some in our society because their capabilities are different. Gardner's multiple intelligence theory (1983, 1999) suggests that there are eight different intelligences, and that these account for a broader conception of what we think about human potential.[1] In a recent keynote address to members of the American Educational Research Association, Gardner stated that he is concerned about educators confusing multiple intelligences with learning styles (2003). Where learning styles are preferences that a learner has in how he is taught, intelligences are learning aptitudes, or ways of thinking about the world around him. The eight intelligences proposed are:

Linguistic/verbal intelligence. This involves abilities with spoken and written language, the ability to learn languages, and the capacity to use language to accomplish certain goals. Writers, poets, lawyers, and public speakers are among those that usually have a high linguistic intelligence.

Logical-mathematical intelligence. This consists of the capacity to think logically, carry out mathematical operations, and investigate issues with a systematic/scientific approach. This intelligence includes the ability to detect patterns, reason deductively, and think logically.

Musical intelligence. This involves skill in the performance, composition, and appreciation of musical patterns. It encompasses the capacity to recognize and compose musical pitches, tones, and rhythms.

Bodily kinesthetic intelligence. This gives rise to the potential of using one's whole body or parts of the body to solve problems. It is the ability to coordinate bodily movements. Gardner sees mental and physical activity as related, since the brain tells the body what to do.

Spatial intelligence. This involves the potential to recognize and use the patterns of wide space and more confined areas. The world around one makes sense because of patterns and organizations that others without this intelligence may overlook.

Interpersonal intelligence. This is the capacity to understand the intentions, motivations, and desires of other people. With this intelligence a person works effectively with others. Educators, salespeople, religious and political leaders, and counselors utilize this intelligence.

Intrapersonal intelligence. This entails the capacity to understand one's own feelings and emotions. With this intelligence a person has a useful understanding of herself and is able to use this information to regulate her life.

Naturalist intelligence. This involves abilities for sensing patterns in and making connections to elements in nature. People with a naturalist intelligence may have a strong affinity to the outside world or to animals, and may show unusual interest in such subjects as biology, zoology, botany, geology, meteorology, paleontology, or astronomy.

Gardner does not suggest that teachers teach to all eight intelligences. He does, however, suggest that teachers will have students who look at the world and understand it in terms of one or more intelligences. The principal implication of this is that teachers should provide a variety of activities that focus on different intelligences. Consider how this might impact you in the classroom. If you were to teach eighth graders in a world geography class, you might have your students read about a particular region in the world (linguistic/verbal), look at a map of that area (spatial), and examine demographic information about that region (logical-mathematical). They could then record their impressions of that region in a journal (intrapersonal) and discuss them in groups of four (interpersonal). What Gardner's theory provides is a challenge for the teacher to help students learn content by thinking about it in ways that benefit the students' strengths.

MAKING IT WORK IN YOUR CONTENT AREA

Along with all of the cognitive developments that occur as adolescents develop is the ability to analyze and evaluate others and themselves. Think of at least one way that you can make use of these emerging thinking skills when teaching your content area. For example, how might a history teacher use students' introspection, analysis, or evaluation abilities when reading a biography of John Adams? How might a chemistry teacher use them during a lab activity?

MOTIVATING STUDENTS TO LEARN

Motivation might best be thought of as a force, or energizer, that helps us accomplish a task. We are motivated by many things, and when we lack motivation we usually accomplish very little. Theories and research about motivation are expansive, so our purpose in this section is to focus on the most salient aspects so that you the teacher can consider how to best motivate your students.

Students will arrive in your classroom with different motivations. Some will have little interest or motivation to attend class, while others will have a high interest in learning your subject. On more than one occasion we have taught high school students who received money from their parents for the grades earned at school (e.g., $50 for an A, $40 for a B, etc.). At the same time, many students will be motivated to simply complete an assignment because they want it to be their best work. As we begin thinking about motivation, it would be interesting for you to consider what motivates you to do various tasks. These are often called *motivating factors*. What factors in your life motivate you? A few might be personal satisfaction, a sense of accomplishment, financial rewards, increased status among peers, or pleasing an instructor/supervisor. These types of motivating factors lead us to consider two different forms of motivation: extrinsic motivation and intrinsic motivation.

Extrinsic motivation is motivation brought on by external factors we believe will provide desirable outcomes, such as praise, a reward, or even avoidance of negative consequences (Pintrich & Schunk, 2002). Extrinsic motivation is a means to an end; we are motivated to do something because the end result will be better. Teachers extrinsically motivate their students in a variety of ways: points for assignments, letter grades, praise for good behavior, assigning after-school detention for misbehavior, allowing free time if students all read silently for 30 minutes, or allowing students to revise their assignment for a higher score.

Intrinsic motivation refers to motivation to engage in an activity because of the satisfaction derived from the activity itself. Students who are intrinsically motivated view the learning process as valuable and genuinely want to understand the content. Teachers are able to encourage intrinsic motivation, though it is more challenging. Researchers suggest that the following types of activities tend to intrinsically motivate learners: challenging tasks that question existing understanding and create a sense of curiosity; tasks where the learner has some control over their own understanding; and tasks that evoke some aspect of our emotions (Lepper & Hoddell, 1989; Ryan & Deci, 2000).

Extrinsic and intrinsic motivation can both be used effectively in the classroom. Although it is important to realize that solely motivating one's students with extrinsic factors may promote learning for the sake of a reward (or for the sake of avoiding punishment), extrinsic motivation is not necessarily bad. For example, most people gain some motivation to go to work for the extrinsic reward of a paycheck. However, teachers need to consider how they might also provide opportunities to promote intrinsic motivation, where students want to learn because they genuinely enjoy the process. Researchers in this area are quick to remind us that motivation is neither intrinsic nor extrinsic exclusively (Pintrich & Schunk, 2002). For example, a student might study so she can receive a good grade and be eligible to play on the basketball team (extrinsic) and at the same time study because the course content is genuinely interesting to her (intrinsic).

While it is important to think about intrinsic and extrinsic factors, as a teacher it is equally important to consider what Brophy calls "motivation to learn" (1998). Brophy describes this as the "students' tendency to find academic activities meaningful and worthwhile and to try and get the intended learning benefits from them" (p. 162). Students who are motivated to learn may not have intrinsic motivation for all tasks, but they see the purpose and value of school. As a result, they are motivated to attend class, think about content, complete assignments, and engage in the activities because they believe that learning will be worthwhile. When you help your students understand how the content and activities are useful and beneficial you promote their motivation to learn. This might be accomplished by modeling to your students your interest in the content, and sharing how you motivate yourself to learn. Creating a classroom environment that exudes your enthusiasm for learning your subject, as well as your interest, care, and concern for your students' learning will both help develop your students' motivation to learn.

"Flow" Experiences and Motivation

An interesting approach for thinking about motivating students comes from a theory of intrinsic motivation called "flow" (Csikszentmihalyi, 1990, 1997). When someone is highly motivated from within, he is in a flow experience. This stems from a general belief that our abilities match the challenge of a task so well that we can simply enjoy the experience. During a flow experience we are unaware of time because we are so involved and concentrated on a task that we are only aware of the present. Additionally, we have confidence in knowing what needs to be done and how to accomplish it. This engagement creates a sense of calm and reward of its own. Most of the people who theorize about flow suggest that people can learn how to create a flow experience. Figure 1.1 below operates on two axes: one is the perceived challenge of a task; the other is a person's perception of his skill or ability to accomplish the task.

Consider how this figure might help you understand motivation and, more important, help you provide appropriate motivating factors for your students. When we perceive that a task presents a low challenge, we will respond with either apathy or boredom, depending on our perception of our skill or ability. If we see ourselves as highly capable, an unchallenging task will bore us. If we see ourselves as having low ability, it will lead us to not care. In contrast, a task that is perceived as highly challenging will promote anxiety (if we do not perceive our abilities or skills as being capable of completing the task), or it will promote a flow experience if we perceive a match between our ability and the challenge (Csikszentmihalyi, 1990, 1997).

This can be directly applied to the middle school or high school classroom in several ways. Low challenging tasks rarely serve to motivate students. According to figure 1.1 below, students will feel varying degrees of apathy and boredom; therefore, one needs to consider how to challenge them. If the task is so challenging that the students believe it is beyond their ability level, then they may be so distressed that they cannot complete the task. Students

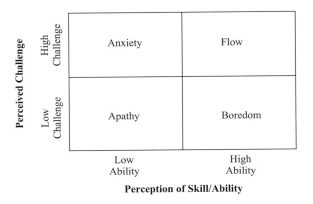

Figure 1.1

also need help in their perceptions. Tasks may appear too difficult when focus is only on the final product. However, when the task is broken into smaller, sequential activities, it becomes more manageable. Likewise, students may at first perceive themselves as lacking sufficient skill for a task. Often with proper modeling or "scaffolding" the students learn that they do have the skills after all. Consider the following examples, and possible ideas for moving students closer to a flow experience.

Boredom. A student who is an advanced reader may show little interest in reading an assigned book that is far below her reading level. She appears bored because the challenge is far below her ability. If the reading task is made more challenging, boredom will be less of a problem.

Anxiety. A shy student may decide to skip class on the day he is scheduled to make a 10-minute presentation to the class, because the stress of standing in front and talking is too great. If the student is coached on how to present, given opportunities to practice, or even allowed to present privately on videotape, he may perceive his ability to be more aligned with the task.

Apathy. A student in an art class may simply give up if he cannot accomplish the first drawing assignment of the year. He thinks that he will never be able to do well in the class, because he has such difficulty with the easiest task. If the teacher expresses her own challenges with drawing, and some of the strategies she has come up with, she provides a model of how to work through problems. If the student is provided with opportunities to practice on specific areas and master those areas he may see his skills improving.

Flow. A low-achieving student who loves to work on the computer is able to provide technical support to her classmates as they develop their personal websites. Classmates' challenges become her opportunities to see how well she can solve problems, and it makes her happy when others begin to rely on her to help with the assignment.

You will not be able to motivate all of your students for every task, but if you think of their motivation in these terms it will help you focus your effort to help them.

Self-Efficacy and Locus of Control

Self-efficacy is our expectation or belief about what we can accomplish as a result of our efforts. This in turn influences our willingness to attempt tasks, and what our expectations are (Dacey, Kenny, & Margolis, 2004, p. 173). Bandura has researched efficacy extensively, and his ideas can be directly applied to the expectations you might have for your future students:

Self-efficacy beliefs determine how people feel, think, motivate themselves and behave. ... A strong sense of efficacy enhances human accomplishment and personal well-being in many ways. People with high assurance in their capabilities approach difficult tasks as challenges to be mastered rather than as threats to be avoided. In contrast, people who doubt their capabilities shy away from difficult tasks which they view as personal threats. They have low aspirations and weak commitment to the goals they choose to pursue. When faced with difficult tasks, they dwell on their personal deficiencies, on the obstacles they will encounter, and all kinds of adverse outcomes rather than concentrate on how to perform successfully. (Bandura, 1994, p. 71)

Self-efficacy is developed through a wide range of factors, including family, peers, cognitive ability, and previous experiences. As a teacher you can work to increase a sense of self-efficacy by modeling successful strategies for students, providing opportunities for success, and helping your students develop strategies for overcoming obstacles. Similar to self-efficacy is the idea of *locus of control*. This is a concept that examines how much control people believe they have over events in their life. If you attribute success or failure to forces beyond your control (for example, you believe you were "just lucky," or "not sure why you failed") you express an *external* locus (location) of control. If you attribute your behavior to forces you can control (for example, you "studied hard for the test," or "won because of practicing") you have an *internal* locus of control. As a teacher, opportunities to help your students develop internal attributions will be beneficial, since control over their achievements/behavior will be from themselves and not from unpredictable outside forces.

MAKING IT WORK IN YOUR CONTENT AREA

Partner with someone who will teach in the same content area as you. Generate examples of how students might behave in your classroom for each of the four student behaviors proposed on Csikszentmihalyi's flow (figure 1.1). For example, how might a student be apathetic in a geometry class, and how would he then behave? How might a student be anxious, bored, or in flow? For the three behaviors other than flow (apathy, anxiety, and boredom), come up with at least one approach through which you could modify either the student's perception of his skill, or the perception of the difficulty level of the task.

DIVERSE CHARACTERISTICS AND NEEDS OF MIDDLE SCHOOL AND HIGH SCHOOL STUDENTS

Your future classrooms will have students who are very diverse. When considering some of the ways in which students might be different from one another, the following provides an adequate but incomplete list: students will have different cultures, ethnicities, primary languages, economic backgrounds, religions, family structures, physical abilities, and learning abilities. These differences are not exclusive, either. For example, some students who are English-language learners are also gifted, and some will have physical disabilities. In this section we will examine several aspects of diversity in your future students so that we can establish several key ideas. The diversity of your students needs to be considered (and embraced) whenever you plan lessons and activities. As a result, we will revisit this topic very specifically when the instructional strategies are examined in section 2 of this book. Your students will learn best when you are informed about their interests, ability and readiness levels, learning preferences, and other areas of their lives that allow you to maximize their specific learning potential (Tomlinson, 2004). As with any examination of adolescents, a caveat needs to be in place about exploring student diversity: generalizations about any group are not intended to create stereotypes. Since there are not universally applicable generalizations about teaching adolescents, it will be up to you to get to know your students as individuals. Diversity is a characteristic of your future students that should be enjoyed and considered for the range of ideas, viewpoints, and experiences that it will provide.

Ethnic and Cultural Diversity

A common term closely tied to diversity is *multicultural education*, which Banks and Banks define as follows:

> Multicultural education is a field of study and an emerging discipline whose major aim is to create equal educational opportunities for students from diverse racial, ethnic, social-class, and cultural groups. One of its important goals is to help all students to acquire the knowledge, attitudes, and skills needed to function effectively in a pluralistic democratic society and to interact, negotiate, and communicate with peoples from diverse groups in order to create a civic and moral community that works for the common good ... *consequently, we may define multicultural education as a field of study designed to increase educational equity for all students that incorporates, for this purpose, content, concepts, principles, theories, and paradigms from history, the social and behavioral sciences, and particularly from ethnic studies and women studies.* (Banks & Banks, 1995, pp. xi–xii; emphasis added)

One implication of this definition is that multicultural education moves students' stories and experiences into the school curriculum. Instead of feeling as though they are not a part of the school and curriculum (often referred to as being "marginalized"), students from ethnic minority groups see their culture, history, and perspectives incorporated into the standard curriculum. In addition, students in the "dominant culture," or the culture of the social or political group that holds the most power in a school and community, need to learn about and embrace stories, cultures, and experiences that are not the same as their own. Ladson-Billings has called teaching with students' culture and background in mind "culturally relevant teaching" (1995). An excellent place to read a summary of culturally relevant teaching is at the website of the Education Alliance at Brown University.[2] For example, the Education Alliance suggests seven principles for meeting the needs of ethnically and culturally diverse learners. Our summary of these principles are represented in the following overview.

PRINCIPLES FOR MEETING THE NEEDS OF ETHNICALLY AND CULTURALLY DIVERSE LEARNERS

1. **Positive Perspectives on Parents and Families:** Parent involvement should not be limited to participation in school functions. Often, religious and cultural differences preclude active participation in school activities. However, parental involvement also includes how parents communicate high expectations, pride, and interest in their child's academic life (Nieto, 1996). Teachers should try to understand the parents of their students, because that will often provide insight into the student at school. This requires communication with parents through such avenues as phone calls and e-mail, school visits from the parent, home visits from the teacher, and even informal conversations at community events. Additionally, teachers can help inform parents of the various social and academic services offered by the school and by organizations associated with the school. If you have not had experience with the culture of a parent, you should learn about cultural activities and beliefs. This will provide a beginning level of knowledge that will help you begin to communicate with parents.

2. **Communication of High Expectations:** All of your students should hear that you expect them to attain high standards in their schoolwork. This message must be delivered by teachers, counselors, coaches, administrators, and other school personnel. Teachers should understand students' behavior in light of the norms of the communities in which they live, which is why the first point above describes the importance of talking with parents.

3. **Learning Within the Context of Culture***:* Schools have a dominant language. Typically this is the standard American English that is common in middle and upper socioeconomic groups. Your students who do not live in a home and/or culture that is close to that of the schools may be inhibited from learning because of "language barriers." Other barriers also exist, including preferences for learning. Some cultures emphasize speaking while others value silence. Some cultural groups put value on cooperation and others do not, preferring individual work. By gaining knowledge of the language and culture of your students you will be able to create lessons that promote learning because they will use contexts with which your students are familiar.

4. **Student-Centered Instruction:** During student-centered instruction, learning is a cooperative venture; students are more engaged in learning the content than when the teacher is the center of attention. This may entail everything from brainstorming topics, to student-led discussion groups, to cooperative learning projects, to

service learning activities in the local community. These types of activities provide opportunities for students to develop their own ideas, and receive feedback on these ideas. Students from diverse backgrounds are able to bring their ideas and cultural perspectives to the classroom, and to work on projects that are culturally and socially relevant to them.

5. **Culturally Mediated Instruction**: Culturally mediated instruction and learning occur in an environment that encourages multiple viewpoints and allows for inclusion of knowledge that is relevant to the students and to their diverse cultures and backgrounds. Your goal should be to create an environment that encourages and embraces culture by using management and learning strategies familiar to students' culture, provides students with opportunities to share their cultural knowledge, and even questions and challenges students' beliefs and actions. Students should learn that there are often multiple ways to interpret a statement, event, or action. By being allowed to learn in different ways or to share viewpoints and perspectives in a given situation based on their own cultural and social experiences, students become active participants in their learning (Nieto, 1996).

6. **Reshaping the Curriculum**: The curriculum should use resources other than textbooks for study. For example, students could research a topic within their community, interview members of their community, or provide information to other students on alternative viewpoints or beliefs on a topic. Students' strengths in one subject area will support new learning in another. If your students use their personal experiences to develop new skills and knowledge, a more meaningful connection between school and real-life situations is established (Padron, Waxman, & Rivera, 2002).

7. **The Teacher as Facilitator:** As teachers, you should develop a learning environment that is relevant to and reflective of your students' social, cultural, and linguistic experiences. You will act as guides, mediators, consultants, instructors, and advocates for your students, helping to effectively connect their culturally based and community-based knowledge to the classroom learning experiences. Teachers should use the students' home cultural experiences as a foundation upon which to develop knowledge and skills. Encourage students to share artifacts from home that reflect their culture, write about traditions shared by their families, or research different aspects of their culture. Teachers should also work to accommodate learning preferences of their students that are linked to cultural background and take into account varying levels of English-language proficiency. This might also occur by using a community speaker, or inviting parents who can demonstrate alternative ways of approaching a subject or a problem to class (Ladson-Billings, 1995; Padron, Waxman, & Rivera, 2002).

Exceptionalities

In your future classrooms you will teach students with unique needs, talents, and interests. One challenge you will face will be to differentiate the curriculum so that every child has opportunities to learn in an environment that is safe and least restrictive. What this means for you is to consider how you might make your daily instruction individualized for each of your students. You can manage this task for many of your students, but you will also have students who will need to receive special services—or special education. These students are frequently referred to as "exceptional students," and teachers have a legal, and we believe ethical, obligation to provide lessons to them that will promote maximum learning. Culatta and Tompkins (1999) developed this list of exceptionalities your future students may have: mental retardation; learning disabilities; behavioral or emotional disorders; communication disorders; physical and/or health impairments; hearing and or vision impairments; severe or multiple disabilities; and giftedness.

Exceptional students may receive special services from an instructional assistant who attends classes with them, or from courses and programs that pull a student out of the general education classroom. When possible, however, exceptional students are kept in the general education classroom. This is known as the "inclusive model" because the general education classroom is a place that includes all students. It is easy to understand that many educators disagree about how to educate children with exceptionalities. Proponents of a fully inclusive model speak to the benefits that all students have when in a room with diverse learners. Students of all capabilities work together to help one another learn. The challenge for teachers is to provide opportunities for learning that account for the wide range of students. Opponents of inclusion suggest that placing students in programs separate from the general education classroom allows for more individualized instruction and learning; they argue that the burden on the classroom teacher will be too great if all students are placed together. The challenge for these "pullout" programs is to ensure that academic expectations remain high. Additionally, boys are identified as needing special services more than girls, as are students of color and students from homes that are disadvantaged economically. Whether these students should be taught separately, included in the general classroom, or taught with some combination of these two is a raging debate in the schools. In any case, you will need to consider how you will help students who have exceptionalities learn when they are in your classroom.

One of the most powerful tools that you will have as a teacher in an inclusive classroom will be your exceptional students' individualized educational program, or IEP. When a public school student needs special services, an IEP must be designed. These are developed by the special education teachers/specialists in your school, with the help of parents, other teachers, school personnel, and at times, the student. An IEP give details about the educational supports and services that will help the child with a disability receive appropriate instruction. An IEP may specify instructional strategies, strategies for managing behavior, motivational techniques, and other insights about how to best help the student learn. Test scores, physician reports, and psychological, cognitive, and/or other medical reports might also be included. By contacting your special education expert(s) in the school you will have powerful strategies for meeting the needs of your exceptional students. New regulations emphasize that the IEP team must consider a student's strengths as well as areas of weakness when formulating an educational plan. An IEP is required by federal law whenever a student has a recognized disability. In 1997 the Individuals with Disabilities Act was passed into law, specifying disabilities and strengthening the expectations of learning for all students. Each state, or in some cases, each district or each school, designs its own IEPs for its students with disabilities. Some students do not have disabilities that require special education services. They might not receive an IEP, but they could receive a 504 Plan, which is a program of instructional services for assisting special-needs students who are in a regular education setting. A student who has a physical or emotional disability, who has an impairment that restricts one or more major life activities (e.g., caring for oneself, performing manual tasks, walking, seeing, hearing, speaking, breathing, working, and learning), or who is recovering from a chemical dependency should receive a 504 Plan.

The instructional strategies that we will examine in section 2 of this book can be adapted to meet the individual needs of students. They allow for all students to learn, whether they are considered general education students, students with learning disabilities, or gifted students. Specifics for differentiating the instructional strategies in order to help your students learn most effectively are described for each strategy.

TEACHING ENGLISH TO STUDENTS OF OTHER LANGUAGES

You might relate to the following reflection from a recent student teacher:

> My university supervisor came to my World History class one day to observe. After class he was encouraging me to consider ways I could include all the students and not only the ones that volunteered to speak-up. He asked if I noticed the three students sitting in the back corner that didn't say a word the entire class. I did notice them. They speak Ukrainian and I had no idea what to do.

The demographics of the United States, including the number of those that speak languages other than English, are changing rapidly. Teaching students that are learning English as their second or third language is not new but it has become increasingly common. Consider this statistic: the total enrollment of U.S. students in grades K–12 grew by 9.5% between 1985 and 1995. At the same time the number of students in the United States with limited English proficiency (primarily immigrants) grew 109% (Olsen, 1997). This trend continues today. A much larger percentage of new students with limited English skills than new students with English as their primary language are enrolling in schools. Statistics that reflect school population change have been used to support what has been referred to as the *demographic imperative*. It is imperative for us to prepare ourselves to teach all of our students.

Obviously, not every new teacher will choose to become a certified expert in teaching English as a second language; however, there are several ways to prepare. An important start is learning about the four basic elements for engaging students who are not proficient in English. First, it is important to be able to understand some basic terms used so that when you are placed in your internship or begin your first teaching position you can ask informed questions. The terminology can be tricky, if not head spinning at times. A person could walk into the teacher's lounge and hear talk of ESLs, TESOLs, ELLs, ESOLs, bilinguals, emergent bilinguals, and LEPs. The following glossary of terms will prepare you with some key words and phrases.

A BRIEF GLOSSARY FOR TEACHING STUDENTS WITH ENGLISH AS A SECOND LANGUAGE

BICS: Basic Interpersonal Communicative Skills. This might be thought of as conversational language. A distinction between BICS and CALP was introduced by Cummings (1979). See CALP.

Bilingual: An ability to speak two languages.

Bilingual education: An approach to instruction that includes the continued development of the student's native language, the learning of a second language, and the use of both languages to teach academic content.

Biliteracy: An ability to read and write in two languages. See Freire (1978) for information about the implications of biliteracy or literacy on issues of social justice.

CALP: Cognitive Academic Language Proficiency. Immigrant children typically take 2 years to acquire a conversational fluency (BICS) in a new language. It may take the same child at least 5 years to reach an academic proficiency (CALP) in the new language.

ELL: English Language Learners or students who are not proficient in English.

ESL: English as a Second Language. A program or system of instruction designed to teach English to those that speak other languages. This system typically will use academic content and is usually thought of as a component of bilingual education.

ESOL: English Speakers of Other Languages. Some prefer this to ESL because it recognizes that English could be the third or fourth language of the student and that this should be acknowledged. For example, a student from Mexico may speak Mixteco (a Native language) as his first language and Spanish as his second language.

Immersion: Technically immersion is a bilingual program developed in Canada where 90% of the early elementary school student's day is in the minority language (the non-mainstream language). Many times, however, this term is used in school to refer to placing a student in a mainstream classroom (not necessarily as part of a well-thought-out program).

LEP: Limited English Proficient. This is usually used as an adjective to describe students, as in "the LEP student." Some prefer not to use this term for the same reason some prefer not to use the word "disability" — it focuses on what a student cannot do instead of what he can do.

TESOL: Teaching English to speakers of other languages OR the professional organization Teachers of English to Speakers of Other Languages.

Second, it is important to know that you are not alone. There usually will be a teacher in your school that specializes in teaching ESL. Her program could look like one of the many possible varieties of teaching English but most likely will reflect current trends of teaching ESL. This means that students of all levels of English proficiency come to her class to either learn the academic subject (ESL content class) or have class time to support them with their assignments from mainstream monolingual English classes; support may be in English or in their first language, depending upon obvious variables. Of course, some students will attend introductory-level English classes as well. This is important to keep in mind, but—without question—conscientious teachers will not shift all of the responsibility for the learning of an ELL onto the ESL teacher.

A third element to consider is the way people acquire new languages. Having a basic understanding of language acquisition theory will help as you try to design or modify lessons. While taking a course on second language acquisition theory would undoubtedly benefit any teacher, here we will focus on two of the components that influence language acquisition in a school context (Cummings, 1997; Thomas & Collier, 1997). Students learning English will tend to begin by learning social language. They learn what they use in everyday conversations. Immigrant children typically take two years to acquire a conversational fluency (BICS) in a new language. Students take much longer to negotiate their way into the more formal academic language. It may take the same child at least five years to reach an academic proficiency (CALP) in the new language. The catch is this: an unknowing teacher may assume that because he hears a student speak English during class that the student is equally proficient in academic language, the language of teaching and learning. This will most likely not be the case. In addition, because textbooks are written in academic language the student's actual proficiency could easily be overestimated and the student not be provided with adequate assistance for understanding what he or she reads for class. Another consideration for teachers is that some students may not have a literacy base at all. In other words, they may not read or write in their first language. This obviously would have an impact on their ability to read or write English even if they are verbally performing well.

The final element for you to consider is inclusive methods of teaching. In the following chapters we will help with ideas for taking what we know about students of ESL and moving into practical ways to include these students in the mainstream class.

Gender Considerations

Campbell and Steinbrueck (1996) write that teachers often communicate different expectations of male students than they do of female. Teachers often give male students more attention and provide them with more opportunities to share during class activities. Others have observed teachers and conclude that teachers tend to praise boys for the intellectual contributions to class, and praise girls for their proper behavior in class (Sadker & Sadker, 1982, 1994). As a result, teachers may reinforce societal norms about gender-biased behaviors that actually limit girls' academic performance and enhance boys' achievements. In recent years a series of programs have encouraged girls' participation in mathematics and science classes, and increases in girls' performances in these areas are starting to be realized. Concern is now beginning to rise about the low number of male students who attend colleges, with some estimates suggesting that in the near future two female students will graduate from college for every male student. Suffice to say that gender differences exist, and you need to reflect on your interactions with students to ensure that gender bias is not affecting your students' opportunities to learn.

The conclusions of Pipher (1994) are compelling and sobering: in early adolescence, girls' IQ scores drop and "their math and sciences scores plummet. They lose their resiliency and optimism and become less curious and inclined to take risks" (p. 19). This could partly be due to changes from the transition from elementary school to middle school, changes brought about by puberty, and/or increased awareness of peer and societal influences on their behavior. Boys are changing as well, repressing emotions and feelings and even using aggressive behavior in order to fit in with societal expectations (Sadker & Sadker, 1994; Thorne, 1994). Boys in middle school and high school engage in more "at risk" behaviors (gang membership, drug use, physical daring, etc.) than girls. Boys tend to receive lower grades, and make up the majority of students referred for special-education services. For example, 71% of students identified as learning disabled and 80% of those identified as emotionally disturbed were boys (Sadker & Sadker, 1994).

For these reasons and more it will be important for you to consider the role gender plays in your content area. Poetry is perceived by many high school students as being feminine even though famous poets throughout history have been men; mathematics is often perceived as being masculine even though women have made significant contributions to that discipline. Women's roles are often omitted from historical accounts; men's conquests dominate the conventional stories. Check your curriculum to identify if you are missing important opportunities for clarifying misrepresentations of women and men, or if you are underrepresenting the roles of women or men in the content your students are studying. When teaching, reflect on the nature of your interactions with students. If you teach in accord with the samples from many studies that McCormick examined in 1994, you will likely give boys five times more attention than girls. Work to provide gender equity in your classroom.

Poverty in Schools

According the United States Bureau of the Census, 37 million Americans are living in poverty. Of these, 13 million are under 18 years of age.[3] The socioeconomic status of your students will likely impact their learning and the educational resources available to you. The National Commission on Teaching and America's Future has issued a report that supports over twenty years of research on poverty and schooling. The commission concludes that

> children at risk, who come from families with poorer economic backgrounds, are not being given an opportunity to learn that is equal to that offered to children from the most privileged families. The obvious cause of this inequality lies in the finding that the most disadvantaged children attend schools that do not have basic facilities and conditions conducive to providing them with a quality education. (NCTAF, 2004, p. 7)

Gorski (2005) follows up on this report, noting that

> schools with large percentages of low-income students are more likely than schools with large percentages of wealthy students to have an abundance of teachers unlicensed in the subjects they teach, serious teacher turnover problems, teacher vacancies and large numbers of substitute teachers, limited access to computers and the Internet, inadequate facilities (such as science labs), dirty or inoperative student bathrooms, evidence of vermin such as cockroaches and rats, and insufficient classroom materials. (p. 3)

Many implications can be derived from these accounts. It is important to recognize the impact of poverty on schooling, both in terms of educational opportunities for your students and the support systems available to them outside of school. You will want to consider whether your assignments and activities unfairly allow students with more resources to have an advantage over those with fewer. Teachers used to be discouraged from finding out the socioeconomic status of their students lest it bias them. Today, the thinking is that teachers must be aware of student differences so they can help each child uniquely. When you know students are living in poverty, you then check if you are assuming that all students come to school from the same background. Poverty is systemic, and it is difficult for schools and teachers to devise a list of strategies for overcoming it. We have developed the following list of topics related to poverty and wealth that we hope you will think about when you are planning your classroom activities. This is not an inclusive list, but a starting point for considering economic diversity in your classroom.

- Some students work for pleasure, some to help pay bills, and some will not work at all.
- The value of education varies dramatically in the homes of your students.
- Opportunities to travel, have access to materials and resources, and use the Internet outside of school are correlated with higher economic status.
- Parent/guardian availability to help with students' schoolwork is widely varied.
- Some students have nutritious breakfasts and lunches, while others will eat little or eat poorly.
- Crime rates and other safety issues could impact students' opportunities to complete schoolwork.

MAKING IT WORK IN YOUR CONTENT AREA

Think of three specific strategies that you might use in your future classroom that will raise the status of students who are typically marginalized due to ethnicity, exceptionality, or gender. Consider the following examples to get you started thinking about this: If you are a woman who plans to teach mathematics, then you could tell girls how you overcame any stereotypes about women and mathematics. If you plan to teach American literature, you might select a story by Alice Walker because African American women are often underrepresented. If you plan to run a mock congress in your civics course, you might consider having students who are not in leadership roles at your school hold offices of class president or ambassador during the simulation.

CONTEXTS OF TEACHING IN A CHANGING AND TECHNOLOGICAL SOCIETY

You will find that in educational circles technology is defined in many different ways. Some, such as the Association for Educational Communications and Technology (1994), define educational technology very broadly so that it includes procedures and resources for learning. This could involve the process one uses while including a tool for learning as itself a type of "technology." Others might define it almost exclusively as the use of resources as tools for learning. Tools might include many resources, from common pencils to sophisticated systems for interactive communication (e.g., laptop computers or cell phones). For the purposes of this text, we will be using the term *technology* to specifically refer to modern electronic resources found in classrooms that can be used for teaching and learning. Most often we will be referring to digitally oriented resources used by and found on computers.

The technology available has changed dramatically over the last twenty years. This is obvious to many of us, but to others that have grown up with the changes it may go undernoticed. The frantic pace of technological change is an unremarkable way of life to many middle and high school students of today; these students have spent their entire lives learning new software, playing video games, updating their computer operating systems, and looking forward to the latest programs with state-of-the-art audio and graphics. Some have described these students as native speakers of the digital environment, or "digital natives." That, by extension, would make those not born into the digital world "digital immigrants"—those trying to grasp the myriad technological changes, those that tire of repeatedly learning new versions of software, those that speak with digital "accents," and those that, according to some, think differently (Owston, 1997; Prensky, 2001).

As long as we are considering this metaphor, it is important to note that some have purposefully decided to stay in the "old country" and not (or try not to) "immigrate" at all. These note how technology does not always have a positive impact on our society and, in fact, takes more than it gives (Oppenheimer, 1997; Postman, 1995). We believe that just as it is important to consider ways to include ESL students while planning lessons, it is also important to consider ways to include the digital language of our students, as well as to take into account our own fluency in that language. Some teachers are naturally apprehensive about using the new language (a computer), while others do not realize that they are speaking with a "heavy accent" and that their students are the "native" speakers (i.e., highly skilled with computers). In addition, it is important to remember that asking your students to use technology implies that students will need access to computers and other electronic devices. Much has been written about the "digital divide," the socioeconomic gap between communities and people who have access to computer technology and those who do not. For example, if you assign students to access the Internet as part of a homework assignment, you are assuming that all students can do this outside of school. If some can, and some cannot, then you are placing students who do not have access at a disadvantage. This is not equitable. Care needs to be taken when implementing student activities tied to technology.

Through the years, as we have discussed using technology with teachers and aspiring teachers, there has been common agreement: most teachers do not want to be "technologists." Teachers are less interested in learning about the gadgets than learning how they can be used in a lesson. One of the most important things a person can discover about using technology for teaching and learning is that the focus in the classroom should not be on the technology, but on how it can be used to promote student learning. "Digital immigrants" can be a skeptical group because most of us have seen the well-meaning use technology in a manner that adds little value to a lesson or, worse, becomes a distraction. Adding technology has become the easy part of teaching, but not necessarily the best part. The question we ask ourselves should not be "How can I infuse technology into this lesson?" but instead "Can value be added to the lesson by using technology, and if it can, then how?"

We have also seen technology used in well-thought-out, valuable ways. Some have argued that technology helps increase student motivation. Of course, any teacher would be interested in something that is motivating. Unfortunately, motivation due to the use of a new gadget is somewhat shallow and often expensive. However, motivation due to increased control of one's own learning is empowering, and technology can help facilitate this. But this takes a rethinking of the way we teach, not simply the addition of more technology to our classes. Technology can also be used to promote, establish, and support dynamic instructional strategies that are designed to meet learning objectives. In fact, in a review of cases studies, the CEO Forum (2001) concluded that technology has the greatest impact when it is integrated into the curriculum for the purpose of achieving clear, measurable educational objectives. In the chapters describing instructional strategies that follow in this book, we show how technology could play an important role when using specific instructional strategies to help students learn.

MAKING IT WORK IN YOUR CONTENT AREA

Think critically about the use of technology in the classroom. Go to the technology-infused lesson-plan database created by in-service teachers in Mississippi at CREATE (http://www.create.cett.msstate.edu/create/classroom/lessons.asp). Choose a lesson to review from the areas of language arts, science, math, and social studies.

What technology is to be used? Do you think the technology will help students learn the content more effectively? If so, why? If not, why did the teacher use technology and what could the teacher have done differently? What caveats would you give any teacher that is interested in trying the lesson?

GUIDING PRINCIPLES FOR CLASSROOM MANAGEMENT AND DISCIPLINE

After many interviews with teachers (both preservice and in-service), we have concluded that classroom management and student discipline are closely linked to the instructional strategy one is using. Each instructional strategy has its own management concerns/issues; the chapters herein on instructional strategies specify how to best manage the classroom while using a particular strategy, and how you might effectively discipline students during each strategy. Therefore, the chapters in section 2 build on the management and discipline principles that we will examine in this section of chapter 1. We intend for this section to provide some general terminology and overviews of key components for managing an effective learning environment.

One of the greatest worries in the minds of many student teachers has to do with management and discipline problems. Preservice teachers often wonder if they will be able to maintain order, earn student respect, oversee group activities, or effectively handle all of the logistical and organizational tasks of the classroom. As well, specific questions arise from working with teachers, such as "Am I really not supposed to smile until December?" or "What should I do if a student says 'no' when I ask him to do something?" These are very real concerns. Many worries fade when you meet your students, but new concerns often arise. Effective teachers are able to manage the classroom and discipline students so that optimal learning can occur. In addition, teaching will be much more enjoyable for you when the classroom is a community of learners in which you and your students are comfortable.

Differences Between Management and Discipline

When preparing to help students learn, you will use a series of instructional strategies. While these strategies will help you determine appropriate ways to assess your students' learning, they will also provide guidance as you identify the activities students will engage in, select materials and resources that you and the students need, and consider the logistics of having the day's events work together to promote student learning. The best-planned lessons can be unsuccessful, however, if you do not think through how you will manage the learning environment, and if you are unable to effectively discipline students who are behaving inappropriately.

We differentiate between classroom management and discipline as follows: *classroom management* is a proactive approach to helping students learn, and *discipline* is a reaction to student misbehavior. Classroom management addresses all of the aspects of the classroom that will promote student learning. You are overseeing all that happens in your classroom. Many educators refer to the classroom as a "community of learners" in which you and your students are committed to making the classroom environment a safe place where knowledge, skills, and dispositions are developed over the school year. As the adult leading that community you need to ensure that students are supported, cared for, challenged, and meeting the learning outcomes for your course. Classroom management involves overseeing the classroom so this happens. *Discipline* specifically refers to how you can effectively control students so their behaviors maintain the sense of community in your classroom. Part of discipline enables students to self-monitor their behaviors (so they literally become self-disciplined), but part of discipline involves the specific action that teachers take when a student disobeys a rule or fails to meet an expectation. While teachers need to discipline students, we suggest that many problems arise simply because the classroom is poorly managed.

Consider the following very real dilemma that a teacher might face: Students are seated in groups of four around the room. One group of students needs the teacher to help in understanding the assignment. A second group of students, on the opposite side of the classroom, is being disruptive and not working on the assignment. The teacher knows that her proximity has a significant impact on disruptive behavior; that is, when she is in close proximity to the disruptive group they quiet down and work. However, this keeps her away from the group of students needing her help. What could the teacher do to manage this situation? How could she address this proactively? What discipline issues are at work?

Relational Teaching

Many conflicts and problems can be avoided if teachers try to build appropriate relationships with their students. The term we use for this is *relational teaching*. As the term implies, relational teaching places high value on the relationship the teacher has with the whole class as well as with each student. Rather than thinking of your students as a group of adolescents that come to your classroom, you think of them individually, with each possessing their own unique experiences, struggles, strengths, and weaknesses. During the school year you look for opportunities to build teacher/student relationships with each member of your class. This takes time and effort, but it is surprising how quickly you can get to know your students. Benefits from a relational teaching approach include: knowing how to assign students to groups because you know each students' strengths and weaknesses; understanding pressures and influences on a student that may affect his or her behavior in class; developing a sense of mutual respect for one another; reducing "acting out" or misbehavior by students because they do not want to harm the relationship you have developed; and, increasing interest in the development and learning of your students as you become more invested in their lives.

Relational teaching also has to do with developing what is often called "with-it-ness." When teachers are "with it" they are described as being keenly aware of all that is happening in the classroom. Sometimes it seems as though a "with it" teacher has eyes in the back of his head, or has an extraordinary sense of hearing and can hear comments whispered on the far side of the room, or is able to preempt a potential problem before it starts. A significant part of being so tuned in to your students that you are "with it" requires developing a positive rapport with them.

Doda, George, and McEwin (1987) devised 10 "truths" about effective schools. These truths attempt to identify how teachers can help to provide a school environment that is effective and helpful to students, and these truths reveal the importance of teacher-student relationships.

Ten Current Truths About Effective Schools

1. Work to reduce the size of student school groups so that as a teacher you are able to build relationships with students.

2. Remember/emulate the climate and tone of the elementary school. Students' work should be on display, and lots of visual stimuli present to promote thinking about behaviors and contents.

3. Spend time with students in noninstructional ways. For example, spend time with them at sports events, as club advisors, or when you see them in the community.

4. Ample rewards and awards help the students feel they are being appreciated for their thinking and work.

5. Reduce the isolation and independence inherent in teaching by interacting with other teachers, parents, and students. See teaching as a collaborative effort among many constituent groups.

6. Do not sit down while you teach. Rather, monitor the classroom by interacting with students and assisting them one-on-one.

7. Make lessons "real" and "hands-on" so students have opportunities to engage in genuine learning experiences.

8. Use/develop your sense of humor. Avoid sarcasm, but be willing to laugh at tense situations and even at yourself.

9. Establish big/high/rigorous expectations for students, but plan and teach in small segments.

10. Look for opportunities to develop a strong rapport with each student.

Approaches to Classroom Management

Every teacher develops his own approach for managing a classroom. A successful teacher will often claim that he does not have management or discipline problems, but when you watch him teach he is continually monitoring and interacting with students to ensure that they are acting prosocially and adhering to classroom expectations. If a student begins to fall asleep, the successful teacher casually walks by and taps her on the shoulder. If two students are passing notes, the teacher does not draw attention to the behavior but simply continues talking while standing next to the two students. His proximity makes them put the notes away. If a challenging assignment is beginning on Monday, the successful teacher has anticipated student questions and is able to address most of them when the assignment is described. In this way students feel as though their ideas and worries are considered. In each of these situations the teacher manages the learning environment with an approach that works. In this section we will describe seven effective and long-standing approaches to classroom management. What you end up using will undoubtedly be a hybrid of these, but an initial examination of these seven will allow you to start thinking about effective management approaches.

Behaviorism   Skinner did not describe an approach to classroom management, but the principles of behaviorism that he established provide some general ideas. The most useful principle for management is *behavior modification*. Behavior modification operates on positive and negative behavior. True to the stimulus-response of behaviorism, a teacher notices a student behaving properly and acknowledges, praises, or in some way reinforces that behavior. The reinforced student, along with his classmates who witnessed the reinforcement, will likely repeat this behavior and perceive it as beneficial. Students who are misbehaving are not acknowledged, and in an effort to earn praise also behave appropriately. Students receive external rewards for behaving appropriately; these often take the form of tokens or other tangible items. For example, a teacher might put a pencil in a mug whenever all of the students are sitting down before the bell rings to start the period. When the mug is full (about 15 pencils), the class receives a "free day" to learn about a topic of their choice, or even to have a pizza party. Rules are established and rewards are provided for following them.

Canter's Assertive Discipline Model   This model (Canter, 1976; Canter & Canter, 1992) provides a set of clear-cut expectations for the classroom. Students can expect teachers to provide a safe learning environment, and teachers can expect students to pay attention and not disrupt the class. The teacher establishes clear expectations, justifies why these expectations are needed, and lists the consequences for misbehavior (not meeting expectations). Once established, the teacher expects adherence to the classroom rules. Students have the choice to behave in accord with the rules or to misbehave. Misbehavior is considered to be a poor choice, and the teacher must be assertive and follow through with the stated consequences. This will teach students to behave responsibly in the classroom. When helping students remember the expected behavior, the teacher should state the expectations to the student ("Chris, remember to bring your book to class"), or to praise a student in front of the class for behaving properly ("Chris remembered to raise his hand. Nice job!"). If a student perpetually misbehaves, then the teacher "moves in" close to the student, establishes eye contact, restates the expectations, and indicates the next consequences of continuing to misbehave.

The Dreikurs/Albert Model   Dreikurs (with Cassel, 1972) suggests that the classroom needs to be democratic, but his ideas became more applicable after Albert (1974) refocused them specifically to classroom management. This has implications for how the rules are decided and for the instructional strategies that are employed. Students impose limitations on themselves for the purpose of directing behavior so that it promotes learning. The teacher and students cooperate to determine classroom procedures, rules, and even the discipline for misbehavior. Democratic teaching is very different from "autocratic teaching" (where the teacher is always in charge of the classroom policies and disciplining students, and where students have no need to develop self-discipline), and it is different from "permissive teaching" (where the teacher does not help enforce the classroom policies and students do not learn about responsibility, accountability, and self-discipline). The democratic teacher engages students in the process, and fosters a sense of self-discipline among the students. Students have goals that they strive to attain, one of which is a sense of belonging to the classroom community. If a student does not follow the class-developed rules, then authentic consequences result. Dreikurs suggests that misbehavior is the result of a student seeking after one of four wrong goals: (1) getting attention; (2) seeking power; (3) getting revenge; or (4) withdrawing and not participating. As the teacher manages the classroom she looks for students who are pursuing these wrong goals and then redirects them by enforcing the natural consequences of breaking rules.

Ginott's Model This model (Ginott, 1972) is built around the key term of *congruent communication*, or communication that is about situations rather than student character or personality. In other words, instead of telling students that they are being rude by interrupting during a classroom discussion, the teacher might say,"This is a whole-class discussion. We need to allow everyone a chance to express their ideas." Students' behavior, thus, is managed by addressing the situations that students are in and inviting students to cooperate. In the teacher's comment, the first sentence addresses the situation (a class discussion), and the second sentence asks for cooperation (letting everyone speak). When the teacher does not attack a student's character or personality, the student may be more willing to discuss his feelings about a situation in the classroom. This open line of communication, along with the teacher modeling appropriate behavior, enables the teacher to change the attitudes and beliefs of students and not merely their behavior. This takes time, and depends on repeated opportunities to communicate with students. Ginott feels strongly about the powerful role that teachers play in students' lives, writing,

> I am the decisive element in the classroom. It is my personal approach that creates the climate... . As a teacher I possess tremendous power to make a child's life miserable or joyous. I can be a tool of torture or an instrument of inspiration ... in all situations it is my response that decides whether a crisis will be escalated or de-escalated, and a child humanized or de-humanized. (p. 13)

As a result, Ginott suggests that communication without attacking the students' character will lead to a well-managed classroom.

Glasser's Model According to this model (Glasser, 1992), the teacher expects all students to produce quality work. Teachers must lead students in learning activities that students and teachers agree are worthwhile and useful. This model suggests that students want basic needs met: survival, belonging, power, fun, and freedom. Survival is not always tied to the school (though it can be if the student feels unsafe), but the other four needs can be met at school. When these basic needs are not met, students are frustrated. When they are met, students are satisfied. If students' needs are not being met, the frustration leads to apathy, and the learning is seen as irrelevant. Teachers must manage the classroom to create an environment that has some fun, allows students a certain amount of power, has some degree of freedom, and helps students feel part of the classroom learning community. This can be partly accomplished when the teacher has high expectations for quality work, and provides opportunities to learn course content in depth. Students then need encouragement to determine their own paths for attaining this level of quality. The teachers role is to encourage quality work by challenging students to problem solve, building relationships with students, and continually being available to help. This can be done individually or during class meetings where expectations for quality work are further refined.

Jones's Model   This model (Jones, 1987) differs from the others in its emphasis on nonverbal communication. The teacher's "body language, facial expressions, gestures, eye contact, and physical proximity" (Charles, 1996, p. 128) all send important messages to the students and help manage the learning environment. The messages from teachers to students about their behavior can be very powerfully sent without saying anything. Some teachers allude to this when they proclaim that when they simply give their students "the look" everyone knows it is time to behave. The importance of proximity is also highlighted by Jones. By simply standing near students who are misbehaving in some fashion, a teacher is able to quickly end the behavior without drawing a lot of attention to the situation. This model also suggests that teachers provide incentives for students that are genuine and will motivate all students in the class. Incentives such as extra credit will motivate select students, while an ice cream party will likely motivate all students. Tied to this is Jones's suggestion to follow "Grandma's Rule": First eat your vegetables, and then you can have your dessert. Translated to the classroom, teachers should remember that students should behave properly before receiving any rewards for their behavior. Teachers must not reward students based on students' promises to behave well.

Aside from nonverbal communication, Jones suggests that teachers should not spend too much time with any one student. Part of managing the classroom is to move around to all students. If a teacher spends too much time/attention on one student, the other students in the class are not monitored—for behavior or for understanding. Also, students need opportunities to work through academic problems without building dependency on the teacher to answer every question. Jones suggests that teachers should provide efficient help to students, and limit interaction to 20-second intervals. He suggests three steps: (1) acknowledge what the student has done correctly, (2) suggest what needs to be done next; and (3) leave the student to work on the details.

Kounin's Model   Kounin's (1977) ideas about classroom management center on teacher behaviors that engage students in the lessons. He suggests that misbehavior rarely occurrs when students are actively learning. Kounin's principal concepts are succinctly described by C. M. Charles (1996, pp. 45–46):

The ripple effect. This is a phenomenon in which the teacher's words or actions are directed at one student, but spread out and affect behavior of other students. Similarly, if misbehavior is ignored by the teacher, the ripple effect could spread a belief that the teacher will not enforce certain rules.

With-it-ness. As described earlier, this term to refers to a teacher's knowing what is going on in the classroom at all times. Students do not think they can "get away" with anything if their teacher is "with it."

Momentum and smoothness. Lessons need to keep moving by not spending too much time on details ("overdwelling"), having smooth transitions from one lesson to another, and varying class activities to keep students engaged.

Student accountability. This term refers to the teacher's efforts to keep students alert and involved in the lessons. This may involve calling on students to answer questions, or other requests that require students to be attentive.

Overlapping. This is Kounin's term for multitasking—the ability to attend to two or three tasks at the same time. For example, the teacher is able to write on the board while answering a question and redirecting a group of students working on a group project.

Satiation. This means that students are done thinking about a topic, and that the teacher needs to change his approach. Satiation can be brought about by boredom, repetition, or frustration.

Valence and challenge arousal. This is Kounin's term for how teachers might make activities more enjoyable/challenging. Variety of activities, teacher enthusiasm, and multimedia presentation are ways to keep students engaged (and not satiated).

Managing the Learning Environment

As we mentioned earlier, exuding a sense of being "with it" and using your proximity to students for making your presence known will help a classroom environment. Establishing classroom rules and routines will also help you manage the learning environment. Rules might be established by students, the teacher, or in concert together, but they need to be consistently adhered to by everyone in class. It is more effective to state your expectation in terms of what should be done, rather than what you do not want. For example, the rule "Do not be late to class" is not as effective as "Be ready to start class when the bell rings." Or the rule "Do not interrupt" is more clearly stated as "Let a classmate finish her thought before you talk." In work that we have done with teachers, it appears that fewer, more general rules and expectations are more effective than many specific rules. "Respect other's opinions" is vague, but it may be a better rule then 10 specific rules about respect. If you are going to ensure that all students follow the rules, then you do not want to provide so many rules that it gets in the way of your planning and instruction. In many ways the teacher who is effectively managing the classroom is like a good baseball umpire: everyone knows he is there and is not afraid to enforce a rule, but he does not allow the rules to overshadow the game. In the case of the teacher, the rules do not overshadow the activities of the day. Similarly, the placement of tables, chairs, and students can help the management of the classroom. The classroom setup needs to vary depending on the instructional strategies you use. For example, you might have students in neat rows during a lecture, but they will need to be sitting in circles during a group project. More specific examples for each instructional strategy are examined later in this book.

Effective teachers also establish classroom routines that help address questions such as when to turn in homework, when to raise hands, what is expected when the bell rings at the start or end of the period, what the procedure is if someone needs to leave class, where class announcements will be posted, or what materials are needed for class (e.g., textbook, binder, pencil). By establishing clear routines, students are able to focus more on the learning and less on the logistics.

MAKING IT WORK IN YOUR CONTENT AREA

To put some of these theories into practice, try completing three tasks.

First, consider how "daily life" in your classroom might operate; examine what you will do regarding classroom management. What routines will you use (e.g., beginning/ending class, homework collection/return, bathroom passes, etc.)? What will your policy be about late work? How will you determine seating assignments and desk arrangements?

Second, create an introductory assignment or student-interest survey that you might use to get to know more about your students. Be creative in what you ask of students; try to find out information that will assist your management of the classroom and give insight into their lives that will help you be a more effective teacher in your content area.

Third, generate a one-page handout that you might give to your students that articulates your classroom guidelines and/or expectations. These can be developed by taking "bits and pieces" from the management theories presented above. Keep in mind the following:

Strive for a suitable level of generality.

State your guidelines positively (say what you expect them to do) and clearly.

Specify your expectations about students' behavior, respect for property, respect for others, academic achievement, safety, and other elements you think are important.

List the positive and negative consequences of not adhering to your guidelines.

CHAPTER REVIEW

Effectively helping adolescents learn is a challenging task because so many variables are at work. Physically, adolescents' bodies are changing rapidly. Cognitive development during adolescence is dramatic. Thinking skills improve and develop, and adolescents begin to have more advanced cognitive abilities. Socially, adolescents begin to negotiate how they will interact with the world around them.

Learning is a "relatively permanent change, due to experience, either in behavior or in mental representations or associations" (Ormrod, 2006, p. 184). Piaget, Vygotsky, and other cognitive psychologists have investigated how our brains function, and not just our behaviors.

Gardner's multiple intelligence theory (1983, 1999) suggests that there are eight different intelligences, and that these account for a broader conception of what we think about human potential.

Motivation might best be thought of as a force, or energizer, that helps us accomplish a task. *Extrinsic motivation* is brought on by external factors that we believe will provide desirable results. *Intrinsic motivation* is motivation to engage in an activity because of the satisfaction derived from the activity itself. A useful approach for thinking about motivating students comes from a theory of intrinsic motivation called "flow."

Self-efficacy is our expectation or belief about what we can accomplish as a result of our efforts. Similar to self-efficacy is the idea of *locus of control*. If we attribute our success or failure to forces beyond our control we express an *external* locus of control. If we attribute our behavior to forces we can control we have an *internal* locus of control.

Your future classrooms will have students with different cultures, ethnicities, primary languages, economic backgrounds, religions, family structures, physical abilities, and learning abilities. *Multicultural education* is a field of study and an emerging discipline whose major aim is to create equal educational opportunities for students from diverse racial, ethnic, social-class, and cultural groups.

In your future classrooms you will have "exceptional students" who have mental retardation; learning disabilities; behavioral or emotional disorders; communication disorders; physical and/or health impairments; hearing and or vision impairments; severe or multiple disabilities; and/or, giftedness. When possible, exceptional students are kept in the general education classroom. Exceptional students are required to have an individualized educational program (IEP) or a 504 Plan.

In the decade between 1985 and 1995 the number of students in the United States with limited English proficiency grew 109%. Students learning English will tend to begin by learning social language; they learn what they use in everyday conversations. Students take much longer to negotiate their way into more formal, academic, language.

Teachers often give male students more attention and provide them with more opportunities to share during class activities. As a result, teachers may reinforce societal norms about gender-biased behaviors that actually limit girls' academic performance and enhance boys' achievements.

We have defined *technology* in reference to modern electronic resources found in classrooms that can be used for teaching and learning. Just as it is important to consider ways to include ESL students while planning lessons, it is also important to consider ways to include the digital language of our students as well as take into account our own fluency, as teachers, in that language. One of the most important things a person can learn about using technology for teaching and learning is that the focus in the classroom should not be on the technology but on how it can be used to achieve something meaningful, to promote student learning.

Classroom management is a proactive approach to helping students learn, and *discipline* is a reaction to student misbehavior. Classroom management addresses all of the aspects of the classroom that will promote student learning. Discipline specifically refers to how to effectively control students so that their behaviors maintain the sense of community in your classroom. Many conflicts and problems can be avoided if teachers try to build appropriate relationships with their students.

Establishing classroom rules and routines will also help you manage the learning environment. It is more effective to state your expectation in terms of what should be done, rather than what you do not want.

NOTES

1. Gardner admits there may be more than eight forms of intelligence, and has more recently considered additional forms such as existential or spiritual intelligence; see Gardner, 1999.
2. For more details about culturally relevant teaching, see http://www.alliance.brown.edu/tdl/tl-strategies/crt-principles.shtml (retrieved September 4, 2006).
3. For U.S. Census Bureau data about poverty, see http://www.census.gov/prod/2003pubs/p60-222.pdf (retrieved September 4, 2006).

REFERENCES

Association for Educational Communications and Technology. (1994). *Instructional technology: The definition and domains of the field*. Bloomington, IN: Author.

Bandura, A. (1994). Self-efficacy. In V. S. Ramachaudran (Ed.), *Encyclopedia of human behavior* (Vol. 4, pp. 71–81). New York: Academic Press.

Banks, J. A., & Banks, C. M. (Eds.). (1995). *Handbook of research on multicultural education*. New York: Macmillan.

Beamon, G. W. (2001). *Teaching with adolescent learning in mind*. Glenview, IL: Skylight Professional Development.

Bransford, J. D., Brown, A. L., & Cocking, R. R. (Eds.) 2000. *How people learn: Brain, mind, experience, and school.* Washington, DC: National Academy Press.

Campbell, P.B., & Steinbrueck, K. (1996). *Striving for gender equity: National programs to increase student engagement with math and science.* Washington, DC: American Association for the Advancement of Science.

CEO Forum on Education and Technology. (2001, June). *The CEO Forum school technology and readiness report: Key building blocks for student achievement in the 21st century.* Retrieved February 21, 2002, from http://www.ceoforum.org/downloads/report4.pdf.

Csikszentmihalyi, M. (1990). *Flow: The psychology of optimal experience.* New York: Harper & Row.

Csikszentmihalyi, M. (1997). *Finding flow: The psychology of engagement with everyday life.* New York: Basic Books.

Culatta, R., & Tompkins, J. (1999). *Fundamentals of special education: What every teacher needs to know.* Upper Saddle River, NJ: Prentice-Hall.

Dacey, J., Kenny, M., & Margolis, D. (2000). *Adolescent development* (3rd ed.). Carrollton, TX: Alliance.

Doda, N., George, P., & McEwin, K. (1987). 10 current truths about effective schools. *Middle School Journal, 18*(3), 3–5.

Gardner, H. (1983/2003). *Frames of mind: The theory of multiple intelligences.* New York: Basic Books.

Gardner, H. (1999). *Intelligence reframed.* New York: Basic Books.

Gardner, H. (2003, April). *20 years of multiple intelligences: Reflections and a blueprint for the future.* Keynote address made to the general membership of the American Educational Research Association, Chicago, IL.

Ginott, H. G. (1972). *Teacher and child.* New York: Macmillan.

Gorski, P. (2005). Savage unrealities: Uncovering classism in Ruby Payne's framework. Retrieved April 4, 2006 from http://www.edchange.org/publications/Savage_Unrealities.pdf.

Jones, F. H. (1987). *Positive classroom instruction.* New York: McGraw-Hill.

Ladson-Billings, G. (1995). But that's just good teaching! The case for culturally relevant pedagogy. *Theory into Practice, 34*(3), 159–165.

Lepper, M. R., & Hoddell, M. (1989). Intrinsic motivation in the classroom. In C. Ames & R. Ames (Eds.), *Research on motivation in education: Vol. 3. Goals and cognitions* (73–105). San Diego, CA: Academic Press.

Litzinger, M. E., & Osif, B. (1992). *Accommodating diverse learning styles: Designing instruction for electronic information sources.* In L. Sharito (Ed.), *What is good library instruction now?* (pp. 72–82). Ann Arbor, MI: Pierian Press.

Lortie, D. (1975). *Schoolteacher: A sociological study.* Chicago: University of Chicago Press.

Marc, P. (2001). On the horizon. *NCB University Press, 9*(6), 1–6.

Nieto, S. (1996). *Affirming diversity: The sociopolitical context of multicultural education* (2nd ed.). White Plains, NY: Longman.

Olsen, R. W. B. (1997). Enrollment, identification, and placement of LEP students increase (again). *TESOL Matters, 7*(4), 6–7.

Oppenheimer, T. (1997). The computer delusion. *Atlantic Monthly, 280*(1), 45–48, 50–56, 61–62.

Ormrod, J. E. (2006). *Essentials of educational psychology.* Upper Saddle River, NJ: Prentice-Hall.

Owston, R. D. (1997). The World Wide Web: A technology to enhance teaching and learning. *Educational Researcher, 26*(2), 27–33.

Padron, Y. N., Waxman, H. C., & Rivera, H. H. (2002). *Educating Hispanic students: Effective instructional practices* (Practitioner Brief #5). Retrieved February 15, 2006 from http://www.cal.org/crede/Pubs/PracBrief5.htm.

Piaget, J. (1970). Piaget's theory. In P. H. Mussen (Ed.), *Carmichael's manual of psychology* (703–732). New York: Wiley.

Pintrich, P. R., & Schunk, D. H. (2002). *Motivation in education: Theory, research, and applications* (2nd ed.). Upper Saddle River, NJ: Prentice-Hall.

Piper, M. (1994). *Reviving Ophelia: Saving the selves of adolescent girls.* New York: Ballantine Books.

Postman, N. (1995). *The end of education: Redefining the value of school.* Westminster, MD: Random House.

Ryan, R. M., & Deci, E. L. (2000). Self-determination theory and the facilitation of intrinsic motivation, social development and well-being. *American Psychologist, 55*, 68–78.

Thomas, W. P., & Collier, V. P. (1997). *School effectiveness for language minority students.* Washington, DC: National Clearinghouse for Bilingual Education.

Thorne, P. (1994). *Gender play: Girls and boys in school.* Piscataway, NJ: Rutgers University Press.

Tomlinson, C. A. (2004). *How to differentiate instruction in mixed-ability classrooms* (2nd ed.). Upper Saddle River, NJ: Prentice-Hall.

Vygotsky, L. S. (1978). *Mind in society: The development of higher psychological processes.* Cambridge, MA: MIT Press.

2

CONSTRUCTING CLASSROOM CURRICULUM

As you work to become an effective teacher you will gather ideas for teaching and consider ways to implement those ideas. Perhaps you have heard about or seen a teaching strategy that you would love to try, and want to learn the best way to plan for using it. This is an issue related to the curriculum. Before helping you do that, however, we first need to address one of the questions asked most often by prospective teachers: How do I know what I should teach?

DEFINING THE CURRICULUM

When teachers think about what they will teach they are thinking about the curriculum. The term *curriculum* is used in many different ways, and has many different definitions. Consider the following examples: a teacher's daily plan that provides detailed information about how he will help students read and understand the works of Langston Hughes is a form of curriculum; a biology textbook is a type of curriculum; when a teacher instructs her students to raise their hands before speaking, she is making a decision related to the curriculum; if half of an afternoon class is excused to attend a cross country meet, that is part of the curriculum as well. Keep in mind that in this text when we use the term *curriculum* we will be using it to help answer questions related to *what to teach* and *how to teach it*. Our use of the term includes the expected learning outcomes of the classroom, the content students will learn, and the lesson plans that provide detailed description for each class period.

There is much more to the school curriculum than deciding what should be included in courses. Before we get to the practical aspects of constructing classroom curriculum, it is important to offer some background on the idea of curriculum for you to consider so you can have added insight when you begin making decisions for your students. We find it helpful to think of the curriculum as having five parts, though some suggest there may be more (Cuban, 1996; Eisner, 1985). While these may have different labels and subheadings, the five basic parts to the school curriculum are: the formal curriculum, the delivered curriculum, the learned curriculum, the hidden curriculum, and the null curriculum. The basic premise behind this partitioning of the curriculum is that to plan curricula you need to be aware that your students will not always learn what you intend. Sometimes they will, and other times they will learn more or less than you planned. Consideration of this will help with planning for your class. A review of each part follows.

The Formal Curriculum

The *formal curriculum* consists of all that educators purposefully intend to teach students. This is also referred to by some as the *intended*, *planned*, *explicit*, or *official curriculum*. This is the part of the curriculum that most think of first and includes syllabi, unit plans, lesson plans, national and state standards, and textbooks. The word *curriculum* is derived from the Latin word meaning "the course of the chariot race." In the movie *Ben Hur*, Charlton Heston has his famous chariot race around the "curriculum." This visual can be used as a helpful metaphor in that while there is a course to be followed, there is also ample room to swerve this way and that, making timely decisions to avoid pitfalls or gain advantage in order to successfully cross the finish line.

The formal curriculum takes many forms. It might be a document that a school district distributes to parents describing the content of a seventh grade earth science course. It might be a calendar used by an English teacher that identifies what his students will learn during each week of the course. It might even be the textbook that a world history teacher will use in her 10th grade world history class. The formal curriculum has been authorized, or formalized, as being the acceptable curriculum. If a school board decides to ban a particular book, then the board is deciding about changes to the formal curriculum. Decisions at this level often result in debates and deliberations, because the changes will become official policy for a school. This curriculum is usually developed without students and sometimes, as you will later see, even without teachers. It is also heavily influenced by theorists and a variety of stakeholders.

The Delivered Curriculum

The *delivered curriculum* is also known as the *taught curriculum*, and can be thought of as the instructional processes or methods used to communicate the formal curriculum. This would include course organization, instructional strategies, and the sequence of learning activities designed for a lesson. In the chariot race metaphor, the swerving of the chariot would be part of the delivered curriculum; there is an "acting out" of the official course of the race. A good teacher does not always follow the formalized written plan, but may decide to change course and follow up on a "teachable moment" for deeper reflection. This may be a spur-of-the-moment decision. Of course, a teacher will need to balance spontaneity with purpose. For example, during a planned lecture about gravity, a student may ask how satellites orbit the earth. The teacher may not have had anything about orbits in his planned lecture, and must make a quick decision about leaving his plan to consider this student's question. For the sake of example, let's say that he spends the rest of the class period talking about this question with the students, and is able to explain gravity from a different perspective that actually enhances his students' understanding. The delivered curriculum may have actually been better than the formal curriculum. However, if the student in the above example proceeds to ask whether the international space station should always have an American astronaut on board, the lecture and discussion will swerve way off the subject, and the delivered curriculum no longer is supporting the intent of the formal curriculum; the question is certainly interesting, but it does not fit in with the overarching curricular plan for the day. The delivered curriculum is heavily influenced by learning theories that we explored in chapter 1. These theories help determine the activities used during class. The teacher and the students also influence the curriculum that is delivered or taught.

The Learned Curriculum

The *learned curriculum* is a representation of all that a student learns in school. Some refer to this as the *realized curriculum*, and it comes into play when assessing the students and the overall curriculum itself. We cannot assume that the planned curriculum or the delivered curriculum will be the same as the learned curriculum. This is one reason that most educators refer to what they intend for their students to learn, and not what they intend to teach. The difference is subtle but important. If you focus on what you will teach, you may be less aware of your students' understanding. If you think in terms of what your students will learn, then you will be focused on how closely your formal planned curriculum aligns with student learning. The learned curriculum has been of major concern to educators in recent years as the accountability movement has given rise to standardized tests used to measure student learning. Test scores are not the only way observers judge the educational system and student performances. A good example of this is the Sputnik era in the 1950s; then, Americans viewed their educational system as lacking because the Soviets were the first in the world to send a manned spacecraft into outer space. This was a perception about the learned curriculum that had far-reaching effects on the educational system for many years. At the classroom level, teachers also play a role with this curriculum as they seek ways to assess their students. They use this information to evaluate both their students' learning as well as their own teaching.

The Hidden Curriculum

The *hidden curriculum* can be thought of as part of the delivered and the learned curricula, but is worth mentioning separately. The hidden curriculum consists of student learnings that are not part of the formal curriculum. It is "hidden" because teachers and other curriculum writers are often not aware of what students may be actually learning. For example, attitudes, values, or beliefs are learned through observation or participation in the normal routine of the school day. This is the curriculum that people "pick up" through immersion in school culture. Jackson (1968) has been credited as one of the first to make educators aware of the hidden curriculum. However, Dewey also has noted that, in addition to course content, students learn values, socialization cues, and other important content simply by being in school together (1938). Dewey thought this "untaught" content might even be learned more than the planned curriculum. Given its hidden status, however, you will want to think about how you can reveal some of the hidden curriculum in your future classroom. Often the hidden curriculum is criticized as a tool for maintaining the status quo in the classroom and in society. Theorists such as Apple (1986) suggest that the hidden curriculum is a misnomer and that it purposefully enables some students (typically those in the dominant culture) and "disables" others (typically those students who are marginalized by socioeconomic status, ethnicity, and ability). Thus, the hidden curriculum is not perceived by all as learning "by accident," but is thought of as a way to perpetuate the current social and power structure of a school. The hidden curriculum might be a teacher calling on boys more frequently than girls in a mathematics class to answer difficult questions (thereby students "learn" that boys may be better skilled at problem solving than girls), or a school canceling classes during the state basketball playoffs so that all students can attend the games (thereby students may "learn" that athletics have equal footing and importance to academics at the school). Both of these examples portray the hidden curriculum as a negative influence. This portion of the curriculum can be a positive learning element, such as when a student learns that hard work pays off or that there are rewards for determination. However, this curriculum is most often referred to when pointing out learnings that reinforce misperceptions, such as the notion that studying hard to get good grades is "acting white," or that girls are not scientifically inclined. Negative elements range from oppressing students (based on gender, ethnicity, ability, etc.) to "sending the wrong message" that one aspect of school is more important than it should be. Cornbleth (1991) suggests the following examples of the hidden curriculum in schools:

grading policies and systems
the separation of schools into subject areas
elevating textbooks as the most accurate and important sources of
    information
the arrangement of the daily school schedule

the distribution of materials and resources
school rituals and traditions

Consider Cornbleth's categories above, and identify examples for each of the categories listed. If you think about it, you will probably be able to come up with several things you have learned along the way through "courses" in the hidden curriculum.

Null Curriculum

The *null curriculum* is simply the content that students do not learn. Consider Eisner's (1994) detailed comment on the null curriculum:

> There is something of a paradox involved in writing about a curriculum that does not exist. Yet, if we are concerned with the consequences of school programs and the role of curriculum in shaping those consequences, then it seems to me that we are well advised to consider not only the explicit and implicit curricula of schools but also what schools do not teach. It is my thesis that what schools do not teach may be as important as what they do teach. I argue this position because ignorance is not simply a neutral void; it has important effects on the kinds of options one is able to consider, the alternatives that one can examine, and the perspectives from which one can view a situation or problem. (p. 97)

This component of the curriculum may send implicit messages to students about the importance of some information over others. As a teacher you cannot teach everything. In our work with future history teachers we often make the obvious point that three and one-half decades of history occur during a thirty-five year teaching career, yet the number of days in a school year will be the same, and teachers need to determine what to include and what to leave out of those thirty-five years of history. It is a difficult task to consider what you leave out when most of your energy is spent trying to determine what you want students to learn. However, it is important to reflect on the range of possible topics that you *could* teach, to ensure that you are planning for students to learn the most important content, skills, and abilities.

MAKING IT WORK IN YOUR CONTENT AREA

We will revisit these components of the curriculum later in this chapter. It is interesting to ask teachers how much control they have in developing their course curriculum. Talk with teachers in your content area, and ask them who develops the following parts of their course curriculum:

the units for their course
the textbooks and/or other supplemental texts they use in class
the videos they show in class
the software they can install on their computers
the tests/exams students take
the daily lesson plans

Do teachers feel a good deal of autonomy, or do they feel constrained by out-side sources? Compare your findings with others.

WHAT SHOULD YOU TEACH?

Decisions about both curriculum and curriculum plans reflect philosophical assumptions about the way adolescents learn and what they should know. We have noted in Chapter 1 that the way we believe students learn affects the way we plan instruction. A constructivist lesson plan will look much different from a lesson plan designed by a behaviorist. A constructivist approach is based on the idea that learners construct, or build, meaning and understanding as they learn. It usually implies hands-on activities in which students spend a good amount of time processing information so they understand it in depth. A behaviorist approach will tend to focus more on the final product and place less emphasis on the process that was followed to attain the information. Decisions about what we teach will be influenced by what we believe is important based upon our view of the purpose of education. These decisions are based upon our educational philosophy. So, for example, in the *Republic*, Plato argues that the purpose of education is to support a just Athenian state. Justice would flow naturally from a well-educated citizenry that is ordered and well-balanced. A just society, then, would display a harmonious balance between different social groups acting in the interests of the society as a whole. Individuals would be educated for service to the state according to the nature of the individual. In Plato's just society, the most intelligent would be taught to become wise leaders, the athletic would be taught to be soldiers for the defense of the state, and so on.

Educational theorists have used ideas like those of Plato to help them decide what should be included in the curriculum. Of course, this can lead to a variety of perspectives. For example, the ideas of Hirsch (1987) and Banks (2003) provide two different approaches to making curricular decisions, though both are influenced by Plato. Cultural literacy is an idea advocated by Hirsch to respond to concerns that American youth are not learning a shared knowledge. According to proponents of this view, the lack of common knowledge adversely affects our ability to communicate with one another, and it weakens the commonalities that hold the country together. Hirsch's core knowledge curriculum attempts to address this concern by detailing a sequential approach to acquiring the knowledge that is essential for becoming a fully functioning citizen.

Critics might contend that the knowledge necessary to be culturally literate is determined by the dominant group. They would ask, "Literate of *whose* culture?" Another curricular perspective is multicultural education, advocated by Banks, who responds to the concern that there has been little respect in the school curricula for the contributions made by the many diverse cultures that make up our country. Banks advocates creating curriculum that moves classrooms beyond merely mentioning the names or celebrating holidays of ethnically diverse heroes and heroines. Proponents of this view intend to transform the curriculum into one that represents a wide variety of perspectives and encourages students to become socially active. Critics of this perspective might contend that this approach contributes to the balkanization of America by focusing students on our differences rather than our commonalities.

You should be aware that making these decisions can be highly politically charged. In general, while new teachers are attentive to the curriculum (what to teach) they are most concerned with the curriculum plan (how to teach). This is interesting because, at the same time, the public eye is focused on the content and skills being learned, and most controversy surrounds this issue. For example, you will make critical decisions about what to teach. As we mentioned in the previous section of this chapter, selecting one topic causes others to be omitted because of the limited amount of time in the school year (this "limit" enforces the hidden curriculum that schools must promote efficient learning). This decision may prove to be highly controversial, such as teaching evolution but not intelligent design, ignoring a certain perspective in history such as the impact of Chinese migration, or choosing one novel over another.

School curriculum should be purposeful and have an aim. Figure 2.1 below may help explain the links between three elements: *schooling*, *education*, and *life*.

The *life* box represents all the time and experiences that people have. A significant part of our life is when we learn, or are educated. This is represented in the *education* box. We learn information, skills, and attitudes in both formal and informal settings. One formal educational setting is school. The

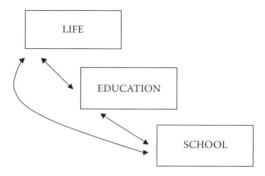

Figure 2.1

school box stands for the time and place in which people receive their formal education. Of course, learning occurs both inside and outside of school. Our focus in this illustration is the link between *school* and *life*. Here, school is separated from life because it provides a time in the day when students focus on learning. Some of the things students learn at school have little or no connection to life but are part of their education. For example, students learn strategies for taking tests. A curriculum problem arises when school and life are separated. Most curriculum theorists argue that school should enable a student to live a good, fulfilling life. The curriculum questions that follow this are simply, "What kind of content, skills, attitudes, and thought processes enable a person to live a good fulfilling life?" and "How can your course curriculum improve your students' lives?" Schubert (1986) contends that this should be the question behind all curriculum decisions.

Understanding assumptions and purposes behind curriculum theory is not merely an academic exercise. Decisions based upon these theories have deep significance, because they will impact your future students.

Expanding Your Thinking About Curriculum

Many different approaches to curriculum development exist that we have not touched upon here. All curriculum development has an aim or intention that is focused on student learning. If you are interested in exploring a range of curricular perspectives, consider the following curricular theorists and/or philosophers:

Michael Apple (1986)
Catherine Cornbleth (1991)
Larry Cuban (1996)
John Dewey (1916)
Elliot Eisner (1996; 1985)
Paulo Freire (1970)
Genva Gay (1988)
Diane Ravitch (1985)
Theodore Sizer (1984)

We list a well-known article, book chapter, or book for each theorist in the references for this chapter; for a quick review of each you could merely search the Internet for their work.

A Hierarchy of Curriculum Influence

Standards and guidelines for curricula exist at the national, state, and local levels. These standards will impact the curriculum that your students learn. Figure 2.2 shows the different levels, or the hierarchy, of the curriculum. National standards are the broadest and farthest removed from the classroom,

Curriculum and Stakeholder Diagram

(Adapted from Garcia, Spalding & Powell, 2001)

Figure 2.2

and lesson plans are the most specific and developed with your students in mind. *Stakeholders* are groups who exercise some influences on the classroom curriculum. Given the level of the curriculum, and the content you are teaching, stakeholders hold different amounts of influence.

Think about the levels of curriculum each stakeholder will most likely influence, and why they are considered stakeholders in the curriculum. For example, what level will parents influence? How about elected officials? Also, consider what stakeholders might contribute to the curriculum, and potential problems that could arise from their involvement.

National Standards

In 1983 the U.S. Department of Education's National Commission on Excellence in Education published the report *A Nation at Risk* (National Commission on Excellence in Education, 1983). As the title states, the report proclaims that our nation is at risk because of problems in education. This report has been heralded by some as pinpointing the key problem with public education: students are not learning. Others criticize the report as unfairly blaming schools for societal problems. Many other publications followed that both refuted and praised the report (Boyer, 1983; Sizer, 1984; Reed and Bergman, 1992; United States Department of Education, 1991) and were instrumental in sparking the national movement toward content-area standards. Professional organizations from each discipline have since published what they consider the essential elements that every student should learn, and these documents have become the national standards for these content areas. Each organization brought together teachers, university professors, and other experts in their discipline to identify the most important content and skills. These national standards will impact your future teaching, because they influence the standards that states have created. State standards influence the local school district standards for your content area and, ultimately, your classroom curriculum.

Before going further, we want you to think about this series of events since 1983. Some believe that the "standards movement" provides an excellent guide for states, districts, and teachers in helping develop the formal curriculum. Some worry that these standards take away from the professional judgment of teachers in determining what their students need to know. As you likely know, the standards movement has led to an "assessment movement" in which most states have developed standardized competency tests for many content areas. These tests assess how well students learn the content identified in the standards; these assessments are praised for holding schools accountable, and criticized for reducing teaching to "test preparation." What do you think about the standards movement? How does a set of national and state standards impact your content areas positively? What negative impact might it have?

The list of educational professional organizations below will guide you to websites where you will find the national standards for each content area.[1] When you visit these sites, search for the "standards" documents. Most of the standards documents are available for free, though some, such as the National Art Education Association, charge a nominal fee. You can also join these organizations. Members receive information about research and teaching in the content area. Usually, membership dues include a subscription to a journal or magazine that provides ideas for helping students learn content and skills in that subject area. We encourage you to "play around" on these websites and locate the standards, as well as to identify how the national organization affiliated with your content area might help you as you prepare to teach. The standards for your content area are an excellent starting point for focusing your lesson plans. They are a planning resource. Near the end of this chapter we describe how an experienced teacher develops curriculum. This teacher suggests that the first step is to read the standards.

Professional Organizations with National Standards

Art: National Art Education Association; http://www.naea-reston.org/stdarteducation.html

Civics: National Standards for Civics and Government; www.civiced.org

Economics: National Council on Economic Education; www.ncee.org

English: National Council of Teachers of English; www.NCTE.org

Foreign Language: American Council on the Teaching of Foreign Languages; www.actfl.org

Geography: National Council for Geographic Education; www.ncge.org

History: National Center for History in the Schools; www.sscnet.ucla.edu/nchs

Mathematics: National Council of Teachers of Mathematics; www.nctm.org
Music: National Association for Music Education; www.MENC.org
Physical Education: American Alliance for Health, Physical Education, Recreation and Dance; www.aahperd.org
Science: National Science Teachers Association; www.nsta.org
Social Studies: National Council for the Social Studies; www.ncss.org

State Standards

National organizations may direct the content taught in your future classroom, but they have no legal authority to determine curriculum. In the same way, the classroom teacher has no legal authority to decide what is taught, as such authority has been granted to the state. Traditionally this authority has been passed along to the local level—to the district, school, department, and on to the classroom teacher. In the last 25 years, along with the national standards movement has come an emphasis by the federal government on assessment and accountability, the rationale being that for federal funds to be expended evidence must be shown of student progress.

As we mentioned earlier, most of the 50 states have crafted their own standards that specify what students are expected to learn. The creations of the standards vary from state to state, but typically are completed through committees of representatives of the various stakeholders. Some states use these standards as guidelines for schools, but most states have accompanied them with a high-stakes testing component. While each state determines how to assess student learning of course content, they are all remarkably similar in how they assess students. Consider how the State of Washington determines whether students are learning course content.

Washington State developed state standards for each content area. These standards are called the Essential Academic Learning Requirements, and they describe the learning standards for grades K–10 at three benchmark levels, one each in elementary, middle, and high school. These requirements were then expanded to include content and skill expectations for each grade level. This provided an additional degree of specificity for each content area. Each spring, students at the three benchmark levels take a standardized test to assess how well they have learned the content. This assessment, called the Washington Assessment of Student Learning (WASL), is used by the district, state, and federal government to determine how well students are learning. The results of these tests are published and can be sorted by school to determine the outcomes of the test. The WASL is thought of as "high stakes" because students that do not pass will not be allowed to graduate from high school. Currently 42.3% of 10th graders tested passed all of the components of the test (Office of the Superintendent of Public Instruction, 2005). Students that fail a portion of the test will be given another opportunity during their junior and senior years. The WASL is also "high stakes" because schools that do not show "adequate yearly progress" can be subject to funding restrictions as well as required staffing changes.

In appendix B of this book we provide a chart that lists each state and a website for downloading information about its standards, the name of each state's academic standards, whether the assessment is "high stakes," and the consequences of the assessment. We include the myriad abbreviations and initials that each state uses to help you become familiar with the jargon the states have adopted relative to their standards and assessments. When we state that a test has "No Child Left Behind (NCLB) consequences" we refer to the fact that the state's test is used to demonstrate partial fulfillment of the federal government's NCLB requirements. Each school and district must demonstrate that they are making "adequate yearly progress" toward meeting their learning goals. The state tests are the source of data most states use to show this progress. You can read more about this legislation at the U.S. Department of Education website (http://www.ed.gov/nclb).

Additionally, the Education World website has an excellent link page to all of the state standards. We find this useful for understanding the learning expectations of each state, and for comparing state standards to national standards. We encourage you to access this site (http://www.education-world.com/standards/state/index.shtml).

Obviously, with these types of pressures, as teachers you will need to tailor your classroom curricula and include time for preparing students in the taking of state tests. You can see then how state influence on the local classroom curriculum has increased dramatically in recent years. However, there still is a great deal of local control and influence over the curriculum.

District Plans

Each school district has at least one administrator that is in charge of curriculum. These coordinators are usually former classroom teachers who are sympathetic to the balancing act a teacher must perform among the various influences on the curriculum. Their role is to help ensure that state initiatives are being implemented by working with department chairs. A curriculum coordinator oversees how the state standards are being addressed in a department. Curriculum coordinators also ensure that the departments' course offerings are aligned and presented in a logical order for students. For example, school districts will often articulate the grade levels at which students will learn American history. Traditionally, eighth grade is when students learn about European contact with the Americas up through U.S. Reconstruction after the Civil War. In 11th grade, American history picks up in the mid-1880s and continues to the present day. By identifying the content (in this case, the chronology of American history), districts help ensure that the content students learn, and the order in which students learn it is the same across the district.

Departmental Plans

At most schools, department chairs work with district administrators, department chairs at other schools, and classroom teachers to outline content and skills for both individual courses and all departmental course offerings. District plans are used by the departments to help facilitate this. In the case of our American history example, the social studies departments at the middle schools and high schools work to ensure that the teachers organize their course curricula around the district plan. Teachers are then in a position to design their course, the units in their course, and their daily lessons to fit within this plan. This type of organization allows for the district to better utilize resources when purchasing textbooks and materials for the classroom. Therefore, daily lessons, units, course outlines, and department or district outlines all are curriculum plans.

Many departments prefer to entrust the classroom teacher with these decisions. Even with the influences that affect the curriculum, most teachers have considerable freedom to develop plans for the classroom because they are supported and trusted at the local level. The curriculum will be a fluid document pushed and pulled by those with keen interests. As with any truly democratic pursuit, parents, students, and the local community have the right to be involved with decisions related to the classroom, and their involvement should be embraced. However, in the final analysis, the teacher is almost always the final gatekeeper of the curriculum and instruction that occurs in her classroom. Thornton (2005) has expanded on the idea that teachers are the curricular gatekeepers who have the final say about how local, state, and federal standards are learned by students. To expand this, it means that you the teacher will determine what your students will learn. This is a sobering yet exciting aspect of teaching: sobering in that the expectation for student learning is great, and exciting because it should make you feel as though you can make professional decisions about the needs and interests of your students. We know many excellent teachers who express the sentiment that "good teachers will meet content standards without too much extra effort; the assessment test will merely confirm what we do." We also have many of our beginning teachers report that state standards provide excellent direction about which content and skills to teach. Many teachers, however, worry whether the assessment tests will accurately determine what their students have learned. Teachers as gatekeepers cannot escape the fact that their teaching is being assessed when their students are tested. In chapter 4 we will discuss classroom level lesson plans in detail.

PRACTICAL SUGGESTIONS FOR DETERMINING CLASSROOM CURRICULUM

Sometimes a new teacher simply needs a practical way to get started. With all the talk of educational philosophy, curriculum theory, and influences it can be somewhat overwhelming. We would like to suggest four practical ways to begin the process:

1. Ask the important questions.
2. Seek advice from experienced teachers.
3. Write out course goals, and yearlong scope and sequence.
4. Determine the role of available materials.

Asking the Important Questions

The most well-known curriculum writing prompts are commonly referred to as the Tyler rationale (Tyler, 1949). Oftentimes, you will see these prompts used to help with schoolwide curriculum decisions, but they are helpful at the classroom level as well. The Tyler rationale is organized around four important questions that we will modify for the classroom level:

1. *What educational purposes should the class seek to attain?* Tyler suggests that these purposes should be determined by considering studies of the student as a learner, the practices of society, and recommendations from subject matter experts. These purposes should then be translated into stated course goals.
2. *What educational experiences can be provided that are likely to attain these purposes?* Tyler suggests that once goals have been formulated the teacher should begin collecting ideas, activities, and materials that can be used to meet the goals. This collection can show alignment with the goals.
3. *How can these educational experiences be effectively organized?* Tyler recommends that each class would have organizing elements upon which to build. This might be related to a value (e.g., respect) in a history class or certain skills in a math course. Considering these elements is useful in the building of lessons, or in integrating several topics or content areas.
4. *How can we determine whether these purposes are attained?* Assessing student learning and evaluating if they have attained the desired aims is a key component of Tyler's rationale. Assessment techniques should go hand in hand with the stated goals of the course.

We find it interesting that this approach is still dominant in schools today—more than 50 years later. It provides a rational and systematic approach for developing curriculum. It is this sequential, four-step process that has made the approach so popular, and provides a starting point for curriculum development (Ornstein & Hunkins, 2004). Tyler's approach is certainly flawed. It is built on behaviorism (which assumes that the taught curriculum will be close to the learned curriculum), and it may oversimplify curriculum development as being a series of small performances. Nonetheless, it is a proven and long-standing approach for developing course curriculum.

Seeking Advice from Experienced Teachers

Another suggested step in making decisions about your classroom curriculum is to seek the advice of experienced teachers. Some schools assign first-year teachers with a mentor, but even if you have no one teacher at your school to lean on you will find that there are many teachers who will be able to offer you insight from their experience. Obviously, each teacher's experience will be unique to some degree. However, it may be helpful for you to read about one high school social studies teacher's process for deciding what to teach in her government course. Jen Reidel's district did not have an outline for her course, and her department had only generally agreed upon classroom based assessment; one suggested by the state. She had the opportunity to create her own curriculum, and describes this process as follows:

> I typically use both state standards (grade level expectations) and the national strands in determining the essential concepts, terms, and ideas to be taught. Often I will also consult education organizations (Center for Civic Education, Foundation for Teaching Economics, Street Law) for their view on what they believe is most essential to teach in that specific discipline. Once I have determined what the essential concepts/terms are to be taught I start investigating what sources of curriculum exist to help me amass materials to teach the course (textbooks, simulations, Internet resources, videos, primary documents, etc. ...). I shy away from running a textbook driven classroom which tends to discourage students' passion regarding the subject. I try to use the textbook as the starting point—not ending point for the teaching of specific concepts and for the kids that need information in black and white to best comprehend it. I do use pocket constitutions though to teach students about the guarantees and structure of the Constitution and I'll use other textbook material as a supplement.

> Consequently, I have created all my own materials to teach about our governmental system, structure, and current issues related to it. This does give me the ability to modify my curriculum as the times change and when a current event is in the news that effectively illustrates what I am teaching. The downside to creating all my own materials is that often I as the teacher become the sole source for knowledge (versus a textbook). This fact alone can cause a teacher to become incredibly worn down creating their own curriculum on a daily basis. I have drawn my materials from the Internet, from conferences I have

attended, from materials purchased from Civic Education organizations, and from materials that I have purchased/located on my own.

For a new or a preservice teacher, I would definitely encourage them to seek some sort of guidance from their district's plan. If the district does not offer one, they can't go wrong consulting the state and national standards for their discipline to narrow down what should be taught. They also might look at both the state and national standards in terms of any potential building or district goals (i.e. increasing reading, writing, math skills or emphasizing diversity). Once the essential concepts that must be taught have been identified, I think then the teacher can choose to teach what they are passionate about concerning the subject. Students more times than not will become most interested in a subject that they see their teacher excited about. My government class is proof of this. I love the subject…and yes I am geeky about it - particularly the court system. So as a result, I have a huge amount of knowledge to draw from when teaching the students. That translates to the ability to give in depth responses to a student's question as well as the fact that I can develop much more meaningful assignments and assessments when I am excited and knowledgeable about my subject.

Reidel's approach is helpful. She suggests that the district curriculum plan, state standards, and national standards will provide you with a starting point for knowing what to teach. Her message is that these standards are not to be feared, but used as a tool for determining critical skills and concepts. When this is determined, the teacher is "freed up" to decide how to best promote student learning. She is the gatekeeper (Thornton, 2005), but she leans on others to help her determine what will be let into her classroom.

Writing Out Goals

A third step is to write out goals and consider a yearlong scope and sequence; this is described in more detail in chapter 4. As Tyler suggests, the creation of written goals is a natural outcome of determining the purposes of the course. Goals, not to be confused with objectives, are broad general statements that allow a teacher to focus. For example, a physicist once wrote, "My goal is simple. It is complete understanding of the universe." Now, that is a broad goal! Goals are usually written for the entire course as well as for segmented sections of the course called *units of instruction*. Course goals will be made more explicit by the unit goals and unit objectives. It might be helpful to think of it as creating an outline for an essay. It might look like this:

Course Goal
Unit Goal
Objective

The idea is to help you focus on your overarching aim while not becoming overly burdened by prescriptive paperwork. Unit objectives will be discussed in detail in chapter 3.

Goals should be written so that they convey broad expectations. For example:

- Students will expand their leisure time activities.
- Students will become familiar with the music developed during the Romantic period.
- Students will appreciate the role of civil rights activists.

State and national standards are filled with broad expectations that could be helpful in determining goals. In fact, sometimes these expectations are thought of as less than helpful when someone is looking for a more specific objective rather than a broad goal. When writing a goal, keep in mind two things: first, that it is something you want students to accomplish over an extended period of time; and, second, that it is something you hope for your students to learn. Because of this it is helpful to consider for a moment which verbs might be used. Some of the verbs we have found to help broaden goals would include:

apply	appreciate	believe	comprehend
demonstrate	enjoy	expand	familiarize
grasp	imagine	know	like
recognize	think	understand	value

If a yearlong curriculum plan is not provided to teachers by the school district or department, then writing this plan naturally follows the development of course goals. Usually a teacher will sketch out the year into units of instruction to begin getting an idea of the amount of time he can spend on certain topics. These topics become the foundation for writing unit plans.

Determining the Role of Available Materials

Determining the role of materials that are available is often undertaken at the same time that plans are being made for the year. For example, math or science courses will often have a textbook that the district has chosen as the formal curriculum guide. The Internet is filled with materials that could be used in the classroom: you will find lesson plans, primary source documents, pictures, audio, and much more. As you sift through this material you will get ideas that will help your curriculum planning. One of the many websites you might visit is the Federal Resources for Educational Excellence site sponsored by the U.S. Department of Education (http://www.ed.gov/free), which organizes hundreds of free lesson plans into content area categories. At the site you can locate your content area, click on its link, and view or download many lessons for future courses. The description from this site reads, "More than 30 Federal agencies formed a working group in 1997 to make hundreds of federally supported teaching and learning resources easier to find. The result of that work is the FREE web site." This is not the only website with lesson and content information, but it might serve as a useful starting point for thinking about lesson planning. We will examine lesson plans in both chapter 4 and section 2 of this book.

MAKING IT WORK IN YOUR CONTENT AREA

Consider for a moment some of the predominant metaphors of schooling. This is important as you develop curriculum because if the "student is the worker" (Sizer, 1984) then what is the role of the teacher? How would this affect the curriculum? Kliebard (1987) has devised three predominant metaphors of schooling for curriculum literature. These are, in other words, three ways to think about education in order to develop curriculum in an educational setting:

1. The Production-Industrial Model
   Teacher = overseer of production
   Student = raw material
   Curriculum = skilled worker who shapes and forms the raw material into a product.
   A rough diamond becomes expensive jewelry. The teacher is able to form students to meet a predetermined goal. In this model, the student is passive, and viewed more as a commodity that brings little to the educational setting except potential. The teacher is the primary determinant for what a student will learn.
2. The Growth Model
   Teacher = insightful gardener who nurtures, feeds, prunes, and nourishes the plants
   Student = the potential-filled plant that relies on the gardener if it is to survive
   Curriculum = the gardener cares for plants and helps them reach their potential
   Unlike in the first metaphor, students in the growth model will develop and learn without the teacher, but they will not reach their full potential unless the teacher interacts and assists the process. The teacher knows what is best, and the students depend on the teacher's insights.
3. The Journey Model
   Teacher = the tour guide
   Student = traveler
   Curriculum = student and teacher are touring knowledge, information, skills, and learning experiences
   The student is a traveler who focuses on many different things depending on their interest, and much of what should be seen is pointed out by the teacher/guide.

Your metaphor for teaching will likely be better than these. Choose a metaphor that seems to fit your perspective, how you envision your class. Share your ideas with a group or the class. After you have written some of your first curricular materials come back to this idea. How does what you have planned reflect your stated metaphor? What do you suppose students would use as a metaphor for schooling? What might students suggest?

CHAPTER REVIEW

We have used the term *curriculum* to include not only the expected learning outcomes of the classroom and the content, but also the plans through which they are delivered.

The five basic parts to the school curriculum are formal, delivered, learned, hidden, and null curricula. The *formal curriculum* consists of all that educators purposefully intend to teach students. The *delivered* or *taught curriculum* can be thought of as the instructional processes or methods used to communicate the formal curriculum. The *learned curriculum* is a representation of all that a student learns in school. The *hidden curriculum* consists of student learnings that are not part of the formal curriculum. The *null curriculum* consists of everything that is not planned, taught, or learned.

Decisions about both curriculum and curriculum plans reflect philosophical assumptions about the way adolescents learn and what they should know.

All teachers will need to understand the existing hierarchy of influences on the classroom curriculum. Teacher decisions are heavily influenced by standards and guidelines for the curriculum at the national, state, and local levels. There are also a variety of stakeholders that have an impact on curriculum decisions.

We have suggested four practical ways to begin the process of constructing your classroom curriculum. First, ask yourself the important prompts found in the Tyler rationale. Second, seek the advice of an experienced teacher such as that given in this text. Third, begin writing out course goals and a yearlong outline, giving thought and attention to the broader picture. These goals should reflect your course aims. Fourth, determine the role of available materials, with careful consideration of how a textbook could have both a positive and negative impact on your classroom.

NOTE

1. Even though this list provides the national standards for each content area, it raises several questions for social studies teachers. If you plan to teach history, geography, economics, or civics you can contact professional organizations in your content area, and you can contact the National Council for the Social Studies (NCSS). The NCSS has a set of 10 standards that attempt to integrate all of the social sciences. We suggest starting with these standards, then visiting a content-specific organization (e.g., a history or economics organization), and identifying the additional content that they suggest should be learned.

REFERENCES

Apple, M. (1986). *Teachers and texts*. New York: Routledge and Kegan Paul.

Banks, J. A. (2003). *Teaching strategies for ethnic studies* (7th ed.). Boston: Allyn and Bacon.

Boyer, E. L. (1983). *High school*. New York: Harper and Row.

Cornbleth, C. (1991). *Curriculum in context*. London: Falmer.

Cuban, L. (1996). Curriculum stability and change. In P. W. Jackson (Ed.), *Handbook of research on curriculum* (pp. 216–247). New York: Macmillan.

Dewey, J. (1916) *Democracy and education*. New York: Macmillan.

Eisner, E. W. (1996). Curriculum ideologues. In P. W. Jackson (Ed.), *Handbook of research on curriculum* (pp. 302–326). New York: Macmillan.

Eisner, E. W. (1985). *The educational imagination: On the design and evaluation of school programs* (2nd ed.). New York: Macmillan.

Freire, P. (1970). *The pedagogy of the oppressed*. New York: Continuum.

Garcia, J., Spalding, E., & Powell, R. R. (2001). *Contexts of teaching: Methods for middle and high school instruction*. Upper Saddle River, NJ: Merrill/Prentice-Hall.

Gay, G. (1988). Designing relevant curricula for diverse learners. *Education and Urban Society, 20,* 327–340.

Jackson, P. W. (1968). *Life in classrooms*. New York: Holt, Rinehart, and Winston.

Hirsch, E. D. (1987) *Cultural literacy*. Boston: Houghton Mifflin.

Kliebard, H. (1987). *The struggle for the American curriculum 1893–1958*. London: Routledge and Kegan Paul.

National Commission on Excellence in Education. (1983). *A nation at risk: The imperative for educational reform*. Washington, DC: U.S. Government Printing Office.

Office of the Superintendent of Public Instruction. (2005). Washington state report card. Retrieved March 29, 2006, from http://reportcard.ospi.k12.wa.us/.

Ornstein, A., & Hunkins, F. P. (2004). *Curriculum: Foundations, principles, and issues* (4th ed.). Boston: Allyn and Bacon.

Posner, G. (2004). *Analyzing the curriculum* (3rd ed.). New York: McGraw-Hill.

Ravitch, D. (1985). *The schools we deserve: Reflections on the education crisis in our lives*. New York: Basic Books.

Shubert, W. H. (1986). *Curriculum: Perspective, paradigm and possibility*. New York: Macmillan.

Sizer, T. R. (1984). *Horace's compromise: The dilemma of the American high school*. Boston: Houghton Mifflin.

Thornton, S. J. (2005). *Teaching social studies that matters: Curriculum for active learning*. New York: Teachers College Press.

Tyler, R. W. (1949). *Basic principles of curriculum and instruction*. Chicago: University of Chicago Press.

United States Department of Education. (1991). *America 2000: An education strategy*. Washington, DC: Author.

Walker, D., & Soltis, J. (1997). *Curriculum and aims* (3rd ed.). New York: Teachers College Press.

CITED WEBSITES

Education World's link page to all of the state standards:
  http://www.education-world.com/standards/state/index.shtml
"Federal Resources for Educational Excellence (FREE)" sponsored by the United States Department of Education:
  http://www.ed.gov/free
Professional Organizations with National Standards:
  Art (National Art Education Association; http://www.naea-reston.org/stdart-education.html)
  English (National Council of Teachers of English; www.NCTE.org)
  Foreign Language (American Council on the Teaching of Foreign Languages; www.actfl.org)
  Mathematics (National Council of Teachers of Mathematics; www.nctm.org)
  Music (National Association for Music Education; www.MENC.org)
  Physical Education (American Alliance for Health, Physical Education, Recreation and Dance; www.aahperd.org)
  Science (National Science Teachers Association; www.nsta.org)
  Social Studies (National Council for the Social Studies; www.ncss.org)
      History (National Center for History in the Schools; www.sscnet.ucla.edu/nchs)
      Geography (National Council for Geographic Education; www.ncge.org)
      Economic (National Council on Economic Education; www.ncee.org)
      Civics (National Standards for Civics and Government; www.civiced.org)
United States Department of Education site:
      http://www.ed.gov/nclb

3

PREPARING LEARNING OBJECTIVES AND ASSESSING STUDENT LEARNING

Learning objectives and assessments are helpful to teachers and students. Objectives provide specific details for meeting the goals of a lesson or unit. We will discuss in this chapter not only how objectives provide a focus for lessons and units, but also that they direct your assessments of your students' learning. Current thinking about student learning suggests that teachers and students must know how they will be assessed before a lesson or unit even begins. This idea is often referred to as a "backward design model," because the teacher designs lessons with the endgoal in mind. Wiggins and McTighe (2000) describe backward design as follows: "One starts with the end—the desired results—and then derives the curriculum from the evidence of learning called for by the standard (learning objective) and the teaching needed to equip students to perform" (p. 8). Thus, objectives and assessment are closely connected, and this is why we will examine them together in the chapter.

THE PURPOSE OF LEARNING OBJECTIVES

Before teaching a lesson you will want to write out learning objectives; these help teachers answer three basic questions related to teaching and student learning:

1. What content do students need to learn?
2. How will student learning be assessed?
3. What activities will students engage in to promote learning?

A concise examination of these three areas helps clarify the content and purpose of learning objectives.[1]

What Content Do Students Need to Learn?

Textbooks, state curriculum guides, and district/school curriculum plans provide direction about what to teach, but teachers are left with the freedom to decide how to best teach the content in the classroom on a day-to-day basis. Consider the following example: If you are going to be teaching a high school biology course you will likely have district goals that are based on local, state and national standards for biology (we explored these in chapter 2). In addition, you will usually have a disctrict-adopted biology textbook and curriculum suggestions. Before the school year starts, you need to consider each of these content recommendations, and then determine the most effective way to help your students learn. If, for example, the standards and curriculum documents lead you to decide that students need to know about symbiosis, you will need to consider how to help your students learn this effectively. Learning objectives help you narrow down the content so you can promote student learning. The number of objectives you have for each day is determined by the complexity of the content your students are learning.

How Will Student Learning Be Assessed?

The second component of an objective helps you determine whether students have learned the content during the activity. It is this area that serves as an assessment of student learning, and helps you know if your students have met the objective. By placing the assessment in the objective, you are ensuring that it coincides with the content to be learned and the activities planned for the class session. Assessments need to be observable, but they do not always need to be graded or quantified into points. Learning is assessed using a variety of approaches. For example, you might have a student present her results of an Internet search activity, take a quiz, or write a book report. As the teacher you determine how well students need to perform on the assessment in order for you to feel confident that they have learned. A score of 100% on a review vocabulary quiz might be your minimum goal because the students have already used the words before. A book report that identifies the theme of a chapter might be what students produce to show they have learned about a particular piece of literature. Therefore, the assessment in an objective has two components: (1) a plan for how students will show their learning; and (2) the degree or the "performance expectations" that students need to meet for you to know they have learned.

What Activities Will Students Engage in to Promote Learning?

Once the content and assessments have been determined you will need to select learning activities for your students. These activities may last 15 minutes (for example, a brief introduction to the day's topic, or a review of previous content), or they may last several days (for example, a research project using online resources). Sequentially, the activities derive from the content you want students to learn, and the activities prepare students to demonstrate their understanding when they are assessed. An old adage among teachers is to change the activity every 20 minutes so that students stay engaged. Although changing an activity every 20 minutes is not required, it is important that you observe students to be sure they are engaged during any activity. Generally speaking, when students learn more difficult content and engage in more cognitively demanding tasks, the activity requires more time. For example, a 20-word vocabulary quiz likely requires less time than a research activity. Often you may find that an activity lasts more or less time than you planned. By reflecting on this you will become more skilled at determining how long an activity will need to last so that all of your students may learn the material. Objectives specify activities that will help your students learn the particular content.

LONG- AND SHORT-TERM OBJECTIVES

Goals provide the general direction for a course. Simply said, they are what you hope your students will learn and accomplish over time. Objectives specify how and when you can help students meet those goals. A social studies teacher might have as a goal the following: *Students will appreciate the personal sacrifices of civil rights leaders.* This does not specify how they will learn about the sacrifices, how they will develop an appreciation for the sacrifices, or how to determine if students meet this goal. These specifics come from the objectives. Objectives can be long term or short term. *Long-term objectives* will be accomplished after a longer unit, semester, or even an entire course. Objectives that are met during an activity or after a few class sessions are *short-term objectives.* These labels are not critical, except to help you understand that long- term and short-term objectives provide a sequential approach to meeting your goals. Figure 3.1 shows the relationship and level of specificity regarding goals and objectives.

Consider again the goal stated earlier: *Students will appreciate the personal sacrifices of civil rights leaders.* Long-term objectives could be:

After learning United States history from 1950 to 1980, students will be able to list two sacrifices that a leader made for the cause of civil rights.

Students will show how they have benefited from the sacrifices of civil rights leaders by stating at least one area of their lives that is better now than it would have been in 1960.

Short-term objectives could be:

In a three-page biography, students will identify three sacrifices that Rosa Parks made during her involvement in civil rights movements.

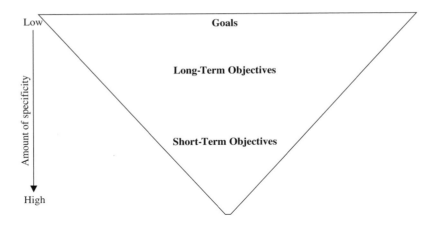

Figure 3.1

During a class discussion students will be able to describe hardships for Marin Luther King Jr. and his family as a result of his involvement in civil rights protests during the 1960s.

Long-term and short-term objectives will need to be restated or revised if students need repeated assistance learning a skill or understanding a concept. For example, adolescents have difficulty criticizing ideas, and not people, during discussions about controversial issues. An objective for developing this skill could be: *During all classroom discussions, students will respect classmates' human dignity by critiquing ideas, not the person bringing forth the ideas.*

This is certainly attainable as a short-term objective, but it is a skill that students will need to continually practice. Therefore, you could restate this objective whenever you plan to have classroom discussions.

MAKING IT WORK IN YOUR CONTENT AREA

Think of a goal that would be appropriate for your content area. In chapter 2 we described the utility of national and state standards, and you may want to refer to those again to help you determine an appropriate goal for a course you will teach. Devise at least one long-term and one short-term objective for this goal. Refer to the examples above on civil rights as a guide for the level of specificity for these two types of objectives. Be sure that the objectives have an assessment component so that you can be sure to help your students meet the objective during the lesson and/or unit.

DOMAINS OF LEARNING

Bloom (1956) and Krathwohl, Bloom, and Masia (1964) have suggested that educators should categorize learning objectives to help focus instruction on specific areas, or *domains*, of learning. This type of focus helps teachers select course content and activities that will promote more specified learning. Since the mid-1960s three domains are generally considered by teachers when writing learning objectives:

1. the cognitive domain
2. the affective domain
3. the psychomotor domain

These three domains provide hierarchies for learning. They move from the less complex (objectives typically easier to attain by your students) to the very complex (objectives more difficult to attain at first). As a teacher, you will write less-complex objectives, but you should continually consider how you might progress to a higher level on each of these domain hierarchies. Bloom and his colleagues worked together to suggest the three domains of objectives, but while they developed in-depth taxonomies for the cognitive and affective domains, they did not develop much for the psychomotor domain. Fortunately, others have examined types of student learning that fit into this third domain, and several taxonomies exist for it. Consider the following descriptions for each of these three domains.

The Cognitive Domain   The *cognitive domain* addresses the thinking skills and academic content to be learned in the classroom. Of the three domains, this is the one that is most common, most easily assessed, and the focus of most educational reforms. When you hear about "getting back to basics," "academic learning," or "concepts and skills," it is usually referring to the cognitive domain. Cognitive objectives are synonymous with research done by Bloom in 1956. His six-level taxonomy classified the types of questions that teachers pose to their students, and the type of thinking that is required when answering these questions. Today, Bloom's work is used for more than categorizing questions. His taxonomy helps evaluate the cognitive tasks in which students engage. Commonly used terms such as "higher-level thinking," or "higher-order thinking skills" have their roots in Bloom's taxonomy. The base level of the taxonomy is called *knowledge*, and the pinnacle of the taxonomy is the level called *evaluation*. As students move in the taxonomy from knowledge to evaluation, the types of questions, activities, and cognitive tasks they engage with are more difficult and require different understandings of course content. The following outline provides a sample question and brief description for each of the six levels of Bloom's taxonomy (Biehler, 1971; Bloom, 1956):[2]

Knowledge   The issue here is *recall of information*. At this level, it is important that students remember what they have read, were told, or saw. This level is crucial because students who do not possess basic knowledge cannot carry out meaningful analyses of language issues, or exercise any disciplined creativity. This is the starting point.

Comprehension   The objective at this level is to ensure that students can *explain ideas*. It is one thing, for example, to be able to identify different regions of the world (knowledge) and another to be able to explain their various influence in international relations (comprehension).

Application   Objectives developed at the application level have as their purpose something practical—use. The issue at this level is whether students can *use* skills, concepts, and information in new situations. For example, in history, one needs to know how to place events in a time sequence (knowledge), to define words (comprehension) for a vocabulary test, and to use these words appropriately (application) in an essay or story.

Analysis   Objectives written at the analysis level are designed to enable students to *see relationships*, make comparisons and contrasts, and look for patterns. *Analysis*, as the term implies, is an attempt to break down whole entities into their component parts. For example, in the study of advertising and other persuasive techniques, students will identify appeals made to status, power, group affiliation, and gender.

Synthesis   Synthesis represents a pulling together or *combining of ideas and elements*. As a synthesis level objective, you might ask students to locate and record the various arguments for and against a controversial issue. Or, having taught your students the mechanics of letter writing, you might ask them to write a letter using the fundamentals they have learned.

Evaluation   Objectives for the evaluation level include those encouraging students to take their own points of view or to express their ideas on issues. A class debate or papers including students' individual *opinions or judgments* are examples of evaluation. At the evaluation level, divergent thinking is encouraged and differences of opinion are to be expected.

Affective Domain   The *affective domain* refers to learning that is tied to feelings or emotions. Learning in this domain does not require students to develop particular feelings or emotions, but it helps students use their emotions and feelings to learn. Where Bloom is usually associated with the cognitive domain, Krathwohl is most often associated with the affective domain (Krathwohl, Bloom, & Masia, 1964). Krathwohl suggests that attitudes, beliefs, and value systems should be identified so that children can learn about them and with them in a cohesive manner. Below is a summary of the affective domain, and examples of activities students may undertake in a classroom:[3]

Receiving   Objectives written at the receiving level are aimed at helping students become aware of or sensitive to the existence of certain ideas, material, or phenomena. Students engage in such actions as looking, asking, accepting, listening, and noticing.

Responding   Responding involves some degree of interaction or involvement with the ideas, materials, or phenomena being learned in class. The interactions promote greater awareness and appreciation than simply "being aware" or receiving the content. Examples include complying, discussing, and supporting.

Valuing   At this level students show a commitment to certain ideas, materials, or phenomena. In short, they are able to find value in them. For example, they may participate freely, share, volunteer, withhold judgment, and support.

Organizing   Objectives written at the organizing level encourage students to defend their values, and to consider how consistent they hold these values when confronted with new ideas, materials, or phenomena. Examples of student activities include theorizing, questioning, comparing/contrasting, and examining.

Characterizing by Value   For this objective students act consistently with the values they have already organized. They are now able to "put into practice" their values. For example, students will adhere to a belief, influence others, verify a feeling, defend a belief, and solve problems.

Psychomotor Domain   The *psychomotor domain* helps students learn the coordinated use of the body's muscular system. Physical education is most often associated with this domain, but any time you want students to learn how to use their bodies you will tap into this domain. For example, a French teacher might employ a psychomotor objective that students will be able to shape their mouth and tongue in a way that allows for clear enunciation of a word. An English teacher may focus on the psychomotor domain when using drama in the classroom. One approach was developed by Dave (1970), and is still very applicable today. Dave's list is also a hierarchy, ranging from how a learner might begin to develop psychomotor skill and ability to a level of proficiency.

Imitation   Objectives for the imitation level are repeated movements from someone else. Students observe and pattern their behavior after someone who usually has more proficiency in a skill than they do. In this way, students can see a model of the behavior or movements. At the imitation level, student performance may be of low quality. Examples of imitation might be enunciating a Spanish word (following the teacher), copying a work of art, or imitating the teacher as she kicks a soccer ball.

Manipulation   At this level, students are able to perform certain actions more autonomously after receiving instructions and given opportunities to practice. Examples of this might be practicing fingering positions on a violin, or working to develop skill at shooting a basketball.

Precision   Objectives at the precision level are simply focused on improved skill in manipulations. Students begin to refine their movements and become more exact. The number of errors decrease noticeably, and performance quality shows significant improvement. Examples of this level include practice on more difficult skills, or working and reworking movement so it approaches being an "error free" level.

Articulation   Objectives at this level involve coordinating a series of actions and movement so that they are synchronized and efficient. Movement and body position approaches that of an expert, and practice sessions emphasize "minor adjustments" rather than significant changes. Examples of this level include developing a tumbling routine for a gymnastics performance, playing in a music recital, or competing against other skilled players in a game.

Naturalization   At this final level, a "high-level performance" is natural. While movement can still be refined and improved upon, body position, actions, and skills become automatic. Students do not need to think about their movement, and they can attend to other stimuli while performing. Examples of this level might be driving a car, playing basketball at a highly competitive level, or performing a dramatic interpretation in front of a live audience.[4]

MAKING IT WORK IN YOUR CONTENT AREA

Consider a favorite topic of yours within your content area—something that you look forward to helping students learn. What would be a cognitive objective for a lesson on that topic? Some content benefits from the affective domain, and others do not. If your topic would so benefit, write one that would explore this area. How about the psychomotor domain? If you expect students to learn a kinesthetic of body movement skills, add an objective for this domain. Refer to the categories for each of the three domains, and try to write objectives that are as high on the hierarchy as possible

IDS: A DIFFERENT APPROACH FOR THINKING ABOUT LEARNING OBJECTIVES

Another way to think about these three domains is in terms of *information*, *disposition*, and *skill* (IDS). When asking students to learn a particular topic, what information will they need and use, what attitudes or dispositions will best serve them, and what skill is required for them to perform effectively?

While schools often adhere to the domains of learning advanced by Bloom and his colleagues, this alternative approach for thinking about what students will learn in your classroom will enhance your learning objectives. This approach does not overturn the three domains just reviewed, but simply attempts to make student learning more specific. In class, your future students will learn academic course content, examine attitudes about learning and the content, and develop intellectual thinking skills. It is therefore helpful to think of the classroom as a place where students attain informational, attitudinal, and skill-based objectives. When you want to be sure students will learn facts, concepts, ideas, or other content-based information you plan with an *information objective*. When your students need to learn processes or thinking skills such as supporting an opinion with facts, searching the Internet, or developing a hypothesis, you plan with a *skill objective*. If your students need to develop skill at working together, cooperating with one another, or supporting each others' learning, then you will develop *disposition/attitude objectives*.

Consider the following hypothetical activity that attempts to demonstrate how using IDS objectives might work: Identify a current event that might have relevancy to your content, and is slightly controversial. Here are a few ideas to get you thinking: a current case of banning books; a recent Supreme Court ruling; a foreign policy decision; recent scientific findings about global warming; the controversy over stem cell research; or a news item about immigration. Next, consider this question, "If a civically minded adult were to develop an informed opinion about this issue, what information, dispositions/attitudes, and skills would he need to have?" Often it is helpful to think of this in terms of a four-column chart delineating *issue/event*, *information*, *dispositions/attitudes*, and *skills*.

Issue/Event	Information	Dispositions/Attitudes	Skills

By completing this chart for several different issues/events, you will find that the attitudes and skills remain fairly consistent, but the information changes depending on the issue. For example, if you decided to complete a chart for global warming, it might look like this:

Issue/Event	Information	Dispositions/Attitudes	Skills

Global Warming (GW)	Causes
	Effects
	Current U.S. policies
	Case studies
	Opposing viewpoints
		Openness to
		  opposing ideas
		Interest in the topic
		Desire to identify
		  truth
		Respect for other
		  opinions
		Belief that sharing
		  ideas is helpful
			Critiquing ideas
			Discussing
			  controversy
			Researching a topic
			Supporting opinions
			Listening to others

If this is what an adult needs when developing an informed decision, then what should you do with your students in your classroom to prepare them for adulthood? More than likely the contents of the "information" column will change as you teach your course. The attitudes and skills, however, can be addressed throughout a course. You may be able to write more specific and appropriate objectives by thinking of the cognitive and affective domains in terms of information, dispositions/attitudes, and skills.

While the traditional domains (cognitive, affective, and psychomotor) of Bloom and his colleagues are commonplace and useful in the public school, the IDS approach allows for diagnostic objective writing: you determine the learning needs of your students, then write out daily learning objectives to target specific information, dispositions, or skills.

FOUR ELEMENTS OF AN OBJECTIVE: THE ABCDs OF OBJECTIVE WRITING

Objectives, when written correctly, will help you design a lesson; they serve as a tool to help you think through what students will learn and what types of activities will help them learn best. Objectives are written as concise statements, and writing them takes some skill and practice. Armstrong and Savage (1994) have proposed that one approach for writing an objective is to think in terms of the letters *ABCD*. Each of these letters represents a part of the objective. Consider the following modified approach for using this technique:

A/B—Audience and Behavior: Who Will Be Learning, and What Activities Will They Engage In?

In this first step you will specify the students' performance and what they will produce by their actions. *Will* is the first verb in the objective. For example:

Students will list reasons for …
Students will write a three-hundred-word essay on …
Students will be able to graph the amount of rainfall during March.

C–Condition: When Will Students Be Undertaking the Activities?

In this second step you will describe the conditions under which students will produce/perform. These conditions might be:

on a test
after being given a ruler and calculator
using class notes

Thought of another way, although your students will be with you during the entire class session, you will not necessarily assess their learning at all times. By including the condition in your objective you are better prepared to determine when your students will demonstrate that they learned the desired content.

D—Degree: How Well Do You Want Students to Perform?

This final step simply states the criteria for the students. While this may be based on predetermined criteria (e.g., your school expects all ninth graders to be able to write out all 10 articles of the Bill of Rights), you will often need to determine your own criteria for student learning. When the students meet your criteria at this level or degree, then you have confidence that the students have learned the content. Examples of criteria might be:

9 out of 10 times
whenever asked to do so
with no spelling errors

These ABCD elements do not need to appear in the order presented above, but any learning objective should have all four of the elements. Consider the following examples:

Students will demonstrate their understanding (A, B) of the parts of a microscope by completing a worksheet (C) with 100% accuracy (D).

After a classroom discussion about the reasons for and against the electoral college (C), students will write a one-paragraph opinion statement (A, B), and support their ideas with at least two reasons (D).

On four out of five story problems (D), students will be able to correctly identify the pertinent information (A, B), and write it down in a mathematical equation (C).

THE ROLE OF OBJECTIVES IN DAILY LESSON PLANS

Objectives focus on the critical content or processes that you will teach during an activity, day, unit, or academic year; they therefore need to be thought about each day. Objectives also help to identify the learning you expect of your students and the specifics for how you will determine if they have learned the content adequately. Learning objectives also help your students: telling them your expectations for their learning, and identifying how the day's activities will help them learn, prepares them for the expectations of your lesson. The previous section explained why objectives use a concise formulaic language. When telling students these objectives you should adjust the wording so that the objectives are easily understood. For example, in the previous section you read the objective, *After a classroom discussion about the reasons for and against the electoral college, students will write a one-paragraph opinion statement, and support their ideas with at least two reasons.* Although you could write this on the chalkboard for your students, it would be clearer to your students if you write, "Discussion on opposing views of the electoral college: one-paragraph opinion article using at least two reasons." You could then tell the students, "We will have a discussion on the opposing points of view about the electoral college. Following the discussion you will have the chance to write a paragraph where you state your opinion about the usefulness of the electoral college, and support your opinion with at least two reasons."

The point is that objectives should be explained and accessible for your students (Slavin, 1999); students should know *what* they will learn, *why* they will learn it, and *how* they will be assessed. This will help them master the content, especially if they know how they will be assessed. Telling students ahead of time how they will demonstrate what they have learned helps them concentrate on what they are learning during the activities. Rather than causing angst or worry in the students, this approach can relieve pressure to perform because the assessment technique is no longer a mystery. Again, in the previous section you read this objective, *On four out of five word problems, students will be able to correctly identify the pertinent information, and write it down in a mathematical equation.* Students know from this objective that they will be expected to identify the pertinent information from a word problem. By being aware of this, they will be prepared to focus their learning on this skill. This not only helps you focus your instruction, but it helps the students focus their attention and learning.

As you teach you will want to consider the relevancy of your course content to your students' lives outside of school. Not everything needs to be readily applicable to the outside world; sometimes students need to learn facts and concepts simply to help their thinking skills and for helping understand more complex content. However, your students will appreciate opportunities to understand how information learned in your class might help them outside the classroom.

MAKING IT WORK IN YOUR CONTENT AREA

Identify a standard in your content that you have not worked with before, and compose three objectives according to the following criteria:

> Write one objective for learning course content (e.g., a key concept, fact, or perspective).
> Write one objective for a skill students will need in your class (e.g., skill in researching a topic, skill in discussing issue with others).
> Write either an affective objective or a social objective (e.g., appreciation for the subject, respect for other opinions).
> Make sure each objective has the ABCD elements.

> You could ask another middle/high school teacher or instructor to critique your objectives, and to tell you when, during the school year, this content is conventionally learned.

AN INTRODUCTION TO ASSESSMENT

Assessment is a key component of teaching. By assessing student learning you can determine how effectively you are teaching, whether you need to reteach a particular area, and how engaged the students are in their learning. Assessment is not merely the assignment of grades; it is a plan that allows you and your students to monitor their progress toward meeting specified goals and objectives. Assessments certainly provide information that can be graded, but—more important—assessment provides a systematic approach for guiding student learning. In this part of the chapter you will be introduced to the basic elements of assessment. As with our introduction to classroom management in chapter 1, specific assessment ideas are addressed later in the book for each of the instructional strategies. Each strategy requires specific assessment approaches. By contextualizing the assessment principles for each of the strategies, you will be in a strong position to appropriately determine your students' progress and learning.

Validity, Reliability, and Usability

Students commonly complain that they have studied information that was not on the test. They also wonder why exams sometimes include "trick" questions—those where the obvious answer is not the correct one. These complaints are challenges of validity. *Validity* means that the assessment is an accurate and appropriate measurement of student learning. An implication of this is that assessments have to be tied to instructional strategies. If you are lecturing to your students and ask them to prepare for a test the next day by studying their notes, then the assessment needs to be closely tied to the content in the notes. If they engage in a debate about the information, or write an essay about a topic loosely related to the notes, the validity of the assessment is questioned.

Objectives help to ensure that an assessment is valid. An infamous phrase in education is "teaching to the test." It is often used as a way to express frustration that some outside authority is determining the content of the tests, and teachers are in the unfavorable position to merely teach students the content of the impending tests. Testing is certainly a significant part of the education scene these days, and many stories circulate about how teachers have needed to abandon their conventional curriculum to prepare students to know the content upon which they will be tested. However, as the teacher, you will have many opportunities to develop assessments for your students. When you develop the assessments/tests based on what you want your students to learn, "teaching to the test" becomes a tool used to help students learn. The ABCD approach to developing objectives is one example of how you might teach to the test/assessment. By being very aware of the condition and degree to which you will assess student learning, you help to ensure that the assessments are valid. If an assessment is not valid, it should not be used.

Along with validity, assessments need to have a high degree of *reliability*. Reliability refers to the degree of confidence that an assessment tool will produce the same results over time. The Scholastic Aptitude Test (SAT) is designed to be highly reliable so that colleges have confidence that all students taking the SAT have been assessed on similar information. Reliability is a concern when teachers grade an essay. If the teacher does not have a rating scale (also known as a rubric, or a series of components she is looking for in the essay), then grading will be less reliable. This is sometimes referred to as "subjective" grading. If you have 75 essays to grade, how assured are you that you will grade the 75th essay the same way as the first? The more assured you are, the greater the reliability.

Usability is simply how difficult an assessment tool is to administer. One of the reasons that the traditional true-false test or multiple-choice test is popular among teachers is because of its ease of use and grading. Imagine that a teacher has three classes of 30 students (90 students total). If students can complete a true-false test in 15 minutes, and the teacher can grade each test in one minute, the teacher uses only 15 minutes of class time and needs 90 minutes of grading time. However, if the students each make 5-minute presentations, and the teacher needs 5 minutes to compose a written evaluation for each presentation, the teacher uses 450 minutes of class time and uses 450 minutes of grading time. The true-false test is a more usable assessment than the presentations. Chances are, however, that the presentations will provide a more valid assessment of student learning than the true-false test will.

All three of these components need to be considered when determining how to assess your students. Assessments must be valid, first and foremost. They must also provide information about your students' learning that is reliable. Finally, assessments need to be usable.

To make the assessment of student learning more valid and reliable, educators are utilizing different techniques for determining how well students have learned. The quiz or test is not the only tool that you have for determining learning, and it is often not the most valid assessment tool. Tests or quizzes tend to emphasize competition among students, and emphasize a student's ability to recall information and/or create a particular product. Instead of using an exam, the trend is to look at the whole picture of student performance in class and during all assignments, and to assess students' understanding of the process they have engaged in to create the product. For example, the National Council of Teachers of Mathematics recommends that teachers have students verbalize the process they went through when solving a problem, and not simply assess the final answer. If the process is correct, the final product will be, too.

Students are engaging in more self-assessments, where they are taught the tools needed to examine and evaluate their own performances. Earlier we mentioned that telling students your learning objectives will help them learn. Similarly, the trend now is to make students aware of the assessments ahead of time, so they can master the relevant content. Assessment is seen not as an end in itself but as a critically important feedback loop for instruction. The traditional test at the end of a unit may not be as valid of an assessment as a presentation three days earlier. If the presentation reveals that a student's understanding is incorrect, then the teacher is in a position to help that student relearn the content. Assessment is now seen as a tool for learning and not just for grading. Hammond (2004) has done considerable work on this subject. The following chart summarizes some of his findings on recent trends in classroom assessment:

From ...	... Toward
Written examinations ...	... Coursework
Teacher-led assessment ...	... Student-led assessment
Implicit criteria ...	... Explicit criteria
Competition with classmates ...	... Cooperation with classmates
Product assessment ...	... Process assessment
Content (facts/concepts only) ...	... Competencies (facts and skills)
Assessment for grading ...	... Assessment for learning

AUTHENTIC ASSESSMENT AND PERFORMANCE ASSESSMENT

What is it that a historian does? What skills does a novelist need to write a manuscript? How does a chemist identify the molecular makeup of an unidentified clear fluid? *Authentic assessments* resemble tasks that might occur outside of the school as well as in the classroom (Hiebert, Valencia & Afflerbach, 1994; Wiggins, 1993). For example, authentic assessments ask students to read real texts such as primary source documents, to write on meaningful topics for authentic purposes such as providing a public opinion to a newspaper editorial page, or conducting an experiment and drawing conclusions in the school science laboratory. In addition, authentic assessment values the thinking behind the work—the process—as much as the finished product (Wiggins, 1989; 1998). *Performance assessment* is a term that is often synonymous with authentic assessment. Performance assessments require students to demonstrate what they have learned and emphasize problem solving, thinking, and reasoning (Mathematical Sciences Education Board and National Research Council, 1993). Even the U.S. Congress determined that performance assessments are valid measures of student learning, and composed the following definition for educators:

> Performance assessment ... require[s] students to construct responses, rather than select from a set of answers, ... are criterion-referenced ... [and] in general, they focus on the process of problem solving rather than just on the end result. (Congress of the United States, 1992)

Authentic or performance assessments are usually longer and more complex than traditional pen-and-paper tests. On authentic assessment, Wiggins comments,

Do we want to evaluate student problem-posing and problem-solving in mathematics? Experimental research in science? Speaking, listening, and facilitating a discussion? Doing document-based historical inquiry? Thoroughly revising a piece of imaginative writing until it "works" for the reader? Then let our assessment be built out of such exemplary intellectual challenges. Comparisons with traditional standardized tests will help to clarify what "authenticity" means when considering assessment design and use:

Authentic assessments require students to be effective performers with acquired knowledge. Traditional tests tend to reveal only whether the student can recognize, recall or "plug in" what was learned out of context.

Authentic assessments present the student with the full array of tasks that mirror the priorities and challenges found in the best instructional activities: conducting research; writing, revising and discussing papers; providing an engaging oral analysis of a recent political event; collaborating with others on a debate, etc. Conventional tests are usually limited to paper-and-pencil, one-answer questions.

Authentic assessments attend to whether the student can craft polished, thorough and justifiable answers, performances or products. Conventional tests typically only ask the student to select or write correct responses—irrespective of reasons.

Authentic tasks involve "ill-structured" challenges and roles that help students rehearse for the complex ambiguities of the "game" of adult and professional life. Traditional tests are more like drills, assessing static and too-often arbitrarily discrete or simplistic elements of those activities. (Wiggins, 1990, p. 1)

Wiggins's mention of "ill-structured" challenges allows for the students to determine the structure and organization of their approach. The notion of a "clearly defined" but "ill-structured" task might help you think through authentic assessments in your content area. For example, student teaching for preservice teachers is a powerful authentic assessment that is both clearly defined and ill-structured: student teachers are asked to promote student learning on par with the cooperating teacher (a clearly defined task), but the planning, organizing, implementing, managing and assessing of myriad classroom elements is left to the student teacher (an ill-structured task). We discussed "backward design" earlier, but if we revisit it again here you can more clearly see how it impacts learning (Wiggin & McTighe, 2000). Consider how a conductor assesses the performances of the musicians in an orchestra. Or, consider how a coach assesses the performance of the players on a basketball team. Both might be based on the performance during the very authentic tasks of playing a musical score and competing during a game, and the performances are clearly understood before the very first practice session. This assessment is much more valid than a paper-and-pencil test (imagine how strange it would seem to not have a concert, but to have orchestra members complete a true/false test about the musical composition). When each of the instructional strategies is described in section 2 of this book, appropriate authentic assessments are contextualized and examined in depth. Each instructional strategy lends itself to particular assessments and a thorough examination of valid, reliable, and usable assessments are addressed for them in the respective chapters. However, some examples of authentic, performance assessments are:

- writing to real audiences such as a newspaper or magazine
- short investigations about a local community issue
- translating text into a foreign language
- developing a museum display
- engaging in a service-learning activity
- portfolios of work showing progress over time and examples of self-selected "best" work
- self-assessment by students of their performance

The following chart compares five different assessment techniques. By looking over the chart you can see that deciding how to assess your students needs to be a thoughtful process that is as important as any other part of the curriculum.

CHART OF FIVE ASSESSMENT TECHNIQUES

Assessment Method	Advantages of the Method	Disadvantages of the Method
Traditional pen-and-paper test (e.g., multiple choice, true-false, etc.)	Students are familiar with format. High in reliability and usability.	Often not a valid test of real-world actions. Time-consuming to develop.
Essays	Highly valid in that it allows students to demonstrate understanding of concepts, opinions, and attitudes. Possibility for student to express a unique understanding is greater.	Reliability: less control, therefore harder to quantify. Usability: time-consuming to write questions and grade responses.
Interviews and oral exams	More relaxed and personal feeling may enhance validity. Confusion can be clarified and jargon defined.	Teacher may not want to be critical on a face-to-face level. Hard to transcribe and quantify.
Performance assessment (e.g., presentation, recital, game, etc.)	Student demonstrates skill. Close to real-world experience. Rubric (rating scales) help focus student performance.	Reliability: can be difficult to grade. Usability: time-consuming because it depends on direct observation.
Product assessment (e.g., homework, research paper, photo portfolio, etc.)	Useful to determine accomplishments. Able to provide a standard to measure by.	Validity: does not show the process, but emphasizes the end result. Reliability—can be difficult to grade.

MAKING IT WORK IN YOUR CONTENT AREA

What is the equivalent of a concert or a game in your content area? In other words, how might students in your content area engage in assessment tasks that are authentic measurements of what they have learned, and that are tasks they might engage in outside of school? Refer to the list of examples in the previous section to get you started, and brainstorm at least three different activities that are authentic and/or performance assessments.

Rubrics

Like any evaluation process, authentic assessments must provide fair and reliable measurements of student learning. A rubric is a tool that lists the criteria for student performance, and describes levels of quality for each of the criteria. For example, the following rubric might be used to assess students' presentations. It clearly lists the criteria and levels of quality in four categories: demonstrated knowledge; use of visuals; explanation of main points; and presentation skills/ mechanics. Students receive a score from zero to three in each category:

	Criteria for Student Presentation				
Categories	*3*	*2*	*1*	*0*	*Points*
Demonstrates knowledge	Shows complete understanding of the content s/he researched, and answers questions accurately.	Shows substantial understanding of the content s/he researched, answers some questions accurately.	Shows limited understanding of the content s/he researched, and has difficulty with questions.	Shows a lack of understanding of the content s/he researched, and is unable to answer questions.	_____/3
Use of visuals	Clear diagram, PowerPoint slide or poster, highlighting main ideas.	Clear diagram, PowerPoint slide or poster, but missing some main ideas.	Inappropriate or unclear diagram, PowerPoint slide or poster.	No visuals.	_____/3
Explanation	A complete response to the main question, with a detailed explanation.	Good solid response to the main question, with clear explanation.	Response to and explanation of the main question are unclear.	Misses key points.	_____/3
Mechanics	Presentation is well rehearsed, fits in the time allocation, and is easy to understand.	Presentation is practiced, and/ or is close to the time allocation.	Presentation needs more rehearsal, and/ or is not close to the time allocation. Difficult to understand main points.	Lack of preparation is apparent. Main points are unclear.	_____/3
				Total:	_____/12

Rubrics help students and teachers define "quality." They increase reliability, and reduce subjective or biased grading. Rubrics also help teachers clearly explain to students why they received a particular score. If students receive a rubric at the beginning of a project they can accept more responsibility for their learning, because they know the expectations of the assessment from the start. If a student needs extra assistance with one area of the rubric, then you will be able to focus on the criteria listed on the rubric for that area. Additionally, when you create a rubric at the beginning of a unit, you are able to plan your lessons in ways that allow your students to meet the criteria stated in the rubric. As we mentioned earlier, this is a form of backward design. We suggest first identifying the categories that you will assess students on by thinking through your expectations. Once the categories are established, you should consider the criteria for two extremes of student work for each category: excellent performances and unsatisfactory performances. The remaining criteria can then be modified for the number of levels you are willing to let students attain. The example above has four levels, so we had to identify different criteria for each. With more levels you will be able to differentiate the quality of student work more, but it will be a more difficult task to create unique criteria for each level. RubiStar (http://www.rubistar4teachers.org) is one of many Internet sites that are designed help teachers design, develop, and use rubrics. We encourage you to visit this site, because it will help you think about the categories and criteria you could have for an assignment. The downside of a website or program that helps you develop a rubric is that it is usually very generic, and does not provide specific expectations for each criteria level. Ideally you will have criteria, and even examples of work, for each of the levels of the rubric. You want the expectations to be clearly understood by students. This is not always possible with ready-made rubrics. We suggest using generic rubrics as a starting point, then adding your own detail, specific to your expectations of an assignment. We will provide more examples of rubrics designed specifically for an instructional strategy in section 2 of this book.

Diagnostic, Formative, and Summative Assessment

Diagnostic Assessment   Although some authors describe diagnostic assessment as a component of formative assessment, most consider it a distinct form of measurement (Kellough & Kellough, 1999; McMillan, 2004). Just as a medical doctor looks at a patient and comes up with a diagnosis for treatment, diagnostic assessments usually occur prior to instruction, and attempt to determine students' strengths, weaknesses, knowledge, and skills. Identifying these helps teachers differentiate the curriculum to meet each student's unique needs. For example, a history teacher might give a pretest on the first day of class to see how much information students remember about the Civil War. Depending on the results, the teacher is able to determine the course content that needs to be learned. At one high school, the mathematics department gives a series of diagnostic measurements to all entering freshmen. Teachers then use the scores to place students into the appropriate mathematics course. The teachers also use the scores to help monitor the progress of each student during their first year of high school.

Formative Assessment   Formative assessment occurs continually during each school day so the teacher is able to monitor student learning. Formative assessment provides information on how students are "forming" their understanding. The National Council of Teachers of Mathematics has developed *Principles and Standards for School Mathematics* (2000), and while it is designed for mathematics, the council's principles around formative assessment transcend content, and are applicable to all subjects:

> Assessment should be more than merely a test at the end of instruction to see how students perform under special conditions; rather, it should be an integral part of instruction that informs and guides teachers as they make instructional decisions. Assessment should not merely be done *to* students; rather, it should also be done *for* students, to guide and enhance their learning. (Paragraph 1; emphasis in the original)

Formative assessment provides information to the teacher about how to appropriately "form" objectives for future lessons, and promote student learning. For example, if several students misunderstand photosynthesis, formative assessments will identify this learning problem and allow the teacher to take strides toward remediation. Formative assessments often are not graded, and allow for the teacher and students to develop a deeper understanding of the curriculum. They provide information for adapting teaching and learning to meet student needs (Boston, 2002). Sometimes formative assessment is labeled *progress monitoring*. When teachers monitor students' progress, and are able to identify where students are having trouble, they can make necessary instructional adjustments, such as reteaching, trying alternative instructional approaches, or offering more opportunities for practice. These activities can lead to improved student success (Black & Wiliam, 1998a). Teachers can formatively assess students' understanding in the following ways (Black & Wiliam, 1998a, 1998b; Boston, 2002):

Have students write their understanding of vocabulary or concepts before and after instruction.

Ask students to summarize the main ideas they've taken away from a lecture, discussion, or assigned reading.

Have students complete a few problems or questions at the end of instruction and check answers.

Interview students individually or in groups about their thinking as they solve problems.

Assign brief, in-class writing assignments (e.g., "Why is this person or event representative of this time period in history?"). A similar strategy is often referred to as an "exit card." Exit cards can be used to determine what students have learned. Students write down one or two main ideas that they learned during class, or they respond to a question from the teacher. As they leave the class they hand this in (it serves as a pass that allows them to exit the classroom).

Summative Assessment   Summative assessment is the attempt to summarize student learning at some point in time. This is the assessment that students, parents, and the public tend to value most because it is so closely tied to grades. Where diagnostic and formative assessments provide direction for future instruction, summative assessments typically do not. Consider this analogy for understanding the difference between formative and summative assessments: When the cook tastes the soup, that is formative assessment; when the customer tastes the soup, that is summative assessment (Stevens, Lawrenz, & Sharp, 1996). Summative assessment occurs at or near the end of a unit, chapter, term, or course. The purpose is to evaluate or grade student learning. The Scholastic Aptitude Test, the Miller Analogies Test, and most standardized exams are also examples of summative assessments. Most statewide assessments are summative (including testing to address such federal initiatives as the No Child Left Behind Act). They are not designed to provide the immediate, contextualized feedback useful for helping teacher and student during the learning process. High-quality summative information can, of course, shape how teachers organize their courses or what schools offer their students. However, it is not often useful for helping teachers work to improve the learning of individual students.

Three More Important Assessment Terms   When thinking and reading about assessment, three other terms will often be used: *norm-referenced assessment*, *criterion-referenced assessment*, and *self-referenced assessment*. *Norm referencing* allows for people to be ranked, put in an order based on their scores. It is competitive. For example, in a class of 25 students, a teacher might use norm-referencing to assign grades to students by determining that the top 20% receive A's, the next B's, and so on. Such a scale looks like this:

A: the five students with the highest grades
B: the next five students
C: the next five students
D: the next five students
F: the five students with the lowest grades

While this is a traditional grading scale, these figures are arbitrary. If the results of any assessment allow you to rank students from high score to low score, then the test is norm-referenced. Many standardized tests are norm-referenced, as is an IQ (intelligence quotient) test. This approach is not used very often by teachers. Rather than having students compete against each other for a grade, teachers would rather have them focus on meeting specific criteria.

Criterion referencing is the term used for assessment against fixed criteria. Potentially, everyone can pass a criterion-referenced assessment—or everyone can fail. While norm-referencing also has criteria (e.g., the criteria for an "A" grade is to have the top five point totals in the class), criteria-referenced assessments determine whether a student has adequately met a minimum level or standard. Criteria are usually determined in advance to ensure that they are valid and appropriate. For example, a driver's license test is often criteria-referenced. It does not matter how well you do, as long as you do not make a pre-specified number of errors. A pass/fail grade might serve as another example. If you earn a specific number of points (e.g., 70% of the total) you pass the course. It does not matter how many points you earn, as long as you meet the criterion. The concern with this assessment is that it identifies only a minimum level of achievement. This is often justified by the advantage of not basing success on comparing scores with others.

Many teachers determine the criteria needed for different grades. For example, a percentage of the total points is needed for an "A" grade. A grade scale that uses multiple criteria could look like this:

A: 90%–100% of the possible points
B: 80%–89% of the possible points
C: 70%–79% of the possible points
D: 60%–69% of the possible points
F: 59% or less of the possible points

Self-referencing is an assessment by the student against himself—or, more particularly, against previous best performances. A computer keyboard or typing class may use this to help a student assess his improvement. A baseline score indicating number of words per minutes is taken at the start of the course, and this is compared with measurements taken throughout the year. Grading with this is problematic because students who have prior knowledge or skill will not be able to improve as much as someone who enters with no prior skill. Self-referencing is most relevant to helping students meet individual goals.

MAKING IT WORK IN YOUR CONTENT AREA

Return to the objectives you wrote earlier in the chapter for your content area. For each objective, develop appropriate diagnostic, formative, and/or summative assessment activities that will help students meet your objective. For example, if you are teaching an earth science course, you might have the following objective: *Students will be able to identify the main minerals in each of the four layers of the earth.* You could diagnostically assess students' understanding by handing out a diagram of the earth on the first day of class and having each student identify the layers. This information will help you know the content knowledge students have prior to the unit. You could formatively assess students during the unit by having them write down the minerals in the first two layers of the Earth, and asking them to explain why these minerals are present. This will allow you to assess how accurately students are acquiring knowledge. A summative assessment could be a PowerPoint presentation through which the student provides slides and descriptions of each of the four layers, and details about the minerals in each layer. This serves as a cohesive plan for helping meet the objective.

Using this as an example, develop assessments for your objectives, and what the purpose of each assessment might be.

CHAPTER REVIEW

Goals provide the general direction for a course. Objectives specify how and when you can help students meet those goals. *Long-term objectives* will be accomplished after a longer unit, semester, or even an entire course. Objectives that are met during an activity or after a few class sessions are *short-term objectives*. Long-term and short-term objectives will need to be restated or revised if students need repeated assistance learning a skill or understanding a concept.

Teachers categorize learning objectives to help focus instruction on specific areas (or domains) of the learner. The three traditional domains are:

1. the cognitive domain
2. the affective domain
3. the psychomotor domain

Another way to think about these three domains is in terms of *information*, *disposition*, and *skill* (IDS).

When writing objectives it is helpful to think in terms of the ABCD approach:

A/B   audience and behavior
C   condition
D   degree

This chapter has also described assessment as a critical component of teaching. Assessment helps to determine how well students have learned. Assessments must be *valid*, first and foremost. They must also provide information about your students' learning that is *reliable*. Finally, assessments need to be *usable*. All three of these components need to be considered when determining how to assess your students.

Assessment is not seen as an end in itself, but as a critically important feedback loop for monitoring student learning and informing your instruction. *Authentic assessments* resemble tasks that might occur outside of the school as well as in the classroom. *Performance assessment* is a term that is commonly used synonymously with authentic assessment.

Assessments should be developed at the beginning of a unit so you can "design backward" by developing lessons that prepare students to meet the assessment expectations. *Rubrics* help students and teachers define "quality." They increase reliability, and reduce subjective or biased grading. Rubrics also help teachers clearly explain to students why they received a particular score.

In this chapter we introduced you to diagnostic, formative, and summative assessments. When you assess students to gain insight into their existing levels of understanding or skill, you will use a *diagnostic assessment* tool. *Formative assessment* occurs continually during each school day so the teacher is able to monitor student learning; it provides information on how students are "forming" their understanding. *Summative assessments* provide a summary of what students have learned.

Assessments are also categorized as norm-referenced, criterion-referenced, and self-referenced. *Norm referencing* compares students based on their score. *Criterion referencing* is the term used for assessment against fixed criteria. Potentially everyone can pass a criterion-referenced assessment—or everyone can fail. *Self-referencing* is assessment against oneself—or, more particularly, against one's own previous best performance.

NOTES

1. The term *learning objectives* is widely used, but it is certainly not the only such term used in education. Synonymous terms that you might hear are *instructional objectives*, *student learning objectives*, or *learning outcomes*.
2. See appendix C for a list of verbs that can be used when writing cognitive objectives at each of the six levels.
3. See appendix D for a list of verbs that can be used when writing affective objectives at each of the five levels.
4. Some of these ideas are adapted from work done by Donald Clark; see http://www.nwlink.com/~donclark/hrd/bloom.html (accessed December 2004).

REFERENCES

Armstrong, D. G., & Savage, T. V. (1994). *Secondary education.* New York: Macmillan.

Biehler, R. F. (1971). *Psychology applied to teaching.* Boston: Houghton Mifflin.

Black, P., & Wiliam, D. (1998a). Assessment and classroom learning. *Assessment in Education, 5*(1), 7–74.

Black, P., & Wiliam, D. (1998b). Inside the black box: Raising standards through classroom assessment. *Phi Delta Kappan, 80*(2), 139–148.

Bloom, B. S. (Ed.). (1956). *Taxonomy of educational objectives: Handbook I; Cognitive domain.* New York: David McKay.

Boston, C. (2002). The concept of formative assessment. *Practical Assessment, Research and Evaluation, 8*(9). Retrieved November 9, 2004 from http://PAREonline.net/getvn.asp?v=8&n=9.

Congress of the United States, Office of Technology Assessment. (1992, February). *Testing in American schools: Asking the right questions.* Washington, DC: U.S. Government Printing Office.

Dave, R. H. (1970). Psychomotor levels. In R. J. Armstrong (Ed.), *Developing and writing behavioral objectives.* Tuscon, AZ: Educational Innovators Press.

Hammond, G. (2004). Testing and evaluation. Retrieved March 2006 from http://xnet.rrc.mb.ca/glenh/outline.htm.

Hiebert, E. H., Valencia, S. W., & Afflerbach, P. P. (1994). Understand authentic reading assessment: Definitions and perspectives. In S. W. Valencia, E. H. Hiebert, & P. P. Afflerbach (Eds.), *Authentic reading assessment: Practices and possibilities* (pp. 6–21). Newark, DE: International Reading Association.

Kellough, R. D., & Kellough, N. G. (1999). *Secondary school teaching: A guide to methods and resources; planning for competence.* Upper Saddle River, NJ: Prentice-Hall.

Krathwohl, D. R., Bloom, B. S., & Masia, B. B. (1964). *Taxonomy of educational objectives: Handbook 2: Affective domain.* New York: David McKay.

Mathematical Sciences Education Board and National Research Council (1993). *Measuring up: Prototypes for mathematics assessment.* Washington, DC: National Academy Press.

McMillan, J. H. (2004). *Classroom assessment: Principles and practice for effective instruction* (3rd ed.). Upper Saddle River, NJ: Allyn and Bacon.

National Council of Teachers of Mathematics (2000). The assessment principle, in *Principles and Standards for School Mathematics.* Retrieved December 2, 2004, from http://standards.nctm.org/document/chapter2/assess.htm.

Simpson, E. J. (1972). *The classification of educational objectives in the psychomotor domain* (vol. 3). Washington, DC: Gryphon House.

Slavin, R. E. (1999). Comprehensive approaches to cooperative learning. *Theory into Practice, 38*(2), 74–79.

Stevens, F., Lawrenz, F., & Sharp, L. (1996). *User-friendly handbook for project evaluation: Science, mathematics, engineering, and technology education.* Arlington, VA: National Science Foundation.

Wiggins, G. (1990). The case for authentic assessment. *Practical Assessment, Research and Evaluation, 2*(2). Retrieved December 6, 2004 from http://PAREonline.net/getvn.asp?v=2&n=2.

Wiggins, G. (1993). Assessment: Authenticity, context, and validity. *Phi Delta Kappan, 75*(3), 200–214.

Wiggins, G. (1998). *Educative assessment: designing assessments to inform and improve student performance.* San Francisco: Jossey-Bass.

Wiggins, G., & McTighe, J. (2000). *Understanding by design.* Alexandra, VA: Association for Supervision and Curriculum Development.

CITED WEBSITES

Donald Clark's homepage about Bloom's taxonomy:
        http://www.nwlink.com/~donclark/hrd/bloom.html
RubiStar (rubric creator):
        http://www.rubistar4teachers.org

4

LONG- AND SHORT-RANGE PLANNING

Planning helps teachers organize what they will teach during the school year, the semester, the unit, and the daily lesson. Planning also helps teachers organize and structure the school day so that student learning is maximized. We believe that many classroom management and discipline problems can be avoided if the teacher is organized and a strong planner. If you have a clear idea of what you intend for students to learn, not only during that day's lesson but for the coming weeks, then you will be in a good position to address student concerns about the content, and have a better understanding of your expectations for student learning.

YEARLONG SCOPE AND SEQUENCE

According to the National Center for Education Statistics,[1] American schools are open an average of 180 days per year. These days are divided by districts and schools into smaller segments such as two 90-day semesters, three 60-day trimesters, or four 45-day quarters. *Scope* and *sequence* are two terms that many educators use; they refer to the breadth of content and skills students should learn (scope), and the order in which students will learn this content (sequence) during these 180 days. *Yearlong planning* is simply the scope and sequence for a course during the school year. Each state usually determines the scope and sequence for courses in each of the grades K–12. Consider these two examples of scope and sequence for two courses:

THE STATE OF VIRGINIA'S SCOPE AND SEQUENCE FOR ALGEBRA 1[2]

Using Algebraic Topics
Linear Equations and Inequalities
Systems of Equations
Relations and Functions: Linear
Relations and Functions: Quadratic

WASHINGTON STATE'S SCOPE AND SEQUENCE FOR U.S. HISTORY (HIGH SCHOOL)[3]

Industrialization and the Emergence of the United States as a World Power (1877–1919)
Reform, Prosperity, and Depression (1918–1938)
World War II, the Cold War, and International Relations (1939–Present)
Post–World War II Domestic, Political, Social, and Economic Issues (1945–Present)

Many states and districts have developed or are developing expectations for the content that should be taught at each grade level to ensure that as students move through the grades they learn content in a predetermined sequence. Many of these are available online, and are usually based on the national standards for each content area. A familiar example of scope and sequence is offered by mathematics courses. Students enroll in geometry, and then proceed to algebra 1 and 2, algebra 3 and 4, trigonometry, and calculus. Not all students complete these levels, but the scope of each course and the sequence in which each course is taught is clearly specified. Most content areas have a scope and sequence for the year as well as the scope and sequence across grade levels. This is a great help for you as beginning teachers because it provides insight into what content students should have learned prior to your class, it suggests the content that students need to learn in your course, and it identifies the content that students will need to know for the years after your course.

School districts and individual schools also develop a yearlong scope and sequence for each grade level. These are tied to the state expectations, but may include additional content that districts or schools believe are important. In our work with schools we have found that some districts provide teachers incredible freedom to develop their own scope and sequence, while other districts require teachers to adhere to a specific program. For example, a common set of topics and concepts for a middle school earth science course is as follows:

geologic time
plate tectonics
plate tectonics
earthquakes
volcanoes
mountains
rocks
fossils

You might teach in a district in which you are expected to teach just these topics, and to teach them in this order. If that is the case, your yearlong scope and sequence is predetermined. You still have opportunities to determine how to promote student learning as you select instructional strategies, but the overall content of the course must meet these expectations. Just as likely, however, you might teach in a district that allows you to add to these topics, and does not specify the sequence in which students learn them. In this latter situation you will need to determine the instructional strategies and the overall topics for the school year.

As the planning moves closer to the daily lesson, the level of specificity increases. As can be seen with the Virginia and Washington examples above, the yearlong scope and sequence are often not very specific. They usually do not specify the number of days to be spent on a topic, subtopics students should learn, assessment tools, or learning objectives. They simply provide an overarching idea of the content students should learn during the school year, and the order in which topics and concepts should be learned.

Textbooks present content in an order that attempts to match the yearlong scope and sequence of a course. For example, history textbooks usually present content in the chronological order that most teachers use when teaching world history. Students, then, are able to read through the textbook as they learn the course content. Mathematics and science textbooks are similar. Language arts and literature textbooks are not as easily organized, and teachers do not necessarily teach courses in the order laid out in the books' chapters. Physical education and music often do not use textbooks at all. Often, textbooks provide superficial coverage of too much information; we suggest that you determine how the textbook might supplement your planning and curriculum, and not depend on the textbook to determine the scope and sequence of your course. As was discussed in chapter 2, textbook publishers are one of many powerful influences on a teacher making curricular decisions. Teachers gather information from these stakeholders, but in most cases you will have considerable freedom to pull the course scope and sequence together by using your professional judgment while collaborating with others in your district.

Scope and sequence usually are used in reference to long-range planning; any time a teacher plans, she should think about the scope and sequence of the content. However, scope and sequence are also important when planning a series of lessons that will comprise a unit plan, and even when planning for a single day's activities. The scope of the content and the sequential ordering of events need to be thoughtfully considered when planning. Teachers develop lesson plans for each day they teach, and these plans are placed in a sequence, or order, that the teacher thinks will help students understand the content. Often a series of lesson plans are placed together to form a unit plan. Unit plans are sequenced together to form a course plan, and the courses are sequenced to form a yearlong plan. We will explore this more as we examine unit planning and lesson planning.

MAKING IT WORK IN YOUR CONTENT AREA

Look at the national standards available in your content area (see chapter 2 for an initial list), and standards that your state may have for teaching your subject/course. For quick access to the standards of all states visit the Education World website, which has links for each state (http://www.education-world.com/standards/state/index.shtml).

Using the state and national standards, write down the yearlong scope and sequence for your course. Talk with a teacher who teaches this course, and compare what you have come up with to what the teacher has developed for the 180-day school year. Consider the following qusations: What is the difference between what you came up with and the teacher's plan? What is similar? How do the two plans reflect the state standards? How do they reflect national standards? How did the two of you go about the process of making your selections?

FOUR COMMONPLACES IN SCHOOL

Awareness of the standards, goals, and suggested scope and sequence for your course is the first step in planning. As we mentioned earlier in this chapter, these will be available to you at the national, state, district, school, and even department levels. The scope and sequence plans provide topics for more focused unit plans, which in turn provide direction for the specific lesson plans. Before we start to describe these unit and lesson plans, however, it is important to consider all that is involved when planning. Schwab (1973) developed the idea that all classrooms have four elements in common; they all have a *teacher*, *students*, a subject matter or *content* that is to be learned, and an environment or *milieu* in which teaching and learning take place. If any one of these four commonplaces is hindered, then learning is thwarted. Any planning or thinking about curriculum—of what should be taught and learned—must consider how these four aspects of every classroom interact.

These four commonplaces should not be thought of as a hierarchy. Though it is tempting in an age of testing and accountability to think of content as the most important aspect of the classroom, Schwab's ideas remind us that all four commonplaces must work together if learning is to occur. As illustrated in figure 4.1, if any of the four sides is removed, the entire structure collapses. Consider how the following examples show teacher, students, content, and milieu codependence affecting teaching and learning:

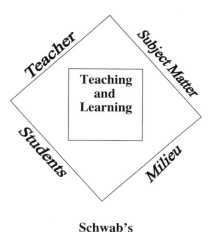

Schwab's
Four Commonplaces

Figure 4.1

If your students already understand the key concepts you want them to learn, then the content will impact what you have planned for the day. Similarly, if the content is too difficult for students to understand (for example, the reading level of a text is too high, the premise of your main point is not accepted by the students, or students do not have adequate prior knowledge), then the learning will be impacted by the *content* commonplace.

If the students are not prepared, not engaged, or distracted, they will not be ready to think about the content you planned for them to learn. This might happen if they did not complete a reading assignment, if your class meets immediately following a school assembly, or even if a noisy lawnmower is cutting grass outside your classroom. In each of these instances the *students* will affect you (the *teacher*), the *content*, and the *milieu*.

If you are discussing a controversial subject in your classroom, students may perceive the milieu as unsafe, and feel uncomfortable sharing their ideas. In turn, this will affect the depth that a topic can be examined, and your selection of an instructional strategy.

If students are making presentations to the class and the desks are positioned in groups of four (so the students are facing each other and not the front of the room), the physical setup of the room, the *milieu*, may distract students from listening to the presentations. This will affect the students' opportunities to learn from the presentations, or to present to classmates who are listening; and you, the teacher, might even get frustrated that students are talking too much.

When we work with student teachers, we will often encourage them to reflect on a lesson after they have taught. The four commonplaces provide focus for that reflection. By asking questions such as "How prepared was I (the teacher) for the lesson?" "Were the students engaged in the learning process?" "Was the content age/ability appropriate?" and "Did the classroom environment promote learning?" teachers are able to critique the class session. For example, consider a case in which students were distracted by a physical education class playing soccer outside the classroom (affecting the *student*), causing the student teacher to became annoyed and frustrated (affecting the *teacher*); this put a damper on the positive tone that had been established (affecting the *milieu*), thus causing the role-play exercise that was occurring to fizzle (affecting the *content*). While reflecting on this lesson a student teacher might mistakenly think that students don't learn much during the role-play exercise and become wary of trying the strategy with another class. Realizing the interdependence of the commonplaces will help a teacher more clearly reflect upon the events of the classroom. This reflective approach could lead to the conclusion that to simply shut the shades quietly without responding emotionally could positively affect the other commonplaces.

Our point for thinking about Schwab's work is simply to remind you that part of planning is taking into consideration all the aspects of the *student* (maturity, diversity, ability, motivation, etc.), the *content* (standards, goals, objectives, etc.), the *milieu* (a perception of safety within a community of learners, etc.), and the *teacher* (a knowledge of the content, an understanding of the students, skill at managing the classroom, a choice of instructional strategies, etc.). These four commonplaces direct your planning, and determine how effective the instruction has been in promoting student learning.

MAKING IT WORK IN YOUR CONTENT AREA

Decide on a concept that you might teach in your content area. Imagine that you will be able to spend about 45 minutes on this concept with your students. After you have come up with the concept, consider each of the following situations that could occur in your classroom, and consider the commonplaces that are most affected (remember that if one commonplace is affected, all four will be).

> Situation #1: Of the 30 students in your class, 20 are in the gifted program at your school. Which commonplace is affected? How does it impact your classroom and all students' learning?
>
> Situation #2: A fire drill occurs for the first 10 minutes of class. By the time you have students back in class, you have 10 minutes left. Which commonplace is affected? How does it impact your classroom and student learning?

Brainstorm other situations where different commonplaces might interact to impact student learning.

THE UNIT PLAN

The *unit plan* is the compilation of lesson plans during a specific amount of time—for example, two weeks—and provides specific focus on course content. By placing daily lessons in a unit, the content students learn is connected. Students are able to recognize relationships in each daily lesson, because of a conceptual or thematic link that the unit plan provides. A few examples help explain this:

> During a unit on China, a geography teacher is able to examine five common geographic themes (location, place, human/environment interactions, movement, and region). Since the unit is on China, students know that the different geographic concepts will all be applied to content about that country.
>
> A biology teacher connects two weeks of lesson activities that include dissecting a frog, watching a video, reading from the textbook, and completing labs on blood-sugar levels and blood pressure when teaching a unit on the circulatory system.
>
> A Spanish teacher presents a series of lessons about beliefs, foods, religion, and traditions during a unit on Mexican culture.

By segmenting the school year into units, you are able to think clearly about needed resources for upcoming units, prerequisite knowledge for each unit, and key concepts and skills that a unit presents. The 180 days of school could be divided into 18 units of 10 days each. We do not mean to imply that units must be about two weeks long. Often they are three or four weeks long, or they can be merely one week long. Rather than thinking of a unit as a specific number of days, think of a unit as helping students learn a specific portion of content and/or develop particular skills.

Essential Questions

Without planned units, daily lessons lack focus. Lessons should be developed because they will help students learn the specific knowledge or skills identified for the unit. As you can see, units are an effective tool for designing lessons that meet your objectives, goals, and curriculum standards. They allow teachers to map out the activities and strategies that will help ensure that students learn specified course content. Erickson (2002) and Wiggins and McTighe (2005) suggest that unit plans should be developed around *essential questions*. Essential questions address the big ideas or fundamental concepts that we want students to think about and learn during the span of a unit. By posing questions, students and teacher are able to focus their attention on content that will help answer the questions. Essential questions, thus, provide a focus for the unit. As an example of how to organize curriculum, we provide a sample unit with essential questions at the end of this chapter.

Components of a Unit Plan

While unit plans can have many components, the following eight are frequently used by teachers when planning:

1. overview and rationale
2. goals and essential questions
3. objectives
4. outline of content (the scope of the content in the unit)
5. calendar (the sequence in which students will learn the content)
6. daily lesson plans
7. assessments and evaluations
8. materials and resources

The following descriptions of these components will clarify their purpose in the unit plan.

Overview and Rationale   The *rationale* for the unit provides a general *overview* and justification for teaching a unit on the topic you are selecting. The overview and rationale allow you to consider your reasons for developing the unit, and to determine how the content will build on your students' prior knowledge and skills. The overview also prepares you to consider available materials and resources, and how the unit fits into the overall scope and sequence for the school year. An overview and rationale often include:

A title for the unit.

The course in which this will be taught (e.g., world history, algebra, Spanish 2).

The grade level (e.g., ninth grade).

A full introduction to the unit that addresses the question, *What is it you will be teaching, and more critically, what is it that students will be learning?* Be specific about the content of the unit and the activities in which the students will be engaged in order to learn the content.

A description of how the unit fits into the existing curriculum. For example, what topic would precede the unit? What will follow it, and why? What existing skills and abilities should students possess before studying this unit? What skills, abilities, and knowledge will the students gain from this unit?

Your rationale statement considers the idea that of all the possible topics you *could* have selected, what you *did* select for this unit, and why you selected it. The rationale also prepares you to answer colleagues, parents, students, and others who might wonder why this content is important for students to learn. You might also consider how students will be able to use content and skills learned in the unit outside of school.

Goals and Essential Questions   *Goals* (which were described earlier in chapter 2) are often clearly connected to a skill or content standard at the state or national level. Unit goals should include both academic content goals and skill goals. Often, *essential questions* come from these goals. These are broad questions that will help the development of the unit. A unit typically has two to four essential questions.

Objectives   *Objectives* are concise, formulaic learning outcomes that you want students to achieve during the study of your unit. Before teachers compose objectives, they often preassess their students to see what content and skills students already have (or what deficits exist). These preassessments could occur during an informal question/answer session or discussion, or from a more formal pretest, survey, or series of interviews. Teachers also use their knowledge and previous experiences of what students typically know when they come to class. Concise, well-articulated, and focused objectives are critical for a well-organized unit, because they focus the unit and will assist in your daily and long-range planning. Many unit objectives are not met until partway through, or at the end of, a unit; therefore, they are broad and not tied to specific daily lessons. Objectives should be written for academic content/information you want students to learn, skills you want them to gain, and dispositions you want them to develop. Follow the criteria for well-written objectives that you utilized in chapter 3, and include the following:

What content will students be learning, and what activities will promote student learning?[4]

How well should students be able to perform to demonstrate they have learned?

Try to list the unit objectives under each learning goal you have established. This will establish a link among the goals and objectives.

Outline of Content   An *outline of content* provides a concise overview, and answers the question, *What academic content will students learn from this unit?* The content outline is not a list of activities or instructional strategies— those will be determined after you determine the content that needs to be learned by your students. The content outline is often referred to as the scope of the content in the unit. You should not feel that you are creating this outline on your own. National and state standards provide guidance, as do some scope and sequence guides, and textbook teacher guides. Unit content outlines do not list everything that students will learn. Rather, they provide key concepts, categories, and topical areas in the unit. For example, part of a content outline for a unit on American Democracy might include the following:

I. Branches of Government
  A.   Executive Branch
      1. President
        a.   Terms
        b.   Requirements
      2. Powers
        a.   Chief Executive
        b.   Chief of Staff
        c.   Commander in Chief
      3. Checks and Balances
        a.   Veto
        b.   Nomination
  B.   Legislative Branch
  C.   Judicial Branch
II. Elections

Calendar   The unit *calendar* gives an overview of the sequence of lessons. It provides the teacher with a "unit at a glance" in regard to content, instructional strategies, and classroom activities; this aids in developing daily objectives and lesson plans. Each day of the unit calendar identifies the topic to be taught, possible instructional activities, and assessments of student learning. The calendar becomes a device for considering the order in which the content will be taught/learned. This is often referred to as the sequence of a unit. The calendar also helps you think about how much time you need to spend on each topic.

By putting the unit objectives into the calendar, you will be able to ensure that your objectives are fully addressed during the unit. Similarly, by listing the instructional strategies you might use, you can check that you are using a variety of activities, both within and across days. The unit calendar could look like the following example for a high school art 1 class. (We have also included one in the unit example at the end of this chapter.)

UNIT TITLE: X-RAY ANIMALS BY KATE OBUKOWICZ

Day 1	Day 2	Day 3	Day 4	Day 5
Topic: Introduction to unit	Topic: Native American Lore	Topic: Norval Morriseau	Topic: Art criticism	Topic: Skit day
Objective: 1.1, 1.2	*Objective: 2.1*	*Objective: 3.2*	*Objective: 2.2*	*Objective: 2.2*
Event: Morrisseau hook. Discussion of the qualities of Morrisseau's paintings. Review color theory and patterns. Introduce X-ray painting assignment, and go over rubric.	Event: Listen to Native American lore read by the teacher, and read on the Internet. Go to computer lab. Internet worksheet.	Event: Read articles on Norval Morriseau and work on art criticism worksheet.	Event: Art criticism. Group time to plan out 3- to 5-minute animal skit.	Event: Skits at the beginning of class. Sketch three possible animal-symbol compositions. Assignment: Journal writing using a web for brainstorming on students' positive qualities and the connections to the animals that represent these qualities.
		Due: Internet worksheet		
Assessment: Formative observation of listening skills.	Assessment: Formative observation of working independently on the computer and exit card.	Assessment: Evaluation. Summative rubric for Internet worksheet.	Assessment: Formative observation of participation in groups.	Assessment: Summative rubric for art criticism worksheet.

Day 6	Day 7	Day 8	Day 9	Day 10
Topic: Color theory	Topic: Work day	Topic: Work day	Topic: Work day	Topic: Written critiques
Objectives: 1.1, 2.1	*Objectives: 1.1, 1.2*	*Objective: 2.2*	*Objective: 2.2*	*Objectives: 1.1, 1.2*
Event: Color theory and pattern worksheet given out. Sketch animal symbol on paper bag.	Event: Work on artwork and color theory, pattern worksheet.	Event: Work on artwork.	Event: Work on artwork.	Event: Work on artwork. Introduce written critique form.
Due: Journal writing using an idea web for brainstorming on student's positive qualities and the connections to the animals that represent these qualities.		Due: Color and pattern worksheet and animal sketches Assign: Journal writing on why they chose the animal they did.	Due: Journal writing on why they chose the animal they did.	

(continued)

UNIT TITLE: X-RAY ANIMALS BY KATE OBUKOWICZ (CONTINUED)

Objectives: 1.1, 2.1	Objectives: 1.1, 1.2	Objective: 2.2	Objective: 2.2	Objectives: 1.1, 1.2
Assessment: Formative assessment using an "exit card" of journal writing.	Assessment: Formative observation of participation.	Assessment: Formative assessment using an exit card of three sketches and summative rubric for color and pattern worksheet.	Assessment: Formative assessment using an exit card of journal writing.	Assessment: Formative observation of participation.

Day 11	Day 12	Day 13	Day 14	Day 15
Topic: Peer critiques	Topic: Work day	Topic: Work day	Topic: Work day	Topic: Sharing of Work
Objective: 3.1	Objectives: 1.1, 1.2	Objectives: 1.1, 1.2	Objectives: 1.1, 1.2	Objective: 2.2
Event: Work in progress; in-class written critiques on peers' artwork. Introduce artist statement assignment.	Event: Work on sketches and artwork.	Event: Work on artwork.	Event: Work on artwork.	Event: Share with the class finished artwork and written artist statement.
Due: In-class written critiques.		Due: Artist statement worksheet.		Due: Artwork and artist statement.
Assessment: Formative observation of participation and summative rubric of written critiques.	Assessment: Formative observation of participation.	Assessment: Formative observation of participation.	Assessment: Formative observation of participation.	Assessment: Summative rubric for final explanation, and rubric for the use of elements of art.

Daily Lesson Plans   *Daily lesson plans* provide the structure and instructional strategies for each day's class. Functionally, the lesson plans are expansions of the unit calendar, providing much more detail about each of the activities, content, assessment, and other particulars needed for each day. The lesson plan is a document that takes many forms. It ranges from fully scripted comments by the teacher to a brief outline for the day. The lessons in a unit need to show in detail how each of the unit goals, essential questions, and objectives are met.

Assessments and Evaluations   What could you do to determine that your students learned what you planned for them? Unit plans should address the range of diagnostic, formative, and summative *assessments and evaluations* you will use during the unit. Assessment principles were described in chapter 3, and assessment will be considered throughout section 2 of this book when each instructional strategy is examined. For purposes of planning a unit, assessments should be taken directly from the unit goals and objectives. Assessments should also be sketched onto the unit calendar to match them with the content students are learning. When we work with preservice teachers we have them describe each assessment tool they will use, and explain why that tool is valid in determining whether or not their students have learned. Assessment is a recursive process, where the teacher and students are continually examining what they are learning and using this insight to help determine future instruction and learning. Assessments are not merely the "final unit test." Rather, they occur throughout the unit, and planning for them ahead of time is crucial.[5]

Materials and Resources   *Materials and resources* include both the sources used in writing your unit and the sources you will need as you write lesson plans, develop assessments, and generally prepare to help students learn the unit content. Some resources will provide materials only you will access, and some will be materials your students will need. Examples of materials and resources include:

a resource list/references
   print resources (books, texts, articles)
   media resources (films, videos, recordings, computer software, Internet sources)
   community organizations, field trip ideas, businesses, guest speakers or other potential resources
a materials list for each day of the unit (e.g., 15 Bunsen burners, 50 ml hydrochloric acid; 30 tennis balls; 30 copies of *The Crucible* handout, etc.)
graphic materials, such as transparencies/overhead projections, charts, graphs, diagrams, photos, and so on; many of these will be developed with each lesson plan

If you have not written a unit plan before, these eight components may seem daunting. Unit plans do require a significant amount of time and energy, but if they are written thoughtfully, individual lessons are then taught in a well-sequenced order that promotes student learning. It is important to develop the skills necessary to write a thoughtful unit. Preservice teachers who have this ability are more likely to be successful during student teaching than those who do not (Harwood, Collins, & Sudzina, 2001).

Although the calendar is important for the reasons we listed above, it often is the most revised section of a student teacher's unit plan. When you actually teach a lesson you may find that it takes more or less time than you planned on the calendar. It is not uncommon for the calendar to be two days off after you finish teaching the first week of a unit! For example, compare the calendar below with the calendar on pages 96 and 97.

UNIT TITLE: X-RAY ANIMALS BY KATE OBUKOWICZ
(CALENDAR MODIFIED DURING TEACHING)

Day 1	Day 2	Day 3	Day 4	Day 5
Topic: Introduction to unit	Topic: Native American Lore	Topic: Norval Morriseau	Topic: Art criticism	Topic: Skit day
Objective: 1.1, 1.2	Objective: 2.1	Objective: 3.2	Objective: 2.2	Objective: 2.2
Event: Unit hook. Discussion of the qualities of Morrisseau's paintings. Review color theory and patterns. Introduce X-ray painting assignment, and go over rubric.	Event: Listen to Native American lore read by the teacher, and read on the internet, Go to computer lab. Internet worksheet.	Event: Read articles on Norval Morriseau and work on art criticism. Due: Internet worksheet	Event: Art criticism. Group time to plan out 3–5 minute animal skit.	Event: Skits at the beginning of class. Sketch three possible animal-symbol compositions. Assignment: Journal writing using a web for brainstorming on students' positive qualities and the connections to the animals that represent these qualities.
Assessment: Formative observation of listening skills.	Assessment: Formative observation of working independently on the computer and exit card.	Assessment: Evaluation. Summative rubric for Internet worksheet.	Assessment: Formative observation of participation in groups.	Assessment: Summative rubric for art criticism worksheet.
			Track meet—half of class gone; re-formed groups and let those present begin planning.	Half of skits presented; those missing yesterday formed groups; skits took longer than expected so finished one quarter of class.

Day 6	Day 7	Day 8	Day 9	Day 10
Topic: Color theory	Topic: Work day	Topic: Work day	Topic: Work day	Topic: Written critiques
Objectives: 1.1, 2.1	Objectives: 1.1, 1.2	Objective: 2.2	Objective: 2.2	Objectives: 1.1, 1.2
Event: Color theory and pattern worksheet given out. Sketch animal symbol on a paper bag.	Event: Work on artwork and color theory, pattern worksheet.	Event: Work on artwork.	Event: Work on artwork.	Event: Work on artwork. Introduce written critique form.

(continued)

UNIT TITLE: X-RAY ANIMALS BY KATE OBUKOWICZ
(CALENDAR MODIFIED DURING TEACHING) (CONTINUED)

Objectives: 1.1, 2.1	Objectives: 1.1, 1.2	Objective: 2.2	Objective: 2.2	Objectives: 1.1, 1.2
Due: Journal writing using an idea web for brainstorming on student's positive qualities and the connections to the animals that represent these qualities.		Due: Color and pattern worksheet and animal sketches Assign: Journal writing on why they chose the animal they did.	Due: Journal writing on why they chose the animal they did.	
Assessment: Formative assessment using an exit card of journal writing.	Assessment: Formative observation of participation.	Assessment: Formative assessment using an exit card of three sketches and summative rubric for color and pattern worksheet.	Assessment: Formative assessment using an exit card of journal writing.	Assessment: Formative observation of participation.
Finished skits from Day 5; skits took longer than expected, so did not begin color theory.	Bumped this work day back one day and began color theory.			

Day 11	Day 12	Day 13	Day 14	Day 15
Topic: Peer critiques	Topic: Work day	Topic: Work day	Topic: Work day	Topic: Sharing of Work
Objective: 3.1	Objectives: 1.1, 1.2	Objectives: 1.1, 1.2	Objectives: 1.1, 1.2	Objective: 2.2
Event: Work in progress; in-class written critiques on peers' artwork. Introduce artist statement assignment.	Event: Work on sketches and artwork.	Event: Work on artwork.	Event: Work on artwork.	Event: Share with the class finished artwork and written artist statement.
Due: In-class written critiques.		Due: Artist statement worksheet.		Due: Artwork and artist statement.
Assessment: Formative observation of participation and summative rubric of written critiques.	Assessment: Formative observation of participation.	Assessment: Formative observation of participation.	Assessment: Formative observation of participation.	Assessment: Summative rubric for final explanation, and rubric for the use of elements of art. Finished unit on Day 16.

UNIT PLAN EXAMPLE

Reading and Writing Short Stories
Tenth Grade English

Partial Overview and Rationale:

This tenth grade short story unit is designed to examine this genre from two angles: reading and writing. Students will read and listen to classical and contemporary short stories, and then they will explore together the literary elements of plot, character, and dialogue. The purpose of these explorations is to discover how different authors used these elements, and for students to consider how they might use them in their own short stories. The second half of the unit will allow students the opportunity to compose their own short stories.

In the process of reading and writing short stories, students will gain skill in state standards of reading, writing, and communication. Additionally, the unit is designed to help students enhance their appreciation and comprehension of literature, and their skill at writing in a particular genre. These are also fitting with state standards and recommendations by the National Council of Teachers of English. Editing will help students refine their understanding of writing styles and conventions.

Ideally this unit will be taught toward the end of the school year, so students can apply their understanding of literary elements. This will allow an engaging opportunity for students to use the skills and abilities they have learned during the year. That said, this unit could fit anytime into the school year, as it is a new exploration into the short story genre, and it does not necessarily build on previous units "setting the stage" for the content explored. The unit is planned to use fifteen one-hour class periods.

Possible Goals and Essential Questions:

Goals

1. Students will explore the short story genre by reading, thinking critically about, and discussing various authors' use of language, style, purpose, and perspective.
2. Students will be able to recognize and understand the following literary elements of the short story: plot, character, dialogue, and theme.
3. Students will compose their own original short stories, and receive and provide feedback on their writing styles and skills.

Questions

1. How do an author's style and perspective affect the plot of a short story?
2. What are effective strategies for developing the characters in a short story?
3. What does an author do with critique and feedback about his/her writing?

Sample Objectives:

1. Upon completion of this unit students will be able to identify the central conflict in a short story, describe the conflict in a journal entry, and support their thoughts with one example from the short story (this ties to Goal #1 & Question #2). Information objective.
2. Upon completion of this unit students will be able to identify all of the short story elements on a written quiz (this ties to Goal #2). Information objective.
3. Upon completion of this unit students will be able to demonstrate their understanding of the writing process by composing their own short stories that fully develop the characters in the story through the use of characterization and dialogue (ties to Goal #3 & Question #2). Skill objective.

Figure 4.2

Partial Outline of Content (the scope of the content in the unit):

I. Introduction: Why do we read and write literature?
   a. Explore cultural values
   b. Cause an emotional response from the reader
   c. Expose us to the world in new way
II. Short Stories
   a. Riki-Tiki-Tavi by Rudyard Kipling
   b. Hills Like White Elephants by Ernest Hemingway
   c. The Father by Raymond Carver
   d. Everyday Use by Alice Walker
   e. etc.
III. Parts of plot
   a. Exposition
   b. Complication
   c. Climax
   d. Resolution
   e. Plot of Riki-Tiki-Tavi (*RTT*)
   f. Plot of the other short stories etc.
IV. Writing short stories
   a. Review of the writing process
      i. Prewriting
      ii. Writing
      iii. Revising
      iv. Editing/Peer Editing
      v. Publishing
   b. Review of literary elements
      i. Plot
      ii. Theme
      iii. Character
      iv. Dialogue
V. etc.

Selected Days From Calendar:

Day 1	Day 2	Day 6
Introduction What is a short story? Begin reading Kipling's *RTT* Homework: Finish Kipling	Lecture: Intro "Plot" Exposition Complication Journal: Elements of plot in *RTT*	Concept Formation: "Theme" Read Everyday Use Groups: discuss possible themes in Everyday Use Homework: Select & read a short story from the anthology by tomorrow.

Day 9	Day 11	Day 15
Review "plot," "dialogue," "theme," and "character" for test on Day 10. Share with a partner the main characters in the story students are composing. Finalize "setting" of their short story	Mini review: writing process Brainstorm session: Appropriate forms of feedback when peer editing Writer's workshop: Feedback on students' short story (at whatever stage of the writing process the students are in). Tell expectations and remind of deadlines for short story assignment (due Day 14)	Student story sharing day! Peer and self-evaluation worksheet completed in class. (Meets Objective #2)

Figure 4.2 (continued)

<u>**Daily Lesson Plans:**</u>

These are described in the lesson plan section of this chapter, and expanded on extensively in section 2 of the book.

<u>**Assessments and Evaluations:**</u>

- Students will be awarded participation points for their journal responses, which include the examples of characters from their short story.
- Students will be formatively assessed on their understanding of plot, dialogue, theme, and character on a test.
- Student's short story will be evaluated for having the elements of a short story. A rubric will delineate these elements.
- Students will provide brief evaluations of peers' short stories, focusing on the stories' plot, character development, and dialogue.
- Students will write self-evaluations of their own short stories, focusing on their stories plot, character development, and dialogue.

<u>**Materials and Resources:**</u>

Graphic/overheads:

- Hemingway background information
- Kipling background information
- Character overhead
- Theme overhead

Print resources:

Atwell, N. (1998). *In the middle: New understandings about writing, reading, and learning.* Portsmouth, NH: Boynton/Cook.
Twenty great American short stories:
   http://www.americanliterature.com/SS/SSINDX.HTML
Classic short stories: Bibliography and on-line full text:
   http://www.classicshorts.com/bib.html

Materials list:

Day One: 30 copies of *Riki-Tiki-Tavi*
               30 copies of Intro to short stories handout, etc.

Figure 4.2 (continued)

Additionally, schools are using block schedules, resulting in extended class sessions. Conventionally, students meet in class for about one hour, five days per week. In a block schedule, students may meet in class for two hours every other day for 90 minutes every day, or for some other combination of hours and days. By the end of the school year, any given course will have met for 180 hours, but you will not necessarily have met every day. Block schedules are varied, and provide excellent opportunities to reduce the number of students you teach, integrate the curriculum, and meet for longer sessions and explore topics in more depth. For these reasons, we suggest that the lesson plans are outlined in the calendar (so you know the order in which the content will be learned, and so you can prepare materials and resources in advance), but the actual lesson plans are finalized about a week in advance.

We include a portion of a unit plan on short stories that could be taught in a high school literature course. Note how each component is applied to this particular content area.

Interdisciplinary Unit Plans

Interdisciplinary unit plans integrate topics from more than one course around a common theme or idea. These are increasingly being used in middle schools and high schools because they allow students to identify connections across several content areas. Teachers develop interdisciplinary units to provide learners with opportunities to think about course content in relation to other courses (or disciplines). The above eight components are the same for an interdisciplinary unit. The unit is more complex because it takes into account more information, and because it needs to describe how the content areas will be integrated. The most common approach for developing interdisciplinary unit plans is to focus the plan around a common theme. Interdisciplinary units are built around a theme that multiple content areas could address. For example, "conflict" might be addressed in a world history course (studying causes of a war), in an English course (studying the use of conflict in plot development), in a mathematics course (learning to graph data related to population growth and conflict with natural resources), and in a biology course (examining the conflict of people and natural resources). These topics would be taught anyway, but the teachers agree to teach them at the same time to help students make connections across disciplines. Some schools promote "team teaching" where students share the same teachers during the course of a day. These teams often represent the core subject areas of mathematics, science, language arts/English, and social studies. This allows teachers to know what was learned in other classes that was related to the theme. Other subject areas (e.g., music, physical education, foreign language) are often electives for students. While these subject areas can join the thematic approach, it is more difficult to have a structure in place that ensures interdisciplinary units.

MAKING IT WORK IN YOUR CONTENT AREA

Think about how you could develop each of the components of a unit plan for a course you hope to teach at a middle school or high school. Think of a topic that would require at least two weeks of curriculum, and has connections to state and national standards. Consider how you would answer these questions: What would you write for a unit introduction and rationale? What Goals and Essential Questions would students meet/answer? What information/content objectives would students meet? What skills will they develop? What dispositions will students form? What would a content outline for the unit include? How could you assess student learning during the unit? Some teachers teach interdisciplinary units; for example, language arts and social studies teachers' content might be combined for a "core" class at the middle school level. Discuss the question above with a colleague from another content area.

THE LESSON PLAN

A *lesson plan* is most commonly thought of as the daily plan. Though a lesson may span more than one day (for example, a mock trial could take three days from start to finish), the plan specifies the "look and feel" of a day in your classroom. In this section we will provide you with the components of a lesson plan, but in section 2 of this book we will return to lesson planning with each of the instructional strategies described.

Components of a Lesson Plan

Many formats for lesson plans are available, and you will develop your own preference for a lesson plan as you prepare to teach. The following eight parts of a lesson are commonplace in the schools, and will provide structure to your class sessions:

1. lesson objectives
2. assessments
3. initiation or start of lesson
4. teacher activities
5. student activities
6. closure
7. materials and resources
8. reflections

Each is briefly described below.

Lesson Objectives   These are the specific learning objectives that you have for the lesson or day. They should meet the criteria described in chapter 3, so we will not go into much detail about objectives here. Include information, disposition, and skill objectives. Students should be able to accomplish these objectives by the end of the lesson. We suggest two to four objectives for each day. You should plan to tell students the daily objectives because they need to know what they will be learning. Some teachers write the objectives on the board so everyone can see them.

Assessments   These are closely tied to the objectives. The assessments may be diagnostic, formative, or summative, depending on when the lesson will be taught in the unit. Formative and summative assessments occur near the end of a lesson, but planning a lesson with a "backward design" (Wiggins & McTighe, 2005) means that you think of the assessment before you plan the lesson's activities. This will ensure that the activities are authentic tasks that prepare students to demonstrate their learning on the assessments. Refer to the descriptions of assessment in chapter 3.

Initiation or Start of the Lesson   Another term for this is *anticipatory set*, or the manner by which you will help the students anticipate what will be happening for the day (some refer to this metaphorically as the "hook" by which you catch the students' attention). This could be a question, a poster, music, or even a short activity. The initiation of the lesson is important to consider because it helps the students focus on the lesson. The initiation should have some connection to the content of the lesson. For example, a biology lesson on the skeletal system might start with a skeleton in front of the class, or a video clip about splinting broken bones, or simply the number "206" written on the chalkboard—the number of bones in the human body. Another way to think about the initiation is this: Students will be coming to your classroom with many things in their minds; what can you do at the start of your lesson to gain their attention and help them start thinking about your course?

Teacher Activities   These are the activities you will undertake during the course of the lesson. By specifying your activities during the lesson, you can think about how you will present information, where you will stand, or the order in which you provide information to your students. These will be described in detail when the logistics for each instructional strategy are outlined in section 2 of this book. When planning what you will do to lead the class, consider student diversity, individualized educational programs (see chapter 1), student motivation, and classroom management. Many beginning teachers choose to write a script for difficult portions of their lessons. If they are concerned about placing students in groups, or about their lecture notes, scripts help teachers think through what they might say. We find that teachers rarely read these scripts, but the process of writing them helps them think through the ideas and content. Scripts can easily be placed in the "teacher activities" section of the lesson. This section of your lesson plan is also a good place to estimate the amount of time each activity will take. At the end of the lesson your estimation can be compared to the actual time needed. For example: How long will it take for the initiation? How long for a quiz? How long for introducing a concept?

Student Activities   The emphasis of any teaching activity is whether students have learned. By specifying student activities you can plan for direct connections between the activities you are engaged in and the activities of your students. It allows you to be clear about your expectations for student behavior that will help maximize learning. For example, if the teacher activity is to present information in a PowerPoint presentation, then what should students be doing—taking notes? listening? If you are facilitating a simulation, then what are the students to do during the simulation? Your estimation of minutes for student activities should also be included. Taken together, the minutes for teacher activities and the minutes for student activities must equal the amount of time allocated for your class session.

Closure   Just as the initiation started the lesson, closure brings an end to the day. When planning the closure, consider how the lesson should be concluded, how the content and skills can be reviewed to be sure students have learned them, or even a comment that will set the stage for the next class session. Sometimes teachers close a lesson with a short quiz or other assessment activity. Exit cards can be used to determine what students have learned. If a lesson has good closure, the students feel confident about the teacher's management of the classroom. The clock should not signal the end of class; the end of the closing activity should. Some lessons need to continue into the next day. If that is the case, then the closure activity should help students see how the day's activities will be revisited the next day.

Materials and Resources   A materials and resources list provides a quick overview of what is needed for the day. It should be safe to assume that your classroom will have paper, pencils, chalkboard/whiteboard, and an overhead projector. Materials and resources are those out of the standard items, and could include handouts for your students, copies of parts of a novel, or other materials that you will use during the lesson. Additionally, materials and resources may include lecture notes, primary source artifacts, a DVD, or anything that you will need to successfully conduct the lesson. The material and resources list will be specific to each lesson, and should be similar to the list you created for the unit plan.

Reflections   It is important to reflect on a lesson after you have taught it. In chapter 2 we described differences among *planned*, *taught*, *hidden*, *null*, and *learned* curricula. By including a space at the end of a lesson plan to reflect on your assessments and objectives you can determine what your students have learned. If you planned something different than what they learned (for example, if the content was too difficult and your students did not meet a learning objective), then you can modify the lesson plan for the next day. Your reflections can also be directed by the four commonplaces: consider the role of the *teacher*, the *students*, the *content*, and the *milieu* on student learning. It is important to reflect and comment on the lesson plan as well, so that you can improve your lesson the next time you teach from it. These reflections could come at the next period, or it could be a year later when you teach from a unit plan again. Every time you teach a lesson it should improve because of the reflections. We will explore reflections more in the last section of this chapter.

The figure 4.3 lesson-plan template is a sample that teachers might use. It identifies each of the components in the plan. In addition, this template includes a title, and names the unit from which the lesson comes. The figure 4.4 lesson plan shows how the template might be filled in by a teacher prior to class.

Preservice teachers often notice that some veteran teachers do not have a lesson plan with them when they teach. It seems as though the in-service teachers simply guide the students without referring to the written document that is

SAMPLE LESSON TEMPLATE

TOPIC FOR THE LESSON: Date:

Grade Level/Course:

Unit:

Lesson Objectives (information, disposition, and skill objectives):
   1)
   2)
   3)

Activities:

Initiation/Opening		Time 4
Teacher's Activities	**Students' Activities**	**Time**
Closure		**Time**

Assessment Tools

Pre-Planning:

Materials/Resources:

__ Camcorder __ VCR/DVD __ Worksheets __ Computer Lab __ Handout __ Notes

__ Other (list items needed):

Instructional Strategies to be Used:

__ Discovery Learning   __ Cooperative Learning   __ Simulations   __ Debate
__ Discussion   __ Concept Formation   __ Questioning   __ Lecture
__ Inquiry   __ Other

Multiple Intelligences:

__ Verbal/Linguistic   __ Musical/Rhythmic   __ Interpersonal
__ Logical/Mathematical   __ Intrapersonal   __ Body/ Kinesthetic
__ Naturalist   __ Visual/Spatial

Reflections/Notes:

Figure 4.3

SAMPLE LESSON PLAN

TOPIC FOR THE LESSON: Probability Unit Introduction   Date: Day 1

Grade Level/Course: Grades 10–12/Trigonometry

Unit: Probability

Lesson Objectives:

1) In groups of four, students will show their understanding of events and sample space by listing all combinations of numbers that are possible when rolling two dice.

2) Students will demonstrate their understanding of "Sample Space" and "Events" by successfully completing a discovery learning activity.

Activities:

Initiation/Opening		Time (min)
Start the class by shuffling a deck of cards. Start talking about different cards, and in the middle "accidentally" scatter the cards onto the floor. Ask students how likely it would be if you closed your eyes and picked out the 10 of hearts. Tell students that their answer requires thinking in terms of "probablility."		4

Teacher's Activities	Students' Activities	Time (min)
Have a student privately select a card from a complete deck, and have the class vote on the color of the card (red or black). Repeat with another student, but ask the class to vote on the suit of the card. Ask why color was easier than suit?	Participate with answers and comments.	5
Lecture on Events and Sample Space as they relate to probability	Write notes in math notebook: Sample Space is an exhaustive list of all the possible outcomes of an experiment. Any subset of the Sample Space is an Event.	10
Introduce group project and help students begin.	Groups of three. Each group has two dice. Write down all of the possible outcomes when someone roles one die, and when someone roles two dice. Share result with the class.	10
Write on board the equation for counting elements in a list: $n - m + 1$ (integers between n and m inclusive). Explore examples.	Write equation in math notebook. Provide examples for the class to consider together.	5
Small group discovery learning activity: List of questions about probability that use the equation. Groups will try to come up with answers quickly and accurately, and will apply the equation. Ask students to share how they came up with the solution for each question.	Students work in groups, answer questions, and share with the class how they came up with the correct answers.	10

Figure 4.4

	Time (min)
Closure	
Review the key concepts by asking questions of the students. Demonstrate the key ideas by using coins (heads and tails). Assign homework that reinforces the introduction to probability.	6

Assessment Tools:

    1) Successful accomplishment of projects in group activities
    2) Homework (to be assessed on Day 2)

Pre-Planning:

Materials/Resources:

__ Camcorder   __VCR/DVD   X Worksheets __ Computer Lab __ Handout __ Notes

__ Other (list items needed):

__ Deck of cards
__ List of questions for group project
__ Homework assignment
__ Two coins
__ 10 pair of dice

Instructional Strategies to Be Used:

X Discovery Learning   X Cooperative Learning   __ Simulations   __ Debate
__ Discussion   __ Concept Formation   X Questioning   X Lecture
__ Inquiry   __ Other

Multiple Intelligences:

X Verbal/Linguistic   __ Musical/Rhythmic X Interpersonal
X Logical/Mathematical __ Intrapersonal   __ Body/ Kinesthetic
__ Naturalist   X Visual/Spatial

Reflections/Notes:

Figure 4.4 (continued)

required of most student teachers. When you observe in-service teachers you may find this to be true. However, we encourage you to consider that the teachers you observe may not *have* a written lesson plan, but they do *use* a lesson plan—that is, their plans may not be written out, but they have thought through the components of such a plan. If asked to, these teachers could usually produce a written plan. The Interstate New Teacher Assessment and Support Consortium and the Educational Testing Service Praxis II and III assessments require that beginning teachers thoughtfully consider and document lesson planning.[6]

Lesson plans provide documentation of what students should have learned in your classroom, and they document how your class is helping students learn content that is tied to district, state, and national content standards. During your student teaching, and when you are observed as an in-service teacher, you will be expected to write lesson plans. By having a written document you will be able to ensure that you deliver all you have planned, that you pace your lesson to maximize class time, that your lesson efficiently moves through the learning activities, and that you are able to assess student learning and determine when your objectives have been met.

THE IMPORTANCE OF REFLECTION WHEN PLANNING

In the previous section on lesson planning we noted that reflection is an important part of the plan. Reflection is a progressive process through which you consider what happened—good and bad—so that your future actions are improved. In this section we suggest that reflection and planning should take place during the lesson, after the students have left the classroom, and when planning future lessons. Killion and Todnem (1991) describe these three types of reflection as "reflection-in-action," "reflection-on-action," and "reflection-for-action" (p. 15).

Reflection-in-Action

Reflection-in-action is the process of monitoring students' work and progress during the class meeting. This involves noting whether time spent on an activity needs to be extended or shortened based on your students' understanding and engagement. The lesson plan is what you take into the classroom, but reflection-in-action is a continual process of determining whether the plan optimizes student learning. The opposite of this type of reflection is being oblivious to the various phenomena occurring in the classroom. Consider how a history teacher might reflect in action; if you are teaching about a historical event and a student brings up a current event that is related and similar, you need to make a quick decision: Is the time needed to talk about the current event an appropriate step to take? You might quickly assess if you have enough time in class, and if the current event will make the historical event more relevant and understandable. You might gauge students to determine if they are interested in the current event. Finally, you might decide to spend the rest of class time exploring the current event, and revisit the historical event the following day. All of these thoughts are reflections while you are teaching. They impact the lesson at the moment, and will modify and adjust what your students are learning.

Reflection-on-Action

Reflection-on-action is defined by Killion and Todnem as "reflection on practice and on one's actions after the practice is completed" (1991, p. 15). This is the most well-known reflection. You ask yourself, *What went well? What needs improvement before the next period starts? What needs to be changed before teaching this lesson again?* This reflection is a powerful way to benefit from your successes and failures. For example, if you allocated 15 minutes to read a four-page article, and your students needed 30 minutes to read it, then you can plan for longer reading times in the future. As we mentioned earlier, Schwab's four commonplaces (1973) are a helpful heuristic tool for reflecting on your practice. These questions could guide you to consider each of these commonplaces:

> How did the teacher impact student learning in today's lesson?
> How did the student(s) impact learning in today's lesson?
> Was the content learned? If not, was the content appropriate? Inappropriate? Too difficult? Too simple?
> How did the classroom environment help or hinder student learning in today's lesson?

Reflection-for-Action

The third type of reflection that is important for teachers is *reflection-for-action*. Reflection-for-action is assumed in the previous two types of reflections, but singling it out helps teachers focus on how to make future teaching promote student learning. We assume that when you reflect while teaching you will also determine what actions to take during class so learning is enhanced. When you reflect at the end of a class, the intent is to improve the lesson. Reflection-for-action simply puts a label to this type of thinking. You reflect with an eye toward improving future actions. Teachers reflect on what they did, on what their students learned, and gain insights from these reflections that will inform future actions. Figure 4.5 outlines this process.

Often, reflections simply identify problems that occurred. Reflection, for example, might help you realize that shy students are not talking during discussions, or that laboratory supplies are being mishandled, or that students lack

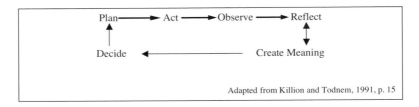

Adapted from Killion and Todnem, 1991, p. 15

Figure 4.5

note-taking strategies. The point of reflection, however, is to create meaning from your observations and reflections, and to develop strategies for your future teaching. Shy students may need more opportunities to share in small groups; rules and expectations for handling equipment may need to be restated; and students may need modeling from you about taking notes.

Many schools have adopted a *peer coach* model, where teachers observe one another and help reflect on lessons; another term for this is the *critical friend* model. The observations are not an evaluation of the teacher, but an opportunity to identify outcomes of your teaching and strategies to improve your teaching—and to ultimately improve your students' learning. It is an effective approach for pinpointing areas of your teaching. For example, Mr. Green and Ms. Lamb, two social studies teachers, have decided to adopt the peer coaching model. Ms. Lamb observes a world geography lesson in which students listen to Mr. Green's lecture on sweatshops in third world countries. The students are then asked to create posters that display examples of sweatshops in various countries around the world.

Ms. Lamb has reflective prompts for Mr. Green that include:

What did you do that effectively impacted student learning?
How did the students positively or negatively impact learning in this lesson?
Were your objectives met in the lesson? How do you know? Did you ask too much from them? Too little?
Was the environment of the classroom conducive to learning today? What could you have done about it?

Mr. Green and Ms. Lamb discuss the prompts on a teacher work day. Mr. Green indicates that the students seemed to "go along" with the lesson but were not overly enthused. He is looking for a way to generate more enthusiasm and also to help students "do something more" with the information. From this discussion Mr. Green decides that a change in instructional strategy will improve the lesson. Next time he will try an inquiry approach (see chapter 11) in which the students, in teams, are asked to create "webquests" (Internet inquiry lessons) on child labor. He decides they could create their own specific questions to pursue, such as "Should you buy tennis shoes made through sweatshop labor?" After completing the webquests, students will have a classroom discussion to help them create a list of possible socially responsible actions related to what they have learned. At the end of their meeting, Mr. Green and Ms. Lamb agree upon a time that he will observe Ms. Lamb's U.S. history class the following week.

Action Research

Action research is another form of reflection that teachers use; it is often defined as a structured approach with which to examine and learn from one's experience. For teachers, action research is a purposeful way to identify a phenomenon in the classroom, determine an approach for gaining insight into this phenomenon, and assess if the approach was effective. When teachers engage in action research they intend to improve upon their practice. Teachers may do so to evaluate their use of particular instructional strategies, or to find a solution to a problem they are facing. Action research is usually carried out by the teacher, and not outside "researchers," and the results/findings of the research are usually limited to the classroom or school in which the teacher works. For example, if a group of students have difficulty comprehending a textbook, then a teacher may devise a strategy for improving comprehension, and develop an assessment tool for measuring the effectiveness of the strategy. This strategy should be based on research findings from other studies, but the teacher often will modify it to fit the needs of particular students in his classroom. After using the comprehension improvement strategy, the teacher then uses the assessment tool to determine the effectiveness of the strategy. In this manner, teachers are engaging in a type of research that relies on their reflections about a problem and systematically analyzes strategies for solving the problem. This gives teachers greater confidence that their planning is going to have a positive impact on student learning.

CHAPTER REVIEW

Planning helps teachers organize what they will teach during the school year, the semester, the unit, and the daily lesson. American schools are open an average of 180 days a year; *scope* and *sequence* are two terms that many educators use to refer to the breadth of content and skills students should learn (scope), and the order in which students will learn this content (sequence) during these 180 days. Many states and districts have developed expectations for the content that should be taught at each grade level to ensure that as students move through the grades they learn content in a predetermined sequence.

Schwab developed the idea that all classrooms have four elements in common: a *teacher*, *students*, a *subject matter or content* that is to be learned, and a *milieu or environment* in which teaching and learning take place (1973). If any one of these four commonplaces is hindered, then learning is thwarted.

The *unit plan* is the compilation of lesson plans during a specific amount of time, or for a specific amount of course content. Unit plans are often developed around *essential questions* that probe the big ideas or fundamental concepts that we want students to think about and learn during the span of a unit. Unit plans commonly have eight components:

1. overview and rationale
2. goals and essential questions
3. objectives
4. outline of content (the scope of the content in the unit)
5. calendar (the sequence in which students will learn the content)

6. daily lesson plans
7. assessments and evaluations
8. materials and resources

Interdisciplinary unit plans integrate topics from more than one course around a common theme or idea.

A lesson plan or daily plan typically has eight parts:

1. lesson objectives
2. assessments
3. initiation or start of lesson
4. teacher activities
5. student activities
6. closure
7. materials and resources
8. reflections

NOTES

1. To access this data and other statistics related to education, visit the Center's website at http://nces.ed.gov/surveys (accessed May 14, 2006).
2. See Virginia Department of Education, 2002.
3. See Washington State Office of the Superintendent of Public Instruction, 2003.
4. As you read about each instructional strategy in section 2 of this book, you will become much more knowledgeable about how selecting appropriate and effective activities will help you meet these objectives.
5. We encourage teachers not to have a test or exam on the last day of the unit. The traditional unit test is often used by teachers as the closing activity of the unit; too often, students will "cram" for the test, and then move on to the next unit. If you want your students to take a test, we suggest having them take it a few days before the end of the unit. End the unit with a simulation, presentation, or some other activity that will allow students to think about the unit content at a higher cognitive or affective level. Studying for the test will not only help the students prepare for that task, but help them as they access the information during a more authentic activity at the end of the unit.
6. The Interstate New Teacher Assessment and Support Consortium standards can be found at http://www.ccsso.org/projects/Interstate_New_Teacher_Assessment_and_Support_Consortium/ (retrieved September 4, 2006).
7. The Praxis II and Praxis III exams are reviewed at http://www.ets.org/praxis (retrieved September 3, 2006).

REFERENCES

Erickson, H. L. (2002). *Concept-based curriculum and instruction: Teaching beyond the facts*. Thousand Oaks, CA: Corwin.

Harwood, A. M., Collins, L., & Sudzina, M. (2001). An examination of student teacher failure: Implications for teacher education programs. In J. Rainer and E. Guyton (Eds.), *Teacher education yearbook* (45–60). Dubuque, IA: Association of Teacher Educators/Kendall Hunt.

Killion, J., & Todnem, G. (1991). A process for personal theory-building. *Educational Leadership, 48*(6), 14–16.

Schwab, J. J. (1973). The practical 3: Translation into curriculum. *School Review, 81*, 501–522.

Virginia Department of Education. (2002). *Algebra I standards of learning sample scope and sequence*. Richmond, VA: Virginia Department of Education

Washington State Office of the Superintendent of Public Instruction. (2003). *Social studies frameworks: Grades 9–12*. Olympia, WA: Washington State Office of the Superintendent of Public Instruction.

Wiggins, G., & McTighe, J. (2005). *Understanding by design* (2nd ed.). Alexandria, VA: Association for Supervision and Curriculum Development.

2

INSTRUCTIONAL STRATEGIES

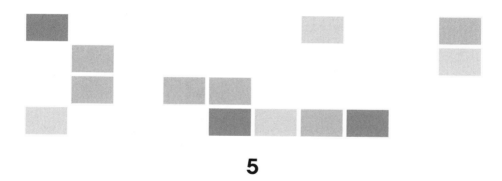

5

LECTURE AND DIRECT INSTRUCTION

OVERVIEW

We have all experienced lectures at which the teacher was a gifted speaker and the students were enthralled by the stories, anecdotes, and details being delivered. Most of us have watched a teacher use pictures, artifacts, video, and/or other visual aids to highlight key points and help us understand the topic. Most of us have also been a student in a class where a guest speaker comes and tells about firsthand or real-life experiences. However, just as likely, we have all had teachers who talk and talk without much regard for their students. Lectures from those teachers and guest speakers become something to endure because they contain an excessive amount of facts, do not engage students' minds or require much thinking, or are simply boring. We suggest that lecturing to students is overused because it is easy for the teacher to control the students and the content being presented. However, lecturing, be it from the teacher or a guest speaker, has the potential to be a powerful strategy that you need to consider using as part of your repertoire of instructional strategies.

Let us define a few terms that will help describe instructional strategies that fit in this chapter. *Lecture* is an instructional strategy with which the teacher presents a specified set of information to students. These presentations take a variety of forms that will be examined in this chapter. *Direct instruction* is a category of teacher-centered and teacher-directed instructional strategies. The teacher directs students purposely to ensure that specific content or skills are learned.

A DESCRIPTION OF LECTURE AND DIRECT INSTRUCTION AND RESEARCH FINDINGS

Lectures and Presentations

We believe that lecturing offers several advantages and reasons for its use in the classroom (Barbetta & Scaruppa, 1995; Heward, 2005). Lecturing allows the teacher to present a specific amount of information quickly and efficiently. It can be used with large or small groups and can be used in every content area. When lecturing, the teacher has a tremendous amount of control over how much emphasis will be placed on certain concepts, facts, and course content. Lecturing enables you to present important content that your students may not be able to learn on their own (for example, a scientific theory that may be too complex for your students could be presented at the appropriate level of understanding during a lecture). During a lecture you control the content and information and use class time to focus student's attention on topics that are particularly important or difficult to learn. Lectures allow you to highlight the key points that students may overlook or not understand during independent reading, working on the Internet, or participating in project-based activities. In addition to the efficiency that lectures allow, if you are passionate and enthusiastic about the topic of the lecture then this excitement for the content is often passed on to the students. We have witnessed a teacher excite students about the U.S. Supreme Court through a simple 35-minute lecture. She talked about the personal lives of the justices, the role of the court in deciding issues that impact our daily lives, and how the court serves as a check and balance to the president and the Congress. More important, however, was her excitement about the topic. She was animated and enthusiastic, brought in personal stories about her interest in the Supreme Court, and generally exuded a passion about the topic. The students' excitement stemmed partly from the content of the lecture, and partly from the affective impact of the teacher's enthusiasm. Lecture is not always thought of as a strategy for exciting students about content, but we contend that it has tremendous potential for this.

As we mentioned earlier, students are often passive observers during lectures, because most lectures do not require students to participate beyond listening, note taking, and asking periodic questions. This passive role is one that many students will enjoy, because it is unthreatening and easy. One of the most consistent and important educational research findings is that students who make frequent, relevant responses during a lesson learn more than students who are passive observers (Brophy & Good, 1986; Fisher & Berliner, 1985). This applies to any teacher-centered activity, and especially to lectures, because students are often passive learners during them. Bligh (2000) suggests that teachers who rely on only lectures may encourage a superficial understanding of concepts and facts. As he states, lecture may "encourage a surface approach and discourage the very intellectual skills that … education claims to foster" (p. 61). Bligh suggests that teachers can help promote more active and "deeper" thinking by providing students with graphic organizers, being aware of students' ability to sit attentively in class, interjecting discussion questions into the lecture, and teaching note-taking skills. We will describe how to engage students during lectures later in this chapter.

The lecture method presents other challenges for students and teachers. The teacher organizes the lecture as she believes is best, but this may not be the order that promotes understanding for every student. For example, a teacher may decided to lecture on the characters in a novel before describing the plot, but some students may want to have an overview of the story line prior to knowing details about the characters. Even more prevalent is the teacher who "moves away from the topic" or "gets off track" from the main topic of the lecture. These occur from a student question or simply because the teacher believes she has an interesting story to tell. While these are opportunities to make the lecture more engaging, students are often frustrated by these stories because they confuse what is important from what is tangential. Similar to this, students often have difficulty keeping track of lecture content in their notes. Even though some teachers have identified strategies for effective note taking (Saski, Swicegood, & Carter, 1983), they seldom teach them to their students. Students are put in the difficult position of receiving a large amount of information without the skill of knowing how to record and remember it (Ormrod, 2006). Students with listening deficits, language difficulties, and writing disabilities are put at even a greater disadvantage (Sandock, 2000). It is a difficult task for all students to identify important lecture content and record it accurately and efficiently in their notes. A student with learning disabilities could easily write one idea in his notes and miss the next two key ideas in the process (Hughes & Suritsky, 1994). We mention these concerns not to discourage lectures, but to point out concerns with relying too heavily on this strategy.

Direct Instruction

Direct instruction meets specific purposes in the classroom, and is an effective approach that helps students learn course content. We use the term *explicit teaching* synonymously with *direct instruction* because both terms imply that the teacher explicitly/directly provides information or step-by-step skills. You do not want your students to practice errors, but to correctly learn skills and key points. Therefore, the instruction is controlled by you, and the students will look to you for guidance about what to do during the class. Direct instruction, however, is a label for a prescribed approach to teaching. Often direct instruction is broken up into "big D.I." and "little d.i."; the former is the label for a scripted and sequential approach for helping students learn, and the latter a general description of teacher-led instruction. While these labels seem informal, we think they are useful in helping understand the complexity of this category of instructional strategies.

Direct instruction ("big D.I.") is an approach that uses scripts, anticipates students' responses and questions, and is based on task analysis and mastery learning. DI allows students to master specific knowledge and skill that has been determined to be important (Engelmann & Carnine, 1991; Kame'enui, Carnine, & Dixon, 1998). The learning theory of DI contends that learning can be greatly accelerated if instruction is clear, removes opportunities for misinterpretations, and facilitates generalizations. The DI model requires that students are placed in appropriate instructional groups based on their performance, and as they progress students are regrouped to stay with those similar to them. This type of grouping is often called *homogenous grouping* because the students are thought to learn best when placed with others of similar skill or ability. To a certain degree, DI is based on behaviorism (you may wish to refer back to chapter 1 for a discussion of this idea): teachers clearly define the tasks they expect of their students, they explicitly teach concepts and skills by telling and demonstrating them to students, students respond with hand signals, choral responses, and other ways to demonstrate their understanding, and the teacher adjusts the lesson to accommodate student learning (Kame'enui, Carnine, & Dixon, 1998). Engelmann and colleagues have developed lessons for reading, writing, mathematics, social studies, and most other content areas that provide the specific scripts and learning objectives needed for a DI lesson.

The other form of direct instruction ("little d.i.") also emphasizes small-group, face-to-face instruction by teachers, carefully articulated lessons, and breaking content and skills into small units that are deliberately taught to students (Rosenshine & Stevens, 1986; Schug, Tarver, & Western, 2001). However, it allows teachers more leeway in creating the lessons, and can be integrated into the whole classroom (as opposed to DI, where instruction is primarily in small groups). Rosenshine has suggested that 10 general principles should be adhered to when writing an explicit or direct instruction lesson plan (Burden & Byrd, 2003, p. 168; Rosenshine, 1987, p. 76):

1. Provide students with a concise statement of goals.
2. Review prior knowledge that is necessary for the day's lesson.
3. Present new information in small chunks, and allow students opportunities to practice frequently with the new information.
4. Clearly explain and describe new skills and information.
5. Provide opportunities for student practice with the skill or knowledge.
6. Check students' understanding by posing frequent questions.
7. Guide students during initial practice.
8. Provide feedback that includes praise and correction on their skill and/or understanding.
9. Provide independent practice through specific activities and seatwork exercises.
10. Continue practice until the skill or content is mastered.

"Big D.I." and "little "d.i." have many similarities. For the purposes of this book, "direct instruction" refers to strategies that serve all the students in a whole classroom more effectively. DI lessons and curriculum are available for helping students learn specific skills. These lessons provide the objectives and scripts for teachers. While we do not provide examples of specific scripts, you may want to examine some examples online at the National Institute for Direct Instruction (http://www.nifdi.org) or the Association for Direct Instruction (http://www.adihome.org) once you have identified specific needs of individual students in your class. Opponents of direct instruction suggest that this approach requires students to focus on memorizing facts and following rigid routines, therefore stifling creativity and preventing students from engaging in higher-order thinking (Poplin, Wiest, & Thorson, 1996). For example, Rosenshine (1987) suggests that direct instruction is most effective when "teaching mathematical procedures and computations, reading decoding, explicit reading procedures … science facts and concepts and rules, and foreign language vocabulary and grammar" (p. 75). Constructivist approaches described in chapter 1 of this book suggest that the teacher provides experiences that encourage the students to uniquely increase their understanding. Direct instruction is very different in that the teacher regulates students' learning and provides the information and skills to the student.

STEP-BY-STEP PROCEDURES FOR PLANNING AND IMPLEMENTING LECTURES

For the remaining sections of this chapter we will move away from direct instruction and focus on helping you consider how to plan and deliver effective lectures. Much of the research and ideas about direct instruction apply to lecturing and several other instructional strategies. Chapter 6, "Questioning," and chapter 7, "Concept Formation," both tap into some of the Rosenshine principles outlined above. Rather than providing step-by-step procedures for a direct instruction model, we chose to introduce it here, and then integrate particular principles of direct instruction into several instructional strategies to improve their effectiveness in promoting student learning.

Teachers use different types of lectures to meet different purposes in the classroom. As mentioned above, lectures can be to the whole class, or to small groups of students. Lectures may be short, as when briefly describing the expectations of a chemistry lab, or they may be lengthy, as when describing the lymph system in the human body. When planning to lecture, teachers are very aware that they need to be prepared for being in front of their students. If you plan to lecture all period, and you teach five one-hour periods, you need to be ready for five hours of talking. This has implications for your content knowledge as well as for your physical stamina and the attention span of your students. In this chapter we examine five key steps for lecturing:

1. planning the topic outline
2. planning the lecture
3. student note-taking skills and preparing the audio/visuals
4. delivering the lecture
5. concluding the lecture

Planning the Topic Outline

We suggest that teachers write a topic outline for every lecture they will present. This outline allows the teacher to think about the sequence in which content should be presented, as well as the level of detail that the students need. If you are lecturing on the elements of fiction, then your topic outline might have the following key points, in this order:

characterization
conflict and rising action
climax
following action
denouement/conclusion

Each key point should then have definitions, minor points, and other details that will help students understand the facts and concepts. This topic outline also allows you to begin estimating how much time you want to spend talking about each point. Beginning teachers often find that a challenge of lecturing is deciding what to leave out. In the above example, you likely know examples of "conflict and rising action" from many different stories (and likely from many different genres of fiction). If you determine that you only have time to describe two conflicts, you will need to omit the many other excellent examples. That is difficult to do. You will often know more information about a topic than you will present in a lecture. The lecture should include only information that is critical for the students to know; this will help keep the lecture focused on important content.

Planning the Lecture

After the content of the lecture has been outlined, you will create a lesson plan that has your lecture notes, opportunities for student interactions, and questions you want to ask during the lecture to assess student learning. Objectives for a lecture will usually fit into one of two categories, *informational objectives* and *skill objectives* (these were explained in detail in chapter 3). Teachers usually highlight the key ideas of the topic outline in their notes, with additional information included to help remind them of the content. These key ideas will comprise the information objective(s) for the lesson. The skill objective of lectures will describe how students will develop their skills at synthesizing information or at note taking. Examples of these two types of objectives for a planned lecture on the construction of the North American transcontinental railroad would be as follows:

> Students will be able to list in their notebooks two reasons why investors were willing to fund the building of the railroad (information objective).
>
> Students will demonstrate their ability to identify key ideas during a lecture by taking accurate notes about the building of the transcontinental railroad (skill objective).

Many teachers will write out an entire lecture (much like a speech) and then bring a script to class. These teachers either read this script to their students or refer to it when they talk about a particularly difficult topic. Scripting is a very effective strategy, because it lets you think through the content and the manner in which you will present it to your students. The process of writing the script helps you estimate the amount of time needed for the lecture, and provides you the opportunity to think through the words you will use to help make an idea clear and understandable. Of course, if you simply read your script to the class you will not be engaging, dynamic, or flexible with the content. Opportunities to interact with the class will be further restricted if you only keep to the written words. We suggest a balance by using scripts when planning a lecture, and outlines or topical notes during the lecture. The scripts can be with your notes, but not the main document you refer to. If you lose track of the topic, or need to present a very technical or difficult concept, then the script is available to read. The rest of the time, the script provides a backup for the detailed outline of the lecture topic.

Student Note-Taking Skills and Preparing the Audiovisuals

The third part of the lecture is to consider the audiovisual components that you will use. Students need help with taking notes and focusing on key concepts. You may want to provide copies of your topic outline to your students. This could provide them with a framework/outline on which they can add points and details gleaned from the lecture. If these notes are so detailed that you are merely repeating the information on the handout, then your students could be less engaged in your lecture. You should also consider making overhead transparencies or PowerPoint slides of your main points. We have watched many student teachers project overhead visuals that are too small or too cluttered. Such visuals should be large enough so that students in the back of the room can read them with ease. If you plan to project a map, picture, or diagram, be sure they are easy to read as well. If an overhead visual is still too complex for easy reading, then hand out paper copiess to the students so that they are able to follow along on their own. If you intend to write notes on the chalkboard, then we suggest planning out the key ideas that you want students to learn from the lecture to ensure that you write them accurately on the board. If your

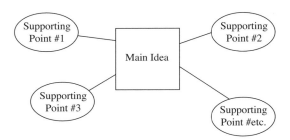

Figure 5.1

students have not had much practice taking notes, then they will need explicit directions from you. Students will record in their notes whatever you put on the board, overhead, or in computer notes, so these notes need to be planned thoughtfully and written logically. Provide students with a format for recording notes, and tell them how to record their ideas. For example, you can tell them, "This is the main idea," or, "This is a supporting point under the main idea that you just put in your notes." An outline format is most common, but teachers might also use a web format, as shown in figure 5.1.

If you will be using audio or video clips, then put a comment in your lecture notes where you want to present those to the students and your purpose for using them (e.g., if you are going to play audio of a protestor who is afraid of a group of policemen, you could tell students, "Please listen to the fear in the voice of this civil rights protestor").

DELIVERING THE LECTURE

Effective teachers use an introduction or "hook" to focus students on the content and help them engage with the content. This hook activity is important because it sets the stage for the ensuing content. These activities will vary greatly depending on your personality, the makeup of your classroom, and the content being examined. We have seen teachers use hooks such as playing a song, reading a poem, showing a video clip, or viewing a webcam. We have also watched teachers dress in costume, display an old artifact or primary source document, and have a human skeleton set up in front of the classroom. In addition to generating student interest, teachers may also introduce a lecture with a brief overview of the content they will examine, a statement of the learning objectives for the day, and the purpose of the day's lesson.

Keep the following things in mind when delivering a lecture: As an instructor, you want to minimize student distraction and maximize student learning. Clearly talk through your notes/scripts. Pace and pause to engage students' interest and to allow them to note important points. Most of the hard work will have been done when preparing the lecture outline and lesson plan. The delivery is now your verbal presentation of these notes. Be sure your voice is clear, that you clearly enunciate your words, and that your mannerisms help your lecture. For example, standing motionless behind the lectern will make you appear separated or nervous. Move and incorporate hand gestures to emphasize particular points and key ideas.

In addition to presenting the information accurately and enthusiastically, the single most important element of lecturing is to be acutely aware of your students. Throughout the lecture, look to see if they are engaged and attentive (this will be evident through body language, eye contact, note taking, and other behavior). Look to see if they are keeping up with you in their notes. When we work with teachers, we encourage them to pause and look at their students' notes to see how closely they align with the teacher's lecture notes. If students are not following, then you need to revisit the content, slow down, or remember who is having difficulty and provide more one-on-one attention after the lecture. This close monitoring of students also provides you with insight about student note-taking skills. It is very important to tell students that they should "include this in your notes," or "write a synopsis of what I just said in your own words in your notes," or to give other prompts to help student note-taking skills. While students are learning academic content from your lecture, you will also need to help them learn the skills of synthesizing information, writing notes, asking questions for clarification, and other advanced thinking skills.

Effective teachers do not merely present; they help students understand what they are presenting. This is more important when students have had fewer opportunities to take notes during a lecture. Therefore, middle school students will need more time spent on these thinking skills than most high school students. As a teacher, the more time you spend on these skills, the less time you will have for lecturing on content. However, by contextualizing note-taking skills into your lecture, you will better prepare students to learn how to best receive information from a lecture. Periodic questions or checks of students' understanding should also be used while you deliver the lecture (questioning is addressed further in chapter 6). These questions should focus on specifics of your topic outline and not be generic. For example, if you just finished describing different cloud formations, a question such as "Could you explain the differences between a cumulous and a stratus cloud?" is a more effective and focused question than "Do you have any questions about clouds?"

Concluding the Lecture

Typically, the conclusion of a lecture will involve a review of the main points that you want your students to remember; you also should remind them of the overall purpose of the lecture. The conclusion is also an excellent place at which to tell students how the information from the lecture will connect with the next day's class. For example, if an earth science teacher just finished a lecture on volcanoes, he may end the lecture by telling students, "This lecture provided you with a general understanding of how a volcano erupts. Look over your notes to be sure you have the following six points listed (teacher lists the six points). You should also have a few details that explain each point in more detail. Does anyone need help with these six points? The information we explored today will prepare us for tomorrow, when we look at Mt. St. Helens in Washington state."

We also encourage teachers to collect students' notes at the end of class, or to have students complete "exit cards." Exit cards are documents that your students must have ready when they leave the class, and are a quick assessment of student learning. These could be lecture notes from the day, answers on a note card (e.g., "Write the titles of the five themes of geography that I described to you"), verbal responses ("As you leave today, tell me one thing you learned that was new to you"), or any other concise strategy for checking students' understanding at the conclusion of your lecture. Assessments will be addressed later in this chapter.

The following lecture/presentation planning chart provides a helpful format for planning lectures. We have adapted this from work by Wingert (2001), and from the University of Minnesota's Center for Teaching and Learning Services (http://www1.umn.edu/ohr/teachlearn/tutorials/lectures/planning.html):

Beginning the Lecture/Presentation	
What would you like your students to do/ know by the end of your presentation (short-term objective)?	
How will you share your objective/goal (including how and why it is important) with your students?	
Introduction: Think of an overview, anecdote, problem/case study, question, demonstration, quotation, relevant fact/statistic.	
Delivering the Lecture/Presentation	
First segment of information (10–15 minutes) List the main points you will present. List the audiovisual aids you will use (handouts, PowerPoint presentation, video, overhead projections, notes on chalkboard, etc.) Active processing/participation activity: What might students do to help them think about the content? Share with a neighbor? Take a brief quiz? Participate in a question/ answer session?	
Second segment of information (10–15 minutes) List the main points you will present. List the audiovisual aids you will use (handouts, PowerPoint presentation, video, overhead projections, notes on chalkboard, etc.). Active processing/participation activity: What might students do to help them think about the content? Share with a neighbor? Take a brief quiz? Participate in a question/ answer session?	

(continued)

Delivering the Lecture/Presentation (Continued)	
Third segment of information (10–15 minutes) List the main points you will present. List the audiovisual aids you will use (handouts, PowerPoint presentation, video, overhead projections, notes on chalkboard, etc.). Active processing/participation activity: What might students do to help them think about the content? Share with a neighbor? Take a brief quiz? Participate in a question/answer session?	
Ending the Lecture/Presentation	
Wrap-up: How will you know students have learned/mastered what you intended? (Refer to the assessment section of this chapter.)	

LOGISTICAL CONCERNS, INCLUDING BENEFITS AND OBSTACLES WHEN LECTURING

Many of the courses you have taken in college have utilized lectures. A lecture hall at a university is a very common structure. Rooms designed for lectures usually have rows of desks or tables that face the front, a screen for a projection unit, chalkboards or whiteboards, and a podium or table for the speaker's notes, computer, or other equipment. These rooms usually seat a large number of students. Thinking about the structure of these rooms reveals much about the lecture strategy: The teacher is the focus of attention; students do not interact much with one another; a large number of people can hear the lecture without much opportunity to interact with the teacher; and audiovisual aids help the presentation.

When you lecture to your future high school or middle school students, you will be in a classroom, not a lecture hall. You will also be talking to a smaller number of students who do not necessarily have the needed note-taking skills or discipline to concentrate during a lecture. As a result, several logistical considerations will help your lectures. The setting of the classroom is an important initial consideration. Determine if all your students can see you and can see your visual aids. Students who have auditory or visual impairments should be close enough to see and hear you.

The following eight recommendations can help make your lectures more effective. They have been adapted from assessments of effective teaching conducted by Cashin (1990, pp. 60–61):

1. Fit the lecture to the audience.

   Be sure that the words you use, the examples with which you illustrate your ideas, and the content of the lecture will engage your students. Middle school students will need direction from you about what to focus on during the lecture, while high school students may have had more experience with lectures. With any age student, recognize that you will be more active then your students during a lecture, so you must be sensitive to their attention spans. There is not an ideal length for a lecture, but the more concise you can be, the better.

2. Focus your topic—remember that you cannot cover everything in one lecture.

   Focus on the key ideas, skills, facts, and/or principles that your students will use after the lecture. Do not think of the lecture as an end in itself, but as a lesson that helps students gain information that they will use during other activities.

3. Organize your points for clarity.

   The topic outline should help you decide the best order for presenting the main points of the lecture. This order should move from less-complex to more-complex ideas so that students are able to build upon their prior knowledge. Hand out notes or a graphic organizer that will help students follow along during your lecture.

4. Select appropriate examples or illustrations.

   As mentioned above, these should help the students understand the information. Therefore, the examples and illustrations should be appropriate for your students' age, experience, and interests.

5. Present more than one side of an issue and be sensitive to other perspectives.

   Since you are leading the class during a lecture, your students are a captive audience. By that we mean that they cannot leave (in general, students will not often question a teacher's authority, and the teacher needs to be aware of this power dynamic). As a result, the teacher must be aware of different opinions, experiences, and ideas that students could bring to the classroom. If an issue is controversial or multifaceted, then you need to consider how to represent multiple perspectives during your lecture.

6. Be aware of your audience—notice their feedback.

   As mentioned earlier, you need to be acutely aware of your students. Watch them during the lecture for nonverbal feedback that will help you know their interest level, degree of engagement, and their understanding of the topics.

7. Repeat points when necessary.

   Students will benefit from your overemphasis of key ideas and points and from your willingness to explain a complex topic multiple times.

8. Be enthusiastic; you don't have to be an entertainer, but you should be excited by your topic.

> If you lack enthusiasm for the topic, students will notice. However, if you model enthusiasm, then students will likely be more interested in the topics examined.

CLASSROOM MANAGEMENT AND STUDENT MOTIVATION ISSUES

During a lecture, the students' attention will be up front and on you (or on the audiovisual aid you are using). Lectures do not require students to talk unless you ask for their insight, ideas, and questions. As a result, your expectations for them to listen must be very clear. Many beginning teachers try to lecture when their students are talking quietly, looking about the room, or simply not paying attention. When you are lecturing you must require that the classroom is quiet, that the students are not distracting one another, and that the learning environment is conducive to listening and taking notes. This means that if several students are talking, you will request them to stop. If the sunshine is making a glare on the chalkboard, then you will close the blinds. If students do not have paper and pencil with which to take notes, then you will either provide that to them or have them get the needed materials.

Your proximity, or location, during the lecture will help with many management issues. For example, if two students are talking to each other during the lecture, then you can move next to them as you talk. Your physical presence will often make the students pay closer attention. If you cannot move next to a student, then stop the lecture and ask the students to please stop and listen (e.g., "I need you two to listen because your talking is distracting me and others who are trying to learn from the lecture"). If students continue to talk, then you may need to rearrange seating assignments. As was mentioned in chapter 1, however, discipline problems this severe usually reveal a relationship problem, and may require more long-term interactions with the students. The bottom line during a lecture, however, is that the classroom needs to be quiet and focused in order for all students to have opportunities to hear what you have to say.

Lecture is a teacher-centered activity. As such you, the teacher, will need to be sure you are ready to "lead the class." Students should clearly understand your expectations of them during the lecture. Possible expectations include:

- bringing pencil and paper to class
- having read any assigned texts
- listening to the teacher
- actively taking notes
- raising hands when questions come up

You should also set high expectations for yourself. If you prepare your notes and are knowledgeable about your lecture topic, move the lesson along at a pace that keeps the students engaged, continually monitor your students' level of engagement (e.g., are they actively taking notes, or gazing out the window?), and show enthusism and excitement about the topic then you will experience fewer management and discipline problems.

Student motivation during a lecture is a significant issue to consider. Many students welcome a lecture because it is an opportunity for the teacher to tell them what they need to know for the test. These students are motivated extrinsically. Thinking about course content is limited to repeating what they heard from a lecture or from assigned readings. However, look for opportunities to communicate to students that a lecture is not merely presenting information for a test. Inform students why you are lecturing to them so that they know the purpose of the lecture. If you are planning to lecture about the safety procedures in the science lab, be sure that your students know why this information is important and how it will be used in the future. Similarly, if a Spanish teacher is lecturing on Mexican holidays, the content will seem more relevant if he also explains why this content will help them understand Spanish language and culture, which will be learned in future units. In each of these cases, the students see the relevancy of the lecture beyond preparation for a test. During a lecture, the teacher is active. Students need to also recognize that they should also be actively listening, thinking, and taking notes. Hearing a lecture can be a very passive activity, unless you remind students to engage with the content. For most adolescents, however, "engaging with the content" is too abstract. Instead, the teacher can facilitate this by asking students to engage in higher-order thinking tasks with the lecture content. For example, they can compare and contrast important information, predict outcomes of events, or write a personal reflection paper about new facts they learned during the lecture. Another approach for motivating students to remain engaged during lectures is to consider whether or not their own experiences might add to the lecture. By knowing your students' backgrounds you are in a position to help incorporate their ideas and stories into your lecture. This could occur as you plan the lecture, or if you allow students to interject their ideas while you lecture. Either approach will provide a greater sense of ownership by the students, which often increases their motivation to learn and helps you manage the learning environment.

APPROPRIATE ASSESSMENT TECHNIQUES TO USE WITH LECTURE

Lectures present students with information, but do not allow students many opportunities to apply the information. As we mentioned earlier in the chapter, this is a criticism of lectures. The relatively passive role of the student also has implications on how you assess student learning. Consider the following example. A middle school art teacher has just finished a lecture on several shading techniques that artists use when drawing portraits. Her lecture was full of examples of many artists' work, detailed notes, and her own demonstrations of several techniques. Students listened at their desks, took notes, and asked periodic questions about the techniques. When this teacher is going to assess her students' understanding of the information presented in her lecture, she must take into consideration the following ideas:

What content did the students learn?
How might they show an understanding of the content that is consistent with how they learned it?

These questions are useful for any teacher to consider when preparing to assess students' learning after a lecture. The general answer to the first question is that students were to have learned the content described in the *topic outline* of the lecture. In the above example, the students learned about shading techniques. The second question, however, is a bit trickier; the teacher will only be able to assess students' understanding of the topic outline by using assessments that are consistent with the lecture technique. A valid assessment technique for the art teacher would be for students to write on a piece of paper two techniques that create depth and shading to a portrait. An inappropriate assessment would be for the students to demonstrate their skill at shading. The lecture presented the facts and skill required, but it did not allow for students to use or apply the facts or skills. Assessments after a lecture, therefore, should be limited to the content presented in the lecture. The following assessments are valid and reliable techniques for determining what students learned from a lecture.

Exit Cards

These were described in the "Step-by-Step" section above. In brief, an exit card is an assessment of the key points a student learned from the lecture. These are usually short and concise assessments (one to five minutes of writing). If you collect students' notes, then you can identify what they wrote down, but you cannot assess what they learned. Having students separately write out what they learned will be a more accurate assessment.

Journal of Facts and Feelings

We encourage students to record a "facts and feelings" section in their notes. This can also be a separate journal that the students keep. Students record new facts and ideas that they learned during the lecture, and then describe their feelings and questions about these new facts. This allows the teacher to assess students' thinking and understanding of the information presented during a lecture. The following is an example from a "facts and feelings" section of a student's notes:

Fact: I never knew that Lewis and Clark were leaders of an official army corps sent by Jefferson.

Feeling: This makes the Lewis and Clark expedition seem more official, because they were on government business. I can imagine that many were excited to hear about what they found. I also wonder if this was the beginning of confrontations between the U.S. government and Native Americans.

The "facts and feelings" entry is also useful for having students write what they consider to be the most confusing or complicated part of a lecture; this often allows you to determine if a portion of your lecture was unclear. It is also a useful technique when students complete a reading assignment, or listen to a presentation.

Think/Pair/Share

This assessment technique is an informal strategy. The teacher provides students with a prompt or question from the lecture, then asks students to "*think* about the question, *pair* with a partner, and *share* your answers." These questions should be about the content of the lecture, but they can push students to apply the content to other situations. For example, after a mathematics teacher has finished a brief lecture on Pythagoras's theorem, she might tell students, "Think of how this theorem is used in our community." The students would then pair and share. The teacher can listen to the pairs' comments, ask students to share their comments after they share with their partner, or ask students to write what they shared on a piece of paper.

Recall of Specific Information

Students can be given a writing assignment where they must recall specific facts and details from a lecture. It could take the form of a true/false test, fill-in-the-blank quiz, or essay exam, but it can also be a written or verbal explanation of information presented during the lecture. These recalls are not necessarily memorization tasks. Students could be asked to compare and contrast information learned during the lecture with information they learned in previous class sessions or readings.

The key point to remember is that if the students have learned the content they should be able to use and apply it in a variety of tasks. However, if the assessment requires skill or knowledge that they have not learned from the lecture, then the assessment is an invalid measure of what they have learned. Consider the following assessments following a lecture on poetic devices:

Finish this sentence so it uses alliteration: "The snake _____ silently through the grass."
Why might a writer use similes?
What is a recent story you read that uses symbolism?
Write a short poem using metaphors and similes.

The first three examples are valid assessments, because all the information was presented in the lecture. The fourth requires writing skills that need practice and cannot be addressed in a lecture; this should not be used as an assessment of what students have learned. Assessments that follow a lecture determine student learning, and they provide insight into how effectively you have presented the information. If all students are confused about the same information, then you should consider how you might revisit that information to promote their learning.

GUIDELINES FOR DECIDING IF A LECTURE IS APPROPRIATE FOR THE CONTENT OF A LESSON

The lecture is a valuable part of a teacher's instructional repertoire if it is not overused and if it is not used when other methods would be more effective. When lecturing to your students, you must have solid knowledge of the content, speak clearly, highlight main points and key concepts, engage students with periodic questions, and monitor student note taking and learning. Since lecturing is a teacher-centered strategy, students can easily become passive learners when you lecture to them. The concern here is that students will not stay engaged in the topic and their attention span will be limited. Good and Brophy (2003, p. 371) have summarized suggested criteria that we believe provide an excellent set of guidelines for determining when to use lecture:

When the objective is to present information that is not readily available from another source, is original, or must be integrated from different sources.
When the material must be organized and presented in a particular way.
When it is necessary to arouse interest in the subject.
When it is necessary to introduce a topic before students read about it on their own or to provide instructions about a task.
When the information needs to be summarized or synthesized, for example, following a discussion or inquiry project.
When curriculum materials need updating or elaborating.
When the teacher wants to present an alternative point of view or to clarify issues in preparation for discussion.
When the teacher wants to provide supplementary explanations or material that students may have difficulty learning on their own.

Many students may not readily learn content that they hear during a lecture, and it is widely accepted at all levels of education that content presented during a lecture is rapidly forgotten by students (Bligh, 2000; Edwards, Smith &

Webb, 2001). This is often called the "curve of forgetting." Cross found that one week after a lecture, students recalled only 17% of the information (1986). This percentage is higher if students use the information after a lecture (e.g., in ways we describe earlier in this chapter). Still, this forgetfulness is a concern, and we believe that the lecture is too often the default approach for teaching. When students' primary language is not the same as the language used for the lecture, and when students have learning difficulties that are exacerbated when listening to someone speak, lecture is not an appropriate strategy. However, the lecture is one of many powerful instructional strategies. Use it when you have confidence that it will enhance student learning more than will other instructional strategies.

A NOTE ABOUT PRESENTATIONS FROM GUEST SPEAKERS AND STORYTELLERS

Guest speakers can provide your students with excellent insights and perspectives. Imagine the information that your students might learn from speakers such as a medical doctor, attorney, therapist, artist, writer, athlete, historian, or politician. Some community organizations have a speakers' bureau that you can contact in order to line up a speaker for your class. If the speaker has made a presentation to adolescents before, she may have a preplanned series of activities for your students. Usually, however, a speaker will come to your class and lecture or present information. Herein is the caveat for inviting guest speakers. You will take many courses in preparation for becoming a middle school or high school teacher. These courses, much like this book, are designed to help you facilitate student learning, and to use class time effectively and efficiently for this purpose. A guest speaker usually does not have this experience. Since she will be speaking to your students, you want to be sure that she is able to teach, and that your students will learn from her comments. Guest speakers should help your students learn information and skills that are different from what you can provide. We suggest that teachers ask the following questions when considering whether or not to invite a guest speaker:

- Will she provide information or skills equal to or more effectively than you?
- What experience has she had speaking to students?
- What evidence do you have that the speaker will help your students learn?
- Do you know the specific content to be presented?
- Can you provide guiding questions or topics for the speaker?
- Does the content fit in with your curriculum scope and sequence?
- Do parents need to be notified?
- Why will your students benefit from hearing the speaker?
- What preparation should your students have prior to the speaker? For example, should students read a text or prepare questions ahead of time?

Storytelling is another type of presentation/lecture that is a powerful supplement to your instructional strategies. Stories incite the imagination and provide narratives and descriptions that help information come alive. Most of us have heard someone who is a good storyteller, who can engage listeners in a unique manner that captivates their attention. There are several organizations that promote storytelling and have a list of storytellers who can come to your classroom (for example, the website http://www.storyarts.org/ provides lesson plans and ideas incorporating storytelling into the classroom; www.storynet.org is the home page of the National Storytelling Network, and provides resources and ideas for teachers). These are usually professional speakers, but the above questions should be asked for them as well.

MAKING IT WORK IN YOUR CONTENT AREA

Consider the subjects you will be certified to teach at the middle school or high school level. Considering Good and Brophy's (2003) guidelines for selecting lecture, determine a topic that you believe will be appropriate for a lecture. Effective lectures are a result of careful planning. Return to the "Lecture/Presentation Planning Chart" earlier in this chapter, and consider the following:

Construct a topic outline for the lecture
Write lesson objectives:
Objectives dealing with the information students will learn.
Objectives dealing with the intellectual skill of taking notes.
Describe the rationale for choosing the issue:
What makes this a good topic for a lecture?
What topics will immediately precede and follow this lecture?
Lesson procedures:
Identify the key topics of your lecture, including at least two subpoints for each topic. Remember that you will probably have more than two subpoints, so you will need to choose the most important topics and subpoints.
Write a script for the opening of your lecture. For the next point/topic of the lecture, write detailed notes. Decide whether you are more comfortable with notes or scripts, and complete the lecture using detailed notes or scripts for the rest of the topics you identified above.
What graphic organizers, overhead projections, slides, or other audiovisual aids will help with your lecture?
Write out some questions you could pose to your class to assess their understanding of your key points. These should be interspersed throughout the lecture to help your students understand your main ideas.
Reread the section on assessing student learning from lectures, and determine which ideas you might use. Consider whether you want to assess them through written work or through an oral review.

CHAPTER REVIEW

The *lecture* is an instructional strategy at which the teacher presents a specified set of information to students. *Direct instruction* is a category of teacher-centered and teacher-directed instructional strategies. The teacher directs student learning purposely to ensure that specific content is addressed. Direct instruction meets specific purposes in the classroom, and is an effective approach that helps students learn course content. We use the term *explicit teaching* synonymously with *direct instruction* because both terms imply that the teacher explicitly/directly provides information or step-by-step skills.

Lectures allow the teacher to present a specific amount of information quickly and efficiently, to highlight the key points that best meet students' interests and needs. Students are often passive observers during lectures, because most lectures do not require them to participate beyond listening, note taking, and asking periodic questions. One of the most consistent and important educational research findings is that students who make frequent, relevant responses during a lesson learn more than students who are passive observers.

Teachers use different types of lectures to meet different purposes in the classroom. Lectures can be to the whole class, or to small groups of students. Lectures might be short, as when briefly describing the components of a chemistry lab, or they may be lengthy, as when describing the lymph system in the human body.

In this chapter we examined five key steps for lecturing:

1. planning the topic outline
2. planning the lecture
3. student note-taking skills and preparing the audio/visuals
4. delivering the lecture
5. concluding the lecture

The following eight recommendations can help make the lecture approach more effective:

1. Fit the lecture to the audience.
2. Focus your topic—remember that you cannot cover everything in one lecture.
3. Organize your points for clarity.
4. Select appropriate examples or illustrations.
5. Present more than one side of an issue and be sensitive to other perspectives.
6. Be aware of your audience—notice their feedback.
7. Repeat points when necessary.
8. Be enthusiastic; you don't have to be an entertainer, but you should be excited by your topic.

Many beginning teachers try to lecture when their students are talking quietly, looking about the room, or simply not paying attention. When you are lecturing you must insist that the classroom is quiet, that the students are not distracting one another, and that the learning environment is conducive to listening and taking notes. Student motivation during lecture is a significant issue to consider: look for opportunities to communicate to students that a lecture is not merely presenting information for a test.

When you assess students' understanding of the information presented in a lecture, take the following ideas into consideration:

What content did the students learn?
How might they show their understanding of the content that is consistent with how they learned it?

These questions are useful for any teacher to consider when preparing to assess students' learning after a lecture.

The following assessments are valid and reliable techniques for determining what students learned from a lecture:

exit cards
a "facts and feelings" journal
think/pair/share
recall of specific information

Good and Brophy (2003) developed eight criteria that we believe provide an excellent set of guidelines for determining when to give a lecture:

1. When the objective is to present information that is not readily available from another source, is original, or must be integrated from different sources.
2. When the material must be organized and presented in a particular way.
3. When it is necessary to arouse interest in the subject.
4. When it is necessary to introduce a topic before students read about it on their own or to provide instructions about a task.
5. When the information needs to be summarized or synthesized, for example, following a discussion or inquiry project.
6. When curriculum materials need updating or elaborating.
7. When the teacher wants to present an alternative point of view or to clarify issues in preparation for discussion.
8. When the teacher wants to provide supplementary explanations or material that students may have difficulty learning on their own.

Guest speakers and storytellers are possible presenters/lecturers that can enhance student learning. These guests to your classroom should be checked on thoroughly before allowing them to make a presentation.

REFERENCES

Barbetta, P. M., & Scaruppa, C. L. (1995). Looking for a way to improve your behavior analysis lectures? Try guided notes. *Behavior Analyst, 18*, 155–160.

Bligh, D. A. (2000). *What's the use of lectures?* San Francisco: Jossey-Bass.

Brophy, J., & Good, T. (1986). Teacher behavior and student achievement. In M. Wittrock (Ed.), *Handbook of research on teaching* (pp. 340–370). New York: Macmillan.

Cashin, W. E. (1990). Assessing teaching effectiveness. In P. A. Seldin (Ed.), *How administrators can improve teaching*. San Francisco: Jossey-Bass.

Cross, K. P. (1986). A proposal to improve teaching or what taking teaching seriously should mean. *AAHE Bulletin 39*, 10–11.

Edwards, H., Smith, B., & Webb, G. (Eds.). (2001). *Lecturing: Case studies, experience and practice*. London: Kogan Page.

Engelmann, S., & Carnine, D. (1991). *Theory of instruction: Principles and applications* (rev. ed.). Eugene, OR: ADI Press.

Fisher, C. W., & Berliner, D. C. (Eds.). (1985). *Perspectives on instructional time*. New York: Longman.

Good, T. L., & Brophy, J. E. (2003). *Looking in classrooms* (9th ed.). Boston, MA: Allyn and Bacon.

Heward, W. L. (2005). Fast facts for faculty—guided notes: Improving the effectiveness of your lectures. Retrieved November 24, 2005 from http://telr.osu.edu/dpg/fastfact/notes.html.

Hughes, C. A., & Suritsky, S. K. (1994). Note-taking skills of university students with and without learning disabilities. *Journal of Learning Disabilities, 27*, 20–24.

Kame'enui, E. J., Carnine, D. W., & Dixon, R. C. (1998). Effective teaching strategies that accommodate diverse learners. In E. J. Kame'enui & D. W. Carnine (Eds.), *Effective teaching strategies that accommodate diverse learners* (pp. 1–17). Columbus, OH: Merrill.

Ormrod, J. E. (2006). *Educational psychology: Developing learners* (5th ed.). Upper Saddle River, NJ: Merrill.

Poplin, M., Wiest, D. J., & Thorson, S. (1995). Alternative instructional strategies to reductionism: Constructive, critical, multicultural, and feminine pedagogies. In W. Stainback & S. Stainback (Eds.), *Controversial issues confronting special education: Divergent perspectives* (2nd ed., pp. 153–165). Boston: Allyn and Bacon.

Rosenshine, B. (1987). Explicit teaching. In D. Berliner & B. Rosenshine (Eds.), *Talks to teachers* (75–92). New York: Random House.

Sandock, B. (2000). Enhancing learning of students with LD without compromising standards: Tips for teaching. Retrieved April 17, 2006 from http://www.ldonline.org/ld_indepth/postsecondary/facultytips.html.

Saski, J., Swicegood, P., & Carter, J. (1983). Notetaking formats for learning disabled adolescents. *Learning Disability Quarterly, 6*, 265–272.

Schug, M., Tarver, S., & Western, R. (2001). Direct instruction and the teaching of early reading. *Wisconsin Policy Research Institute Report, 14*(2), 1–27.

Wingert, D. (2001). Basic presentation skills. Retrieved April 19, 2006 from http://www1.umn.edu/ohr/teachlearn/tutorials/lectures/planning.html.

CITED WEBSITES

Association for Direct Instruction:
> http://www.adihome.org

Story Telling:
> http://www.storyarts.org

> http://www.storynet.org

National Institute for Direct Instruction:
> http://www.nifdi.org

University of Minnesota's Center for Teaching and Learning Services:
> http://www1.umn.edu/ohr/teachlearn/tutorials/lectures/planning.html

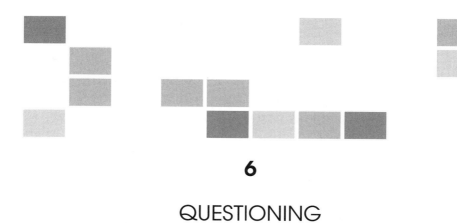

6

QUESTIONING

OVERVIEW

During the years of schooling, the average student has been asked over a million questions. Some researchers have found that a teacher may ask as many as three to four hundred questions in a single day (Wilen, 1991). Others have found that questioning is one of the most dominant teaching strategies used in middle and high school classrooms, second only to lecturing (Gall, 1984). Of course, many believe that both of these strategies are overused, and often misused. In this chapter we will offer a description of questioning as an instructional strategy, propose procedures for planning and implementation, and discuss logistical concerns, classroom management, and assessment issues. Finally, we will propose guidelines to help you decide if questioning is appropriate for the content of a lesson.

Defining Questioning

While you have heard, answered, or asked innumerable questions at school, you probably have not considered the significance of using questions for learning. Not all teacher questions used during a lesson are part of questioning. The instructional strategy of questioning, as used in this text, is a teacher-centered approach that encourages students to think more deeply. Some might call this strategy a question-and-answer session, or "questioning to learn." The teacher uses a series of questions to lead the class or the student toward the lesson's objectives. Often, questioning is either blended or confused with discussion. While questions are certainly a part of a discussion, in this text we will speak of these as different strategies with different purposes—the primary distinction between the two being that questioning is teacher-centered and discussion is student-centered. During a discussion the teacher may choose to move to the background; during questioning, the teacher remains an integral part of the strategy. Discussion is a strategy used to give students opportunities to engage in substantive dialogue while exchanging ideas and examining a variety of perspectives. Questioning is a strategy used by a teacher to help students develop and use a variety of thinking skills. Some teachers have designed and used methods to merge the two strategies in order to help achieve lesson objectives (Henning, 2004). The instructional strategy of discussion is presented in detail in chapter 10. Additionally, some teacher questions are used as an assessment technique and not as part of an instructional strategy; these questions will be addressed later in this chapter.

In the same way, there is also a distinction between student questions and the questioning strategy. Student questions are usually either an essential part of inquiry learning, another student-centered strategy (see chapter 11), or are used simply for clarification purposes. It is possible that some student-generated questions will help a teacher move the class toward lesson objectives related to higher-order thinking and, in that case, may be examples of the highest form of questioning. At some point the distinction between all these types of questions blur. Of course, the common denominator is that what we really want as teachers is improved, thoughtful, oral participation on the part of students. However, a clear understanding of what we mean by questioning as an instructional strategy is important as we move toward using it effectively.

A DESCRIPTION OF QUESTIONING, AND RESEARCH FINDINGS

Purposes for Teacher Questions

As we have noted, there are many reasons teachers purposefully ask questions. Most of these questions will fall into one or more of three categories: (1) as part of instruction; (2) as part of classroom management; and (3) as part of assessment. Questions are used to help students move between what is commonly referred to as higher- and lower-order thinking, or as an attempt to encourage student participation and investment in learning. Questions can be used for classroom management purposes to create an open and inviting atmosphere, to encourage self-monitoring of behavior, or to manage the pace or direction of the class. Finally, questions can be used formatively during a lesson to check for student understanding, summatively as a test, or to help a teacher reflect upon the effectiveness of a lesson.

Myths About Teacher Questioning

As a new teacher, you may be tempted to go by your intuition when it comes to using questions. After all, you have seen this strategy in practice many, many times over your years of schooling and may have developed some strong opinions based upon your observations. Our purpose in the following paragraphs is to help you glean highly effective uses of the questioning strategy, as noted by research on teachers using questions. Wilen (2001) proposes nine common myths about the questioning of students, and offers research-based principles for a pedagogically sound approach to counter the "myths."

Myth 1: Questioning Is a Natural Teaching Behavior that Does Not Require Planning To effectively lead students beyond recitation of factual information teachers should plan most questions but allow for some spontaneous questions related to student answers. Planning questions provides structure and direction, increased engagement, and increases the likelihood that thinking and understanding will occur. Challenging students to think deeply has been found to increase and enhance participation and interest (Newmann, Wehlage, & Lamborn, 1992; Wilen, 1990).

Myth 2: The More Questions a Teacher Asks, the More Students Will Learn Research by Good and Brophy (2000) has shown that frequent questioning *does* help students recall factual information. It does not show that frequent questioning helps students think at higher levels. The *quantity* of questions is not as relevant as the *quality* of questions in situations where students would need to analyze an issue or evaluate a response. Unless a teacher wants students to recall factual information, it is better to focus on fewer questions of a higher quality that lead to higher-order thinking.

Myth 3: There Are No Bad Questions Good questions are easily understood and stimulate student thinking. These questions are usually brief, naturally phrased, adapted to students in the class, and sequenced to help students reach objectives. Bad questions are those that frustrate or intimidate students. These questions call for yes/no responses or guessing, give little direction, or intimidate a student into agreeing with the teacher (Gamoron & Nystrand, 1992; Groisser, 1964).

Myth 4: Higher-Level Cognitive Questions Are More Critical than Lower-Level Questions A person might think that with the emphasis on moving students toward higher-order thinking this might be true; but it is not so. In fact, lower-level questions can be more important at times because they can help a teacher diagnose a student's readiness to move into higher-order thinking. In addition, recall of factual information might be the objective for a particular lesson, and thus lower-level questioning might be appropriate. Ultimately, the goal for adolescent students is to be able to solve problems and make decisions that will assist them in becoming competent citizens. Being able to answer critical and evaluative questions must be based upon lower-level thinking (National Council for the Social Studies, 1994; Wilen, 1990).

Myth 5: Higher-Level Cognitive Questions Elicit Higher-Level Answers Several studies have uncovered this to be untrue (Costa & Lowery, 1989; Hunkins, 1995; Mills, Rice, Berliner, & Rousseau, 1980). It is interesting to note that it has been found that the cognitive level of student responses align only 50% of the time with the cognitive level of teacher questions. Students tend to answer at a lower level, while teachers tend to assume student answers are at the same level as their questions. Teachers do not always inform students of their own expectations for student responses or explain why they are questioning them. Teachers should inform students of the types of questions they will be asked, and why they are being asked them. Teachers that use action verbs in their questions that correspond with a particular cognitive level more clearly express their expectation for student responses. For example, it is helpful to use verbs like *identify*, *compare*, *predict*, or *judge* in a question to lead the student to a particular cognitive level. Using these approaches will assist a teacher in establishing a stronger relationship between the cognitive level of the question and the response.

Myth 6: Teachers Should Ask Lower-Level Cognitive Questions Before Progressing to Higher-Level Questions Many see the use of Bloom's taxonomy as hierarchical in that one level cannot be reached until the previous level has been reached. Because of this, many believe that a student should start at the bottom and work his way up, as if climbing rungs on a ladder. It may be necessary to review the basic facts and concepts before proceeding. For example, it would be difficult for students to compare the Russian Revolution with the American Revolution before they understand the basic facts of each. At times, however, starting a lesson with a higher-order question could be appropriate if there is no need for review or a teacher wants to use the question as a lesson "hook" to stimulate interest (Bloom, 1956; Good & Brophy, 2000).

Myth 7: Teachers Give Students Enough Time to Answer Questions Researchers (Newmann, 1992; Rowe, 1986) have found that while this may be true for factual recall questions it is not the case for questions that call for more complex thinking. In classrooms where teachers gave students enough time to think through their responses it has been found that the quality of student responses increased dramatically, student participation increased, and responses were more thoughtful. Rowe (1974) and Tobin (1986) found that waiting as long as three to five seconds for a response to difficult questions will have positive results.

Myth 8: When Questioning Students, Teachers Should Call Only on Volunteering Students This myth probably stems from classroom experience in which a student is painfully embarrassed or intimidated. On the other hand, research findings (Kelly, 1993; Wilen, Ishler, Hutchinson, & Kindsvatter, 2000; Wilen & White, 1991) show that students learn more when actively involved in class, that answering questions gives students an important opportunity to practice oral communication skills, and that there is a positive relationship between calling on students who do not volunteer and achievement gains. Some argue that students, as all citizens, have an obligation and responsibility to engage in public dialogue and so should practice this process in the classroom. The classroom expectation should be that all students participate, especially in cases of recitation. However, students should be given the option of nonparticipation if questions are of a sensitive nature and they feel their privacy is threatened.

Myth 9: Teachers Encourage Students to Ask Questions   Research findings (Brice & Johnson, 1999; Dillon, 1988; Hunkins, 1995) have shown that adolescent students do not ask many questions in class and that they do not expect to ask questions in class but to answer them. This is primarily because many teachers spend over 75% of class time talking. With so much of the class time centered on teacher talk there is little time left for student talk. One main reason students do not ask many questions is because they are not encouraged to do so by teachers. Questioning by students increases interactive involvement and student thinking, and can be encouraged by teachers who model how they pursue answers to their own questions and by teachers who value student questions.

STEP-BY-STEP PROCEDURES FOR PLANNING AND IMPLEMENTING QUESTIONING

As we have seen, good questions can serve to engage, motivate, and challenge students. On the other hand, poorly designed questions can frustrate students and turn them off. Have you ever been in a class where no one responds to a teacher's question because the answer is embarrassingly obvious? We mention other common questioning errors later in this chapter. There are a variety of proposed schemas designed to help you create effective questions that help students think critically. We will focus on one that is research based, and build upon what has been described in this text about the way students learn.

Framing Questions and Prompts

Chapter 3 noted that Bloom's taxonomy has been widely used to help design instructional objectives. In the same way, it has been a primary means by which effective questions for learning have been constructed. You will recall that this taxonomy covers six cognitive levels ranging from lower order to higher order—knowledge, comprehension, application, analysis, synthesis, and evaluation. Questions designed for the lower levels, especially for knowledge and comprehension, will focus students on recitation (Dillon, 1988). Questions at the other levels will ask students to move increasingly into more complex and difficult thinking (Dantonio & Beisenherz, 2001). Below we offer sample questions at each of the cognitive levels to help you consider the type of questions you might ask in your content area. Notice how any of the action verbs that reflect a particular cognitive level can easily be turned into a question or be used in "command" form to ask a question through the intonation of the teacher's voice. For example, "List the main characters in the play" can become "Can you list the main characters in the play"? or "Who are the main characters in the play"?

Knowledge

Overarching question: Can students recall information?

Sample action verbs that reflect this cognitive level: *list, locate, define, describe.*

Sample questions: What is the formula for the Pythagorean Theorem? Who are the main characters in the play?

Comprehension

Overarching question: Can students explain ideas?

Sample action verbs that reflect this cognitive level: *explain, describe, estimate, paraphrase.*

Sample questions: How does communism differ from socialism? How would you describe the life cycle of a cell?

Application

Overarching question: Can students use ideas?

Sample action verbs that reflect this cognitive level: *chart, predict, compute, classify.*

Sample questions: How could you use the formula for a triangle's area in a real-life situation? How would you say "I would like to eat at the restaurant" in Spanish?

Analysis

Overarching question: Can students see relationships?

Sample action verbs that reflect this cognitive level: *analyze, compare, contrast, solve.*

Sample questions: What are some positive and negative characteristics of Lady Macbeth? Why did the Soviets side with the Nazis and not with England?

Synthesis

Overarching question: Can students combine ideas?

Sample action verbs that reflect this cognitive level: *arrange, compose, formulate, hypothesize.*

Sample questions: What would happen if we mixed these two chemicals? What other times and settings might you use for *Hamlet*, and why would the other time period work?

Evaluation

Overarching question: Can students make judgments?

Sample action verbs that reflect this cognitive level: *judge, diagnose, apprise, assess.*

Sample questions: Should Truman have ordered the dropping of the atomic bomb? Who are the five greatest composers of all time, and why?

Additional verbs corresponding with each cognitive level can be found in appendixes C and D. A diagram that may be helpful is the question construction wheel designed by the St. Edwards University Center for Teaching Excellence. Notice how the figure 6.1 wheel offers not only the verbs for question construction but also contains project suggestions for lesson enhancement.

While you are becoming comfortable using Bloom's taxonomy to help guide your questioning, it might be helpful for you to become familiar with a simple technique. Many teachers use the idea of convergent and divergent questions to begin planning. *Convergent questions* are those that allow for only one or a few correct responses. These questions tend to be lower-order questions; for example, "What year did the Civil War begin?" or "How many spark plugs are in a six-cylinder engine?" *Divergent questions* are those that require greater deliberation and encourage broader responses. There could be a number of appropriate responses to these types of questions and typically they require higher-order thought processes; for example, "In the musical score we just heard, what is the composer trying to communicate by choosing to feature the flute with the French horn in the second movement?" Keeping these two types of questions in mind when you begin to plan your questioning can be a helpful way to get started—or to think quickly on your feet during class. It could help a new teacher avoid the "deer in the headlights" look as she stands in front of the class while processing the six cognitive domains.

Leading Effective Questioning Sessions

You might hear questioning sessions called *Socratic seminars*, after the Greek philosopher/teacher who made this instructional strategy famous.

Even Socrates had to begin developing his questioning expertise at some point—we just don't have a record of all the mistakes and gaffes he made while learning. To help lead you more quickly into effective use of the questioning strategy we offer the following suggestions.

Plan Your Questions Carefully You may recall that the first myth of using questions relates to planning. Consider your lesson objectives. Do they call for recitation? Do they call for higher-order thinking? What is the purpose of the

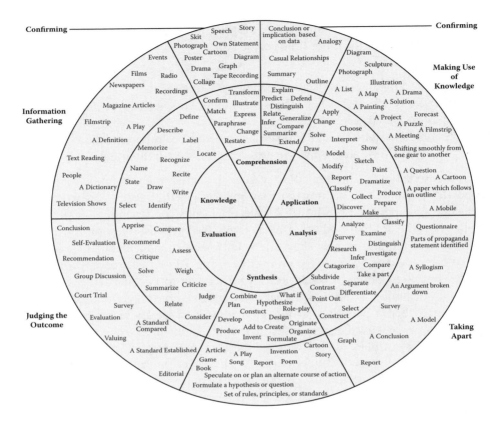

Task Oriented Question Construction Wheel Based on Bloom's Taxonomy. ©2001 St. Edward's University Center for Teaching Excellence, www.stedwards.edu/cte/resources/bwheel.htm. Used with permission.

Figure 6.1

questions? Are you trying to build classroom atmosphere in this way? Thoughtfully write down as many questions as you can that will help lead students to the lesson objective. You may need to ask questions from all cognitive domains, or you may need to ask questions from only one or two. Remember as you plan that the purpose of this strategy is not to start a discussion, but to help students share orally their thinking at higher levels or to recite factual information.

Don't Be Afraid to Depart from Your Written Questions While Staying with the Plan   If you have planned carefully you will know where you want to go with this strategy. You will be more prepared to come up with questions spontaneously in response to students in a natural way. This can be done while staying with your overall plan as defined by your objectives.

Consider Who You Are Teaching   What time of day is it? Are the students tired? What about those who are learning English or have other special needs? Think about ways you can encourage shy students without being intimidating. What kind of relationship do you have with your class? How can you use this strategy to improve your classroom atmosphere?

Consider Classroom Management and Assessment Techniques Every objective will call for an assessment. How will you assess students' oral communication? Every instructional strategy has its own unique issues related to classroom management. Have you thought this through? We will discuss this further later in this chapter.

Close the Lesson on a Strong Note As with any lesson it is important not to allow any teaching session to fizzle. What can you do to close the lesson? Is there some type of interesting closing activity that uses another learning style such as pictures or music? Is there a bookend to a "hook" you may have used at the beginning? Can you debrief orally or ask a student to summarize?

The Role and Purpose of Student Questions

While the questioning strategy is teacher-centered and focuses on teacher-generated questions, we cannot overlook the importance of student-generated questions. These are important for a variety of reasons, the most important being that curious students learn. In this text we have chosen to dedicate chapter to inquiry learning, which deals with the development of students' questions and the process of helping them find answers to those questions. However, a good teacher will constantly be encouraging student curiosity and the environment of that teacher's classroom will promote questioning. We have all noticed how younger children are full of a constant stream of questions—questions that at times seem they will never end. Sadly, for adolescents the desire to ask questions at school has been discouraged by peer pressure or instructional practice. Teachers can help counter this by encouraging students to ask questions in class, by allowing time for written questions, or having students work with a partner to devise questions.

THE TECHNOLOGY CORNER

You will likely be able to locate some drill-and-practice software or websites that may be useful as part of your questioning strategy, but keep in mind that they rarely function beyond lower-order questioning. It might also be difficult to find software or websites that relate to the exact topic you are addressing with your lesson.

Instead, consider the following activity for generating student questions. This is an example activity that could be modified for other content areas.

After reading a chapter in the book *All Quiet on the Western Front,* have students go to the computer lab. Ask students to write a question that they would like to explore further or would like to have clarified. Instead of writing a simple question, students should be encouraged to write nonstop about the question until it leads them to a conclusion or perhaps another question. Why did they think of it? Is it related to an event or character? Why is it relevant? Why is it important to them? After several minutes of writing, ask them to switch computers with a partner and continue the writing on that partner's computer. Here the students should write an exploratory response to the other student's initial question and continue the writing until another question emerges. Continue the exchange of computers so that students read, respond to, and add to the comments of other students. This type of writing is helpful for the generation and exploration of ideas, all of which comes from the students themselves.

As with most effective uses of technology in the classroom, the focus is not on the technology itself but on your lesson objectives.

LOGISTICAL CONCERNS AND QUESTIONING

We have indicated the importance of planning when preparing an effective questioning seminar. At some point, however, it will come down to how you perform in the classroom. Having the skill to ask your good questions is something that will take practice. You can quicken your development if you think through several logistical issues.

One way for you to improve your questioning technique is through attention to an element researchers have called *wait time*. This refers to the amount of time teachers wait after asking a question (called *wait time 1*) or before responding to a student or asking another student to respond (called *wait time 2*). The concept is simple, but most new teachers struggle with it, thus stifling participation and learning. When it comes to asking questions, teachers tend to be a very impatient group. In fact, Rowe (1974) and Wilen (1991) have found that it is common for teachers to wait less than one second before speaking again to rephrase the question, answer it themselves, ask another question, or fill the quiet in some other way. Perhaps in the many years of your own schooling you can recall instances in which you were about to respond to a question when the teacher began talking.

Waiting for students to respond has been shown to have a number of positive effects. When teachers increased wait time to just three to five seconds, there were positive results according to research done by Rowe (1974) and Tobin (1986), who found that:

the length of the student response increased
the number of times students failed to respond decreased
students asked more questions
students were more confident
unsolicited responses increased
students with a broader range of abilities participated

It is interesting that something as simple as being aware of and applying principles of wait time can have such impact on classroom interaction.

Improving your wait time is something that will take practice. Keeping this in mind will likely help you develop good habits from the start. Some teachers choose to count to themselves for four or five seconds after asking a question and before allowing themselves to speak again. Some choose to do the same before responding to a student. Others will tape-record themselves to help self-assess their technique. You will need to decide what will work for you given all the variables of a classroom. Of course, you should understand that just waiting for a few seconds will not necessarily produce dynamic classroom interaction. In fact, there are times when a "popcorn" approach (having students pop up and respond very quickly) can be effective, such as during recitation lessons or times when exploring affective thinking. Clearly, however, when students are asked to think at a more complex level they need time to respond.

Good questioning seminars depend upon a positive environment in the classroom. You will need to create an atmosphere in the class where students want to participate and interact. If you happen to student teach in a classroom where students are not encouraged to speak (the proverbial lecture class) it will be difficult for you to have a high-quality questioning seminar or discussion. If you haven't established this questioning atmosphere in your first class session it will likewise be difficult. It may take some time for you to establish an atmosphere conducive to verbal interaction in a lesson. You will need to share your expectations with the class, as well as let them know that it is psychologically safe for student talk. This becomes a function of classroom management clearly related to the questioning strategy.

CLASSROOM MANAGEMENT ISSUES

There are a number of different elements related to classroom management that have a profound impact on the effectiveness of this instructional strategy. You will recall that in this text when we refer to *classroom management* we are not only speaking of controlling or redirecting a student's behavior, but are also speaking of creating and maintaining a positive climate for learning. There is no formula by which you can create this atmosphere. However, implementation of these elements will help you create an atmosphere more conducive to using questioning strategies with your students.

Responding to Student Responses

The way a teacher responds to students is very important and impacts further student participation specifically and classroom atmosphere in general. We would like to include a good flow chart for how to respond to students (if they say *this*, you should say *this*), but in reality productive responses will depend on careful listening and quick thinking. There is probably no better analysis, synthesis, and evaluation practice for a teacher. With that in mind, there are two basic types of responses to students that enhance learning.

Prompting   Students will often need to examine further their responses. Their responses may show that they misunderstand, or that they have not responded at the level of thinking that you require. Do you think that a student gives an incorrect response because she misunderstands your question? Do you think she needs to work on her analysis? Does she want to apply a principle without careful consideration of implications? Does she evaluate a situation but not show that she has a complete understanding of the facts? Maybe you should rephrase the question, gently redirect it to another student, and ask that student to ask a clarifying question of another student, or quickly paraphrase the pool of information the student would need to respond correctly. Perhaps you need to restate their answers while allowing time for them to clarify.

Expanding   At other times students need to be asked to extend their thinking beyond the original response, or to be challenged. Do you think the student is correct and can go further? You might want to ask the student to analyze or evaluate information. For example, if a student has stated that the Nazis allied themselves with the Soviets you might ask why they formed the alliance, or what would have happened if they had not formed such an alliance. Do you think a student offers an in-depth evaluation? It might be helpful to challenge the student by asking another student for an opposing evaluation or a differing view from outside of class. For example, "How would you respond to the writer of this article, who disagrees with your evaluation"? Remember, however, that engaging in a direct disagreement with a student in which you "win" the argument rarely enhances a lesson and can shut down others who were thinking of responding. Of course, even this will depend upon the atmosphere that has been established and to what degree the students trust you. Do you think a student's response is off-the-charts amazing? Most of the time praise should be reserved for private conversations. The environment in your classroom that enhances a questioning session can be destroyed by comments that aren't respectful of students. Obviously, comments that intimidate or embarrass students will not encourage participation. Sometimes a teacher does not realize how his tone or nonverbal responses to students can impact the class. A frown, smirk, roll of the eyes, or blank stare all communicate as much as a smile or an interested look. In much the same way, tone of voice can turn the same statement from an encouraging prompt to a put-down.

CLASSROOM APPLICATIONS

Using Tone to Communicate

If you emphasize the underlined word in the sentences below it will change the meaning of the entire sentence each time. Can you hear all four different meanings?

I like that answer.
I *like* that answer.
I like *that* answer.
I like that *answer.*

Next, try changing the following two sentences from pointed commands into questions or encouraging statements using tone.

Combine those two points of view.
Criticize that argument.

Now, try changing the meaning of the sentence "Someone add to Michael's answer." Start by making the sentence a put-down and change it to an encouraging question just by changing the tone and not the words.[1]

Participation Patterns

One reason teachers use questioning sessions is to give students an opportunity to participate orally. However, many times those who participate are the usual volunteers or those "go-to" students the teacher uses when a correct answer is needed. One way to help assess your pattern of questioning is to employ an observer grid, through which an impartial observer uses a seating chart to place a check mark by the name of each student who participates. It is interesting for a teacher to note after a lesson that most of the responses came, for example, from the right front corner or from the boys in the class. Feedback from this type of observation can help the teacher create a more equitable and encouraging classroom.

The eighth myth of questioning claimed that only volunteering students should participate. Research implications show that, within reason, all students should be encouraged and expected to participate. For example, a teacher should expect all students to respond during a review of factual information in a reading assignment. A teacher may opt to allow a student to pass if, for instance, he is asked a question related to his political beliefs regarding a presidential candidate. Some teachers choose to do this through random calling. This could be done through the use of two decks of cards: each student is given a card from the first deck, and the teacher has another deck from which she randomly draws a card that corresponds with the card of the student who will participate. Other teachers will simply choose students at random, trying to get all students involved. Some will go around the room, having students respond one by one but allowing for a student to pass. As you consider when you will call on volunteers and when you will solicit responses you will also be deciding whether you want your students to "raise their hands," answer without permission, or be called upon by the teacher. This logistical issue goes hand in hand with your thinking about participation.

One final consideration about student participation is related to culture. White (1990) has found that different ethnic groups communicate orally in different ways. In the classroom, as much as possible, consideration should be given to the student's cultural background when encouraging oral participation. In addition, students who speak English as a second language (ESL) may have considerable difficulty participating at a high level in a questioning session. Alternative strategies should be used to reach this population, or perhaps questions could be provided in written form. Students could follow the text during class or be able to use the text with a helping partner or during an ESL-supported study hall. It may also be helpful to give additional wait time to allow such a student to comprehend the question. Students could also be given several minutes of free-writing time after some questions; this would improve responses from all students without singling out some.

Common Classroom Management Errors

As we have noted, there are many different elements to consider while establishing or maintaining an atmosphere conducive to an effective questioning session. Below we offer some common errors that are made in this area.

Questions aren't clear, so students become frustrated.

The "guess what's in my brain" game, in which the student must try to verbalize what the teacher is thinking. This becomes a "give me what *I'm* looking for" session.

The teacher calls on favorites or the reliable few with answers, and does not include the whole class.

Negative uses of questions, thus intentionally or unintentionally embarrassing or intimidating students.

Asking more than one question at a time.

Not giving enough time for responses.

Poor follow-up, which stifles students' desire to respond.

The questions are so simple that no one wants to respond because it's embarrassingly obvious.

The teacher commonly answers his own questions, and students are thus confused about responding.

Questions leave out a large portion of the class.

The teacher fails to frame learning through the use of questions that build to higher-order questions.

The teacher is not listening well. Perhaps she is thinking about the next
   question, or a response the students might give or should have given.
Negative nonverbal cues. The teacher uses cues such as looking at papers,
   at the clock, raising eyebrows, rolling eyes, and so on to show disinter-
   est or displeasure in a response.
Rewording an answer into an idea the teacher *wants* to hear.
The teacher talks too much.

APPROPRIATE ASSESSMENT TECHNIQUES
TO USE WITH QUESTIONING

Assessing questioning can be difficult, as can assessing any oral participation
strategy. The written objectives for the lesson will again be key in determining
how to go about assessing students. You may have had a number of purposes
in mind when choosing to question the students. The lesson objective may
be related to critical thinking skills, participation, or practicing verbal skills.
A rubric similar to the one shown in chapter 10, "Classroom Discussion and
Debate," could be used to assess any of these objectives. This would be done
with a checklist-style rubric that could quickly be used to rate a response. However, unlike with discussion, this strategy is teacher-centered. There likely will
be little time to fill out a rubric while fully participating in leading a questioning seminar. Instead, a teacher will commonly use the strategy to support
objectives that call for a different type of assessment. Take, for example, this
objective: *Students will be able to show their ability to evaluate the effects of
the Vietnam War on foreign policy decisions during later presidential admin-
istrations by writing a two-page editorial according to guidelines on the provided rubric.* Here the objective indicates that the point of the lesson is to teach
students to evaluate. The teacher may have chosen to use questioning to help
students practice their evaluation skills. However, the formal assessment of
those skills will be completed during the written assignment. The teacher will
formatively, through listening and observation, assess student ability to evaluate during the oral questioning seminar. Most assessment for questioning will
be formative and eventually used to modify future lesson objectives or prepare
for a summative assessment.

   One reminder may be important here, and that is that questions are commonly used as an assessment strategy. For example, a teacher may ask questions as part of a lecture to assess student comprehension. This use of questions
specifically for assessment is not part of a questioning seminar.

GUIDELINES FOR DECIDING IF QUESTIONING IS APPROPRIATE

Questioning for learning is thought to be a useful strategy for the promotion of
higher-order thinking skills. If you decide that your students need assistance

moving from recitation of memorized fact to being able to analyze or evaluate information, this strategy can be helpful. A skilled questioning seminar leader can have a strong influence on student thought processes. Students often need this guidance to be able to think critically. Simply *asking* a student to evaluate isn't *teaching* a student to evaluate. For example, a student might "evaluate" a character's action as "dumb" by simply depending on his own impressions or emotions. Questioning can help a student go back and look at the factual information and make judgments based on supporting evidence. This interaction between teacher and student can have long-lasting positive results.

The unique student characteristics of a class should also be considered when deciding if this strategy is to be used. If your class has a high percentage of ESL students it would be problematic to consistently use questioning. In addition, consideration should be given to the types of learning styles that you have in your classroom. Most experienced teachers will tell you that any group of students forms a unique personality. Some seem to be more verbally oriented than others. However, within this class personality there will be students who do not have the same learning style as others. Because this strategy is so verbally oriented it may or may not be the right choice for habitual use. Using a variety of instructional approaches is key to being able to attend to the needs of the diverse group of learners that will be in your class.

At times, questioning is used to encourage student participation and investment in learning. Studies have shown that when students become more actively involved rather than passive recipients that they learn more. This strategy is one that encourages teacher-led student participation and thus could assist a teacher with purposeful student engagement. Keep in mind, however, that these teacher-centered activities have been commonly overused with adolescents.

MAKING IT WORK IN YOUR CONTENT AREA

Questioning for Cognitive Variety

Review the "Framing Questions and Prompts" section in this chapter. Choose a topic for your content area. Write an objective for that topic that requires evaluative thinking. Create at least six questions (one from each cognitive level) that you could ask students in order to help lead them from knowledge through evaluation during one lesson. Share this with a colleague from the same content area and ask for feedback.

Feedback prompts might include:

How will the questioning session you design help your students achieve the lesson objective?
Were you able to create a question from each cognitive level? Would any need clarification? Would it affect student achievement of the objective if you skipped one of the levels?
How will you assess learning?
How do you envision these questions fitting in with a lesson?

CHAPTER REVIEW

Questioning is a teacher-centered strategy used to support students as they move from lower-order to higher-order cognitive thinking. Questions can be asked for many reasons, but this chapter focused on using questions for learning.

We also discussed the research response to the nine common myths about questioning:

1. Questioning is a natural teaching behavior that does not require planning.
2. The more questions a teacher asks, the more students will learn.
3. There are no bad questions.
4. Higher-level cognitive questions are more critical than lower-level questions.
5. Higher-level cognitive questions elicit higher-level answers.
6. Teachers should ask lower-level cognitive questions before progressing to higher-level questions.
7. Teachers give students enough time to answer questions.
8. When questioning students, teachers should call only on volunteering students.
9. Teachers encourage students to ask questions.

There are different ways to think about question design that are helpful. Here we offer the use of Bloom's taxonomy as a schema for designing effective questions. Questions can be designed for each cognitive level as appropriate. Simplified, this can be thought of as using divergent and convergent questions.

To be effective in questioning strategy, use the following guidelines:

Plan your questions carefully.
Don't be afraid to depart from your written questions while staying with the plan.
Consider who you are teaching.
Consider classroom management and assessment techniques.
Close the lesson on a strong note.

Wait time has been shown to have an impact on student responses. Students will need more time for higher-order questions than they will need for lower-order questions. When responding to students, consideration should be given to questions that *prompt* and *expand*; these are questions that encourage students to clarify or extend their thinking when giving responses.

It is important to think about how you might get all the students involved with the strategy when appropriate. There may be some students that are reticent to participate due to cultural backgrounds. Some suggestions are given to help expand participation patterns in a classroom. Some common errors made related to classroom management while using this strategy are discussed in this chapter.

Many times questions are used as an assessment technique for another instructional strategy. Teachers ask questions to formatively assess learning. Commonly, a teacher will use questioning to support objectives that call for a different type of assessment. For example, there may be a written form of assessment to determine if a student has learned to think critically about an issue after using this strategy.

To determine whether or not questioning is the right strategy to use, ascertain if your students need your guidance to support their ability to think critically. Are they able to support their analysis of an issue through the appropriate use of factual information? Do your students need to practice their oral communication skills? What type of English language skills do your students have? What are the dominant learning styles of the class? Has your classroom become too teacher-centered?

NOTE

1. This exercise is modified from an activity idea in Tanner, 1972.

REFERENCES

Bloom, B., Englehart, M., Furst, E., Will, W., & Krathwohl, D. (1956). *Taxonomy of educational objectives, Handbook 1: Cognitive domain*. New York: David McKay.

Brice, L., & Johnson, L. (1999, November). *Discourse as a critical pedagogical form in social studies teaching and learning*. Paper presented at the annual meeting of the National Council of Social Studies, Orlando, FL.

Costa, A., & Lowery, L. (1989). *Techniques for teaching and thinking*. Pacific Grove, CA: Midwest.

Dantonio, M., & Beisenherz, P. (2001). *Learning to question, questioning to learn*. Boston: Allyn and Bacon.

Dillon, J. T. (1988). *Questioning and teaching: A manual of practice*. New York: Teachers College Press.

Gall, M. (1984). Synthesis of research on teacher's questioning. *Educational Leadership, 42*, 40–47.

Good, T. L., & Brophy, J. E. (2000). *Looking in classrooms* (8th ed.). New York: Longman.

Gamoran, A., & Nystrand, M. (1992). Taking students seriously. In F. Newmann (Ed.), *Student engagement and achievement in American secondary schools* (40–61). New York: Teachers College Press.

Grossier, P. (1964). *How to use the fine art of questioning*. Englewood Cliffs, NJ: Prentice-Hall.

Henning, J. (2004). The "bow tie": A conceptual tool for opening up classroom discourse. *Curriculum and Teaching Dialogue, 6*, 59–67.

Hunkins, F. P. (1995). *Teaching thinking through effective questioning* (2nd ed.). Norwood, MA: Christopher-Gordon.

Kelly, T. (1993, April). *Calling on non-volunteers in the classroom: Democratic imperative or misguided invasion?* Paper presented at the annual meeting of the American Educational Research Association, Atlanta, GA.

Mills, S., Rice, C., Berliner, D., & Rousseau, E. (1980). The correspondence between teacher questions and student answers in classroom discourse. *Journal of Experimental Education, 48*, 194–204.

National Council for the Social Studies. (1994). *Curriculum standards for social studies.* Washington, DC: Author.

Newmann, F. (1992). Higher order thinking and prospects for classroom thoughtfulness. In F. Newmann (Ed.), *Student engagement and achievement in American secondary schools* (62–91). New York: Teachers College Press.

Newmann, F., Wehlage, G., & Lamborn, S. (1992). The significance and sources of student engagement. In F. Newmann (Ed.), *Student engagement and achievement in American secondary schools* (11–39). New York: Teachers College Press.

Rowe, M. (1974). Wait time and rewards as instructional variables, their influence in language, logic, and fate control: Part one—wait time. *Journal of Research in Science Teaching, 11*(2), 81–94.

Rowe, M. (1986). Wait time: Slowing down may be a way of speeding up! *Journal of Teacher Education, 37*, 43–50.

Tanner, F. (1972). *Basic drama projects.* Pocatello, ID: Clark.

Tobin, K. (1986). Effects of teacher wait time on discourse characteristics in mathematics and language arts classes. *American Educational Research Journal, 23*(2), 191–201.

Wilen, W. (2001). Exploring myths about teacher questioning in the social studies classroom. *Social Studies, 92*, 26–35.

Wilen, W., Ishler, M., Hutchinson, J., & Kindsvatter, R. (2000). *Dynamics of effective teaching* (4th ed.). New York: Longman.

Wilen, W., & White, J. (1991). Interaction and discourse in social studies classrooms. In J. P. Shaver (Ed.), *Handbook of research in social studies teaching and learning* (483–495). New York: Macmillan.

Wilen, W. W. (1990). *Teaching and learning through discussion.* Springfield, IL: Charles C Thomas.

Wilen, W. W. (1991). *Questioning skills for teachers* (3rd ed.). Washington, DC: National Education Association.

White, J. J. (1990). Involving different social and cultural groups in discussion. In W. W. Wilen (Ed.), *Teaching and learning through discussion* (pp. 147–157). Springfield, IL: Charles C Thomas.

7

CONCEPT FORMATION

OVERVIEW

In early August, Steve signed a contract to teach five sections of U.S. history at a local high school. The school district specified that the 11th-grade U.S. history curriculum starts with the revolution, reviews the events leading up to and following the Civil War, and proceeds with history from the late 1800s to the present day. During the year Steve developed units around the conventional historical eras (e.g., the progressive era, the "roaring twenties," the Depression era, etc.), but he also explored the concept of *authority* during each era. He asked students to think about who had authority during different times in American history, how they had authority, and why they had power. Throughout the year his students examined the relationships among power, authority, and the government,[1] and compared the differences between authoritarian and authoritative governance. The level of interest and insights by his students convinced Steve that anchoring his teaching to a concept helped students learn the course content.

A concept is the same as an idea. We create concepts to help categorize or classify the world. As Parker (2005) explains, concepts are

> abstract categories or classes of meaning. For example, island is the word label for a geographic phenomenon consisting of land completely surrounded by water. Kauai is one specific example of such a set of

conditions. There are thousands of other specific examples of the concept island...concept definitions, therefore, tell us only about those qualities or attributes that a group *has in common*. They do not tell us about the unique features of particular examples. (p. 191; emphasis in the original)

Many of the words we use refer to an idea, and not to specific or tangible "things." For example, *books*, *liquids*, *artifacts*, *cultures*, *rules*, *theorems*, and *characters* are all concepts. Usually, when we use a word such as *book*, people around us know what we mean: books all share specific attributes that most people agree make something a book. In your future classroom, however, you will be helping students learn concepts that they have not learned. Then, as they explore specific examples of a concept, they will become better able to categorize and organize this information.

The purpose of the concept formation strategy is to help students form a robust understanding of significant concepts in the content area. Too often we use concepts and have limited understanding of what we mean. Middle school students may be able to use the concepts of *democracy* and *freedom* in a sentence, but often cannot articulate the meaning of these terms. Consider, for example, the difference between the words *bravery* and *courage*. Most people will acknowledge that they are not synonyms but will find it difficult to specify the differences. Some have referred to this as the "rattle of empty wagons" (Parker & Perez, 1987; Taba, 1967). With this metaphor, wagons are thought of as the word, or label, we use for a particular concept, and the content of the wagon is the understanding of the concept. When we use concept labels without fully understanding their meaning, we rattle along like a wagon would without any contents.

Each of the instructional strategies described in this book promote student learning of facts, skills, and concepts. In this chapter, however, we examine a specific strategy that helps students form a deep and flexible understanding of a concept that the teacher determines is critical for students to understand. We believe that helping students gain conceptual understandings—literally understanding big ideas—is a critical element of any instructional strategy. Helping middle school and high school students learn concepts is important because it helps them organize information. Concept formation is an approach to learning where students examine examples of a concept and draw conclusions about those examples. In addition to learning about the concept formation strategy, we also intend for this chapter to challenge you to think about concepts that are important in your content area. As we explore this strategy, continue to consider those ideas that are important for your students to learn during the school year, and consider the instructional strategies that will promote student learning of these important ideas.

A DESCRIPTION OF CONCEPT FORMATION, AND RESEARCH FINDINGS

We often present the following idea to preservice teachers: *Thinking is how people learn. Therefore, always be aware of who is doing most of the thinking/learning in your classroom.*

Imagine that a local high school or middle school teacher in your content area asked you to come in and teach for 55 minutes. This teacher gave you a concept that she wants her students to learn, and you have three days to prepare. Preparing for this will require several hours to determine valid assessments of student learning, preparing learning activities, and writing the lesson plan. Additionally, you will also spend a significant amount of time thinking about the concept, and finding relevant examples of it. It is during those hours of thinking and exploration that you develop a robust understanding of the concept you will be teaching. If you have only 55 minutes of class time, students cannot spend the same amount of time you spent preparing. And you would not want them to. What activities can you have your students do that will help them learn the concept that you learned while preparing? Often, teachers spend time preparing a lesson and learning the content, and then use class time to simply tell students what they learned. This is what we call *concept telling*; you tell students about a concept. The problem with concept telling is that deep conceptual understanding occurred during the hours of preparation that *you* spent before you taught. By simply coming to class and telling students about a concept, they miss out on the opportunity that you had while preparing—the opportunity to think about and learn the concept.

Concept formation is a strategy that takes your students through a process whereby they work to understand a concept. Rather than you telling them, the students form their understanding of a concept. This approach taps into Vygotsky's theory of learning (1978). You may recall from chapter 1 that Vygotsky suggested that a "zone of proximal development" exists between our current understanding of something and the next, more robust level of understanding. Usually we need help attaining this new level. According to Vygotsy's theory, people learn when they have proper scaffolds in place to help them reach this next level of understanding. This strategy provides a step-by-step process for helping students learn a new concept.

Consider figure 7.1 as a graphic description of different levels of learning.

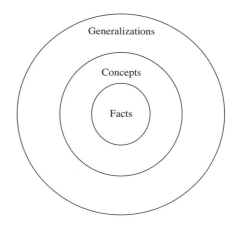

Figure 7.1

Facts, concepts, and generalizations rely on each other to help promote deeper understanding. A *fact* is something that can be verified through observing, experiencing, reading, or listening. Facts are necessary for building conceptual knowledge and generalizations. They are the building blocks of concept development. As we stated earlier, a *concept* is an idea for organizing and classifying experiences and facts into groups with common qualities. Concepts are timeless and abstract. *Conflict, change,* and *perspective* are three concepts. Examples of the concept *change* can be found in social studies (historical events), earth science (erosion), literature (character development) and music (tempo). *Generalizations* are descriptive statements of relationships between two or more concepts. To state that "social change often brings about conflict" is a generalization about two of the concepts stated above. You can make this statement only if you understand the concepts of *change* and *conflict*, and if you have examined many examples and facts about social reform movements. *Generalizations*, as the word implies, are "generally true. They can also be called conclusions" (Parker, 2005, p. 201).

Before we proceed to the step-by-step procedures for helping your students form their understanding of concepts, we need to define five key terms:

Concept: A concept is an idea.

Concept label: Since concepts are ideas, they exist only in our minds. Words are labels that we use to talk about the ideas. A concept label is the word or phrase that people use when referring to a particular concept. Consider the concept of *cooperation*. We all have an idea of what cooperation is, but in order to talk about it we need to use the word/label.

Critical attributes: These are the traits or characteristics that every example of a particular concept will have. If we return to cooperation, we would conclude that every example of this concept involves at least two people who are working together toward a common purpose. For something to be an example of cooperation it must have these three attributes—therefore, they are critical to the concept.

Examples of a concept: Every example of a concept has all of the critical attributes. An example of *cooperation* might be a group of four students helping each other complete a task assigned by the teacher. Another example might be a football team successfully executing a play. Both are examples because they have all of the critical attributes.

Nonexamples of a concept: Nonexamples simply lack one or more critical attributes. If any of the critical attributes of cooperation do not exist, then it is not an example.

This quotation by Parker (1987) provides an additional example of how these terms work together:

For instance, the idea *sentence* (or democracy, equation, mammal, or experiment) does not exist physically, but there are numerous examples of sentence, such as the one you are now reading. What makes it an example is that it has the critical characteristics all sentences must have in order to be called by the label *sentence:* it has a subject, verb, and direct object, either present or implied; it expresses a complete thought; it has a beginning, ending, and, as needed, transition signals. (p. 57)

Before we explore the planning procedures for a concept formation lesson, it is important to understand where a concept's critical attributes come from. *Epistemology* is the study of knowledge that seeks to explain how we know—literally how we obtain, use, and think about knowledge of the world around us. Concepts help us think about and understand the world, so studying concepts is an epistemological venture. When you help your students learn a concept, you are helping them think and study how they know something to be true. Concepts help us categorize the world. As a result, anyone is able to create a concept that helps him do this. Concepts are proved to be accurate ideas when they are tested. In other words, when we have experiences that require us to make judgments using a concept, we either verify or discredit the concept. Left to our own devices, we might create concepts that appear accurate simply because our individual experiences have not allowed for many judgments using the concept. When others use our concepts, they increase the number of experiences, and prove or call into question our category. Consider, for example, the concept of *democracy.* Two important attributes of this idea are that democracies require a free and fair election process. It is not all that important to know who decided this, as much as it is important to know whether these are defining attributes with which we all agree. As a society, we test the idea of democracy by making judgments about different systems of governance. If examples of this concept all include free elections and a fair election process, then the critical attributes are confirmed, and the concept is valid. On the other hand, there has been much debate over the concept of *family.* The debate is about the critical attributes of a family, and whether these attributes are accurate when we determine if different scenarios are examples of a family. We all agree that *family* is a good concept label, but many disagree on the critical attributes. There is not an overall agreement on what defines a family. In the next section we refer to *established* and *dynamic* concepts as one approach for determining if the experiences of the greater society have verified the critical attributes. It will be helpful for you to engage in some epistemology and think about how well you know the key concepts in your content area, and how these concepts have emerged.

STEP-BY-STEP PROCEDURES FOR PLANNING AND IMPLEMENTING CONCEPT FORMATION

Concept formation is an inductive approach that will help students learn the critical attributes of a given concept. As we suggested earlier, telling students the attributes that we, the teachers, have discovered does not promote mastery learning as effectively as helping students engage in a process whereby they actually think about the concept. In brief, concept formation provides students with the opportunity to examine several examples of a given concept in light of the critical attributes, and then draw conclusions about the similarities and differences among these examples. Students' conclusions about the similarities are then generalized to be true about other examples of the concept they examined. To promote the type of thinking that will engage students, concept formation follows a sequential eight-step process.[2]

Step 1: Selecting a Concept

The first step in developing a concept formation lesson is selecting a concept that students need to know. Teachers often tell us that this first step is the most difficult part, because the teacher needs to determine the concept on which the students will focus. Think about a few powerful ideas and issues that you want your students to build on and explore in your class. It might be helpful to follow this process: First, given all the potential topics that could be mentioned during the 180 hours you will have in class with your future students (far too many topics to teach well), identify five or six topics that are critically important for your students to learn. In previous chapters of this book you thought of many topics that you might teach in your future classroom; you might return to one of those. When you are teaching you will also have curriculum guides that provide many topics. Next, reflect on these topics and identify concepts that are an integral part of each topic. Think of concepts that you believe students must know well, and upon which other course content can be built. It is from this select list of concepts that you will select the big ideas, the important and powerful concepts for your students to explore. In a course on American government, you might select the topic *constitutional government*. With this topic, the concepts of *democracy*, *checks and balances*, or *e pluribus unum* are all significant concepts. In an earth science course you might decide on the topic *rock cycle*. Possible concepts could include *sediment*, *erosion*, or *weathering*. Select concepts that are difficult for students to grasp, and that are ideas you can build upon in future lessons. For example, a teacher might decide that the concept of *authority* is critical for understanding U.S. history. This concept will help students compare and contrast authoritarian forms of government with forms of government that gain their authority from the people (an authoritative government). The concepts should also have critical attributes upon which your local community has some agreement. While we all could agree on the critical attributes of *symbiosis* or *improper fractions*, we would have more difficulty agreeing on the critical attributes of *love*. We refer to concepts with easily agreed upon attributes as *established concepts*, and concepts with more disagreement as *dynamic concepts*. Concepts are established to help us make sense of the world around us. As a result, previously agreed upon attributes may change as societal expectations change. Dynamic concepts are often learned best through inquiry projects, lecture, or classroom discussions (please refer to the chapters on these instructional strategies).

Step 2: Studying Examples and Gathering Data

Once an established concept has been selected, you will need to develop a graphic organizer of some form to help students gather and record information about several examples of the concept. This organizer can take any form, but must contain two components: (1) a list of three to five examples for students to study; and (2) a set of three to five focus questions that direct students' attention to the critical attributes of the concept. As such, you will need to come up with examples of the concept, identify the critical attributes of the concept, and develop questions that address each of the critical attributes. Many times teachers feel perplexed as they try to identify examples and attributes of a concept. It is hard work, because you must think in depth about the concept. We find that you can identify the most critical three to five attributes efficiently by looking up the concept label in dictionaries or web sources (such as http://www.wikipedia.org), having conversations with fellow teachers or other experts on the concept, and closely examining examples of the concept. Consider the following sample of a chart that a high school social studies teacher developed for the concept *social caste*, and possible student responses to the focus questions. The critical attributes for *social caste* are that it is (1) hierarchical; (2) tied to occupation; (3) based on ideas of purity/cleanliness; and (4) inherited and rigid. As you look at the chart below you will notice the four focus questions across the top, and their relation to the critical attributes of this concept. Down the left column are three examples of the concept that the teacher located online and modified so that his students could understand the descriptions better.

Providing students with this chart helps them study particular examples of the concept (examples that have relevance to your course content), and helps students consider the examples in light of the critical attributes. This is undertaken as they think to answer the focus questions. These charts will not necessarily use descriptive paragraphs such as the chart above. They may present students with examples of a concept by providing video clips (e.g., clips of different examples of cell division in a biology class), words or phrases (e.g., examples of racism in the media during a current-events unit), pictures (e.g., examples of contrast in a graphic design class), or even skits (e.g., examples of compromise). One teacher gave his students three examples of *appeasement* along with five focus questions, and then had the students spend a day in the library researching each example and answering the questions.

The focus questions can follow each example, or be placed in a chart. The graphic organizer (adapted from Ehrenberg, 1981, p. 37) on page 171 could be useful for the simple concept of *fruit*.

DATA-GATHERING CHART

Data	Is this country's social organization hierarchical?	Is the social organization tied to occupation?	How does the idea of purity/ impurity contribute to a separation of the social groups?	Can people move out of the social groups into which they were born?
The burakumin are a social group in Japan whose occupations consist of unwanted jobs. These jobs include executions, disposing of dead animals, and sweeping and cleaning. Historically, the emperor was the exact opposite in Japan. The people believed that he was a deity. In between the Emperor and the Burakumin were several social groups. During the middle ages, at the height of this social system, an individual was born into his social group and could not leave it.	Yes	Yes	Burakumin perform unwanted jobs.	No
In India, one social group called the panchamas, or untouchables, are required to perform work that is considered to be "unclean." A higher social group in India, known as the brahmans, performs religious duties. Members of both groups are born into these roles, and individuals cannot change their membership in a group. In order to maintain "purity," marriage among members of different groups is not allowed. In addition to these social groups, there are others in India. The origins of this social structure are based on religion.	Yes	Maybe	Untouchables perform work that is considered "unclean."	No
Members of the ñeeño social group in Senegal inherit their status from their parents. The ñeeño are characterized by their occupations, such as blacksmiths, leatherworkers, and griots (musicians and storytellers). The geer, members of a higher social order, traditionally has discriminated against the ñeeño. Historically, the idea of pollution and impurity prevent intermingling between the ñeeño and other social groups. The ñeeño and other social groups are fixed within their social status.	Yes	Yes	Ideas of pollution and impurity prevent intermingling between groups.	No

Mango

Where does this grow on a plant? What purpose does this part serve for the plant? Does this contain seed(s)?

Tomato

Where does this grow on a plant? What purpose does this part serve for the plant? Does this contain seed(s)?

Pumpkin

Where does this grow on a plant? What purpose does this part serve for the plant? Does this contain seed(s)?

Step 3: Reporting Information

During this step the students report to a group or to the whole class what they found out from thinking about the examples and answering the focus questions. By reporting on the data they collected, students compare their findings with others. This allows students to clarify any questions they could not answer and verify their findings with others in class.

Step 4: Noting Differences

At this point in the lesson the teacher talks with the whole class about the examples they have examined and their answers to the focus questions. During this step, the teacher helps the students focus on the differences among the examples. An effective prompt for this is, "Look at the examples, and describe how these are different from each other." This is an important cognitive step because it requires students to consider how examples of a concept can have very different attributes but still be examples. In the above example of fruits, attributes such as the color, climate in which they grow, or size would not be critical attributes. Or, consider all of the different examples of dogs, which all possess the critical attributes for a canine.

Step 5: Noting Similarities

After contrasting the examples in step 4, you as the teacher will proceed to have students compare the examples and identify how they are similar. An effective prompt for this is, "In what ways are the examples all alike?" This question directs students' attention to the answers (data) they provided for each focus question. You should list these on the board for use in the step 6, "Synthesizing." These similarities match the critical attributes that you came up with when preparing the focus questions. You have not told them to your students, but they have come up with them on their own as a result of thinking about the different examples. You will keep asking them to identify similarities, and the students will identify all of the critical attributes by using their own thoughts and words. Look again at the data-gathering chart we gave for "social caste"; you can imagine how the attributes are identified by sharing similarities.

Step 6: Synthesizing

In this step the students form the concept by combining the similarities into a sentence or statement. At this point the students write their own definition of the concept, being sure to incorporate all of the similarities, on the chalkboard. The students then share aloud their sentences, and check each other to ensure that they have mentioned each similarity; the teacher engages with the students to check their definitions. These definitions will be accurate descriptions of the concept, but will be in the students' own words and not be given to them by the teacher. Instead, the students will have developed these through their own thinking about the examples.

Step 7: Labeling

Although concepts are abstract, the word or label that we use when referring to a concept is tangible. The concept label *cooperation* makes a lot of sense because the label is closely related to the critical attributes (*co-* means "more than one," and *operate* means "to do something"). The concept label *fruit* makes less sense because the label does not seem closely related to the critical attributes. At this step in the lesson, students think of labels that they believe capture the essence of the critical attributes. These labels do not need to be the actual words for the concept. In fact, the teacher focuses more on the reasons a student selected a label than the actual label. Labeling is another type of synthesis, and it ensures that the students understand the gist of the concept. An effective prompt by the teacher might be, "Think of a word or phrase that you think captures the idea of your definition and the similarities we listed on the board. In a minute I will have you share what you came up with, and why that word is a good choice." Consider for a minute the concept of *compromise*. A student may suggest that a good label is "give and take," and another may suggest the label "negotiation." Both labels are acceptable *if* the students are able to explain why they are related to the critical attributes of the concept. After several students have the opportunity to state and explain their labels, the teacher provides them with the conventional word for the concept. Just as the students did, this is also a good place to add any insight into why this word is used when referring to this concept. In other words, see if you can provide any etymology for the word. This allows students to add to their understanding of the concept by learning the word that "adults use" when referring to the concept they have just explored. One final note on labeling: Students may say the conventional word when they are thinking of a label. That is great; the teacher should follow up with the same request that students explain why they think this is an appropriate label.

Step 8: Assessing with Classifying Tasks

At this point, the concept has been formed and labeled. Now the teacher assesses students' understanding by asking them to engage in a series of classifying tasks. We will highlight three tasks that become increasingly complex and that give you increased confidence that the students have learned and can use the concept. These tasks are addressed in the next section of this chapter.

APPROPRIATE ASSESSMENT TECHNIQUES TO USE WITH CONCEPT FORMATION

Assessment is so closely tied to the concept formation strategy that it really is an extension of step 8, above. To assess students' understanding you will determine if students can note how nonexamples may resemble examples, but more importantly how they differ from them (Ehrenberg, 1981). You are also checking to see if students can make the generalization that all examples of a concept must have all of its critical attributes. For instance, if they finished forming the concept *war*, they should be able to identify why the "Vietnam Conflict" was close to, but not officially, a war (that is, they should be able to identify which attribute of "war" is missing).

The most efficient and valid assessment of your students' conceptual understanding is to engage them in the following three types of classifying tasks: (1) distinguishing examples from nonexamples; (2) producing examples; and (3) correcting nonexamples (Parker, 2005, p. 198). The great advantage of these three types of concept practice is that they get students thinking about the critical characteristics of the concept. We describe each type below.[3]

Type 1: Distinguishing Examples from Nonexamples

In this classifying task you present the students with a list of examples and nonexamples all at once. For the concept *fruit* the following mixed list might be used: *avocado*, *celery*, *carrot*, and *pinecone*. The instructions are, "Study these items and decide which ones are examples of *fruit*, and which items are nonexamples. Also, note the items that you cannot determine. In a minute, I will ask several of you to support your decisions." Or, you might have them write their support as part of the assignment. Whichever way you prefer, be sure to give lots of students, if not all of them, the opportunity to support their decision.

Type 2: Producing Examples

This task is different from type 1 because you do not provide any examples or nonexamples. Rather, you give students only the concept label and ask them to come up with an example of the concept. This time, the instructions are, "Now that we have studied the concept called (state the concept label), I want you to find (or make/write/produce/construct/look for, etc.) an example of it. Remember, in order to be an example, it must have all the critical attributes we identified in our definition. After you have produced your example, be ready to support it by telling us why it is an example and not a nonexample." The students' support for the concept they produced is what you use to accurately assess their conceptual understanding.

Type 3: Correcting Nonexamples

Most teachers consider this the most difficult type of classifying practice, which is why it is the final classification task (the first type is considered the least difficult). Unlike in type 1, where you give students the label of several items, and type 2, where you only give them the label, in type 3 you give them the label of a nonexample. Now the instructions are, "Here is a nonexample of the concept we call (state the concept label). Your task is to make the necessary changes in this nonexample in order to make it into an example. Then, I'll ask several of you to support the changes you made." Cognitively, your students will be comparing the critical attributes of the concept with the critical attributes of the nonexample, *and then* they will identify which attributes are missing and make the needed changes. Earlier in the chapter we commented that *courage* and *bravery* are related but different concepts. If the concept the students learned was *courage*, then having them change an example of *bravery* to be an example of courage would be a type 3 task. Or, if the concept was *interdependence*, then being able to correct a nonexample of interdependence would require them to understand the concept well enough to identify the missing critical attributes of the example and make the needed changes.

Of course, other assessments could be used in which the students engage in tasks that require them to use their conceptual understanding. For example, students in a chemistry class could demonstrate their conceptual understanding of neutral, acidic, and base chemicals. You might ask them to test 10 different chemicals, using purple cabbage water and turmeric-stained parchment, categorize the chemicals into one of the three areas, and provide a rationale. The emphasis of all these assessments is to have students work with examples of the concept, and to demonstrate their understanding of the critical attributes that are part of each example (and that are missing in nonexamples).

LOGISTICAL CONCERNS, INCLUDING BENEFITS AND OBSTACLES

As we mentioned before, preparation before the lesson is extensive. First, you need to select an established concept upon which you can explore future course content, and identify the three to five critical attributes common to every example of the concept. Next, you need to compose focus questions that address each critical attribute, and locate three to five examples of the concept. We described ideas for developing the examples earlier in the chapter, but some general thoughts bear repeating here, under logistics. Often the concept and examples will determine how students will gather data. For example, if students are exploring the concept of *propaganda*, then the examples will likely be statements, phrases, and or images, because these are usually the forms propaganda takes. These may best be viewed online or as a handout. If the concept is *theme*, then the examples will be fully developed themes of stories that the students need time to read. The examples need to provide enough information so that the students can answer the focus questions. As a result, you need to consider your students' prior knowledge as you prepare the examples. If you are teaching the concept *civilization* to sixth graders, you should not have as an example the term *Mesopotamia*. While this is a fine example of the concept, your students will not know enough about Mesopotamia to answer the focus questions. Instead, a paragraph description of Mesopotamia that emphasizes the key characteristics of all civilizations will facilitate students' forming of the concept. Therefore, you need to allow student opportunities to find and use information about the example. At times this can occur simply from the examples given on a data-gathering chart. At other times this may require more in-depth examinations of the examples.

Listing the similarities (step 5) requires patience on your part as the teacher. Remember, you have already thought about the concept, but this is the first time your students will do so. The temptation is to turn this step into a question-and-answer session in which the students feel they are trying to guess what you want. If you are patient, the students will come up with a list of similarities that very closely resembles the list of critical attributes you identified during your preparation. If students find this step difficult, prompt them with, "Look closely at the focus questions across the top and see if any of your answers reveal how the examples are alike." You might also need to model this for the students. For example, if the concept is *photosynthesis*, then you might model for your students how to identify similarities in this manner: "When I look at my answers to the focus question about sunlight, I see that I have the same answer for all the examples. So, one way these examples are alike is that they all require sunlight. How else are they alike?" Again, since you know the similarities, you need to exercise patience and allow your students the thinking time required to form the concept. The similarities must be listed on the chalkboard for use in step 6, synthesizing.

The synthesis step may require more time than you originally think. During this step, students write their definition of the concept from the list of similarities. Students will originally do this independently, and revise their definitions to ensure that they incorporate all of the critical attributes. You should have many students share their definitions. As they do, encourage the class to cross-check the definition with the similarities listed on the board, noting any gaps. After a student shares, initial definitions may need revisions. Allow time for this, so that all students eventually have a definition that incorporates all of the similarities.

CLASSROOM MANAGEMENT ISSUES

All of the eight steps in the concept formation strategy guide the students in their understanding of the critical attributes. The principal classroom-management issues involve ensuring that you are monitoring the students, guiding them through the steps, and providing ample opportunities for them to share their ideas. It is during the sharing that you can assess their learning, and that they can learn from each others' ideas. Therefore, concept formation requires the teacher to facilitate students' independent work and whole-class interactions. The independent work will occur when students gather data, write their synthesized definitions, develop labels, and engage in the classifying tasks (steps 2, 6, 7, and 8, respectively). The whole class interactions occur when students report their findings, consider differences and similarities, share their labels, and explain their classifying decisions (steps 3, 4, 5, 7, and 8, respectively).

When students work independently you may want them to work individually or with a partner (*independent* work is not always the same thing as *individual* work). We suggest limiting the size of these work teams to two or three, because the steps of the lesson require students to think on their own about the examples and focus questions. The use of partners is to assist this thinking and help with understanding the critical attributes. If students are in large groups they may rely on others for answers, and not think as deeply about the examples and attributes of the concept. During the independent work period the students must have time to answer the focus questions and think about the topic. By watching students closely you will be able to decide when they have had adequate time to think. We have worked with teachers who have not allowed enough time (the result is that students do not gather adequate information to accurately form the concept), and with teachers who provide too much time (the result is that the lesson loses momentum, and the students disengage). Because the data gathering precedes a classwide reporting session, you do not need to wait until all students have fully completed the data gathering phase.

However, you should be aware of who is not finished, and watch them closely so you are able to ensure that they complete their data gathering as the class reports on its findings.

The whole-class interactions need to allow as many students as possible the chance to share their ideas. To manage this, it is often helpful to ask for volunteers and to call on students. The only times you need to be up front writing on the chalkboard or on an overhead projection is when students report similarities and when they suggest labels for the concept. The rest of the time, you can walk around the room and encourage student participation. Since students may work with partners and share their ideas with the entire class, consider how the desks might be arranged to facilitate both. The conventional rows of desks/tables facing the front will work well (students then lean across the rows to interact with a partner), but so will any seating configuration in which students are facing the front of the room: they must be able to easily see the board/screen during the synthesis step.

During the entire lesson you will want students to listen to and critique their classmates' thinking. When students gather data, be sure you are interested in what they are finding. You will need to work at this, because you have already thought about the concept and its critical attributes in preparation for the lesson. You do not want to give the impression that your students are trying to guess what you want; rather, you need to impress upon them that you want them to think about the examples and come up with their own answers to the focus questions. It is a subtle difference, but one that helps motivate students to think for themselves, and not think for the teacher. For example, if you present students with a data-gathering chart, be careful that they do not think it is merely a worksheet that they need to mindlessly complete. Instead, promote the idea that they need to think about the examples and questions. Show enthusiasm and curiosity for their answers as they report their findings, note differences, and suggest similarities.

GUIDELINES FOR DECIDING IF CONCEPT FORMATION IS APPROPRIATE FOR THE CONTENT OF A LESSON

The concept formation strategy is an effective tool for helping your students think through the critical characteristics of a concept. It should not be used to teach vocabulary words to your students, but should be used to explore a few important concepts that will provide a foundation for future learning. One teacher we know uses the concept of *tradition* when teaching a unit on Japanese culture because she believes that exploring this concept in depth will helps students understand the nuance of Japan's history and culture. Another teacher begins a geometry course by engaging students in a concept formation lesson about vectors. If understanding a complex idea is important for learning additional content in your course, then consider introducing the idea with the concept formation strategy.

Earlier we mentioned the difference between *established* concepts and *dynamic* concepts. The critical attributes of established concepts are agreed upon by most people, but this is not the case with dynamic concepts. If you cannot identify three to five critical attributes that are clearly established, then this strategy will not be effective. Consider the important concept *culture*. Would you consider it dynamic or established? Your answer will help determine the appropriateness of the concept formation strategy. Similarly, reserve the concept formation strategy for those significant and/or more complex ideas that students have difficulty understanding, or for those ideas that students often misunderstand. For example, *institutional racism* is more complex than *prejudice* and may be the better concept of the two to explore with this strategy.

Because concept formation lessons take time to develop and teach, be sure you have the time to develop the lesson fully. If the focus questions are not complete, or if they do not focus students on the critical attributes, then the students might miss an important attribute. Use this strategy after you have double checked that the critical attributes are clearly identified, the examples are descriptive and appropriate, the focus questions are clear, and you have enough class time to develop the lesson. Usually, a concept formation lesson requires 40 to 50 minutes. If students are engaging in extra research on the examples, then the lesson could take two days.

MAKING IT WORK IN YOUR CONTENT AREA

In step 1 of the step-by-step lesson procedures we had you consider a process for selecting a concept you might teach in your content area. We want to build on that a bit more in this section. Our intention is for you to identify how to use the concept formation strategy to help students learn at least one "big idea" in your content area. We will restate what we put in that section, and then build on that activity. Work through the following twelve steps on your own or with a partner.

1. Given all the potential topics that students need to learn in your future classroom, identify five or six topics that you believe are critically important for your students to learn. Next, reflect on these topics and identify ideas/concepts that are an integral part of each topic. From this select list of concepts, select one that is complex and powerful enough for your students to explore.
2. State the concept that your students will learn (actually list the concept label).
3. Ascertain the origin of this label; often the origin, or etymology, provides insight into the label's critical attributes.
4. Ascertain your rationale for asking students to build on this idea. Why is it significant in your content area? What will precede this lesson? What will follow it?
5. Identify the critical attributes, and list them.

6. List three or four examples, and briefly describe how students will learn about these examples—for example, will they read about the example, or view a video clip?
7. List three or four nonexamples for the classifying tasks.
8. Decide which format will be best for the data-gathering chart. Will it be a matrix? Paragraphs and questions? A webpage?
9. Develop a data-gathering graphic organizer that lists examples and focus questions.
10. Develop a list of at least two examples and two nonexamples of your concept that students can explore during the first classifying task.
11. Come up with a nonexample of your concept that students can change into an example during the third classifying task.
12. Write lesson objectives for a concept formation lesson that incorporates the ABCD structure (see chapter 3). It is important to note that objectives should be written before the lesson is written. Since concept formation has the single objective of helping students learn an important concept, we are here having you write the objective after you have thought through and applied each step of the concept lesson. In future concept lessons, however, you should write the objective(s) at the beginning.

CHAPTER REVIEW

Concepts are ideas. We create concepts to help categorize or classify the world. Many of the words we use refer to ideas, and not to specific or tangible "things." In your future classroom you will be helping students learn concepts that they have not learned before. The purpose of the concept formation strategy is to help students form a robust understanding of significant concepts in your content area. Helping students gain a conceptual understanding, literally an understanding of big ideas, is a critical element of any instructional strategy.

Concept formation has roots in Vygotsky's theory of learning (1978). Vygotsky suggested that a "zone of proximal development" exists between our current understanding of something and the next, deeper level. Usually we need help attaining this new understanding.

Facts, concepts, and generalizations rely on each other to help promote a deeper understanding. A *fact* is something that can be verified through observing, experiencing, reading, or listening. A *concept* is an idea for organizing and classifying experiences and facts into groups with common qualities. Concepts are timeless and abstract. *Generalizations* are descriptive statements of relationships between two or more concepts.

Five key terms in the concept formation strategy are:

Concept: idea.

Concept label: a word or phrase that people use when referring to a particular concept.

Critical attributes: traits or characteristics that every example of a particular concept will have. For something to be an example of a concept it must have attributes that are critical to the concept.

Examples of a concept will have all of the concept's critical attributes.

Nonexamples of a concept will lack one or more critical attributes.

Concept formation is an inductive approach that will help students learn the critical attributes of a given concept. To promote the type of thinking that will engage students, concept formation follows a sequential eight-step process.

1. selecting a concept
2. studying examples and gathering data
3. reporting
4. noting differences
5. noting similarities
6. synthesizing
7. labeling
8. assessing with classifying tasks

The most efficient and valid assessment of your students' conceptual understanding is to engage them in the following three types of classifying tasks: (1) distinguishing examples from nonexamples; (2) producing examples; and (3) correcting nonexamples. The great advantage of these three types of concept practice is that they get students thinking about the critical characteristics of the concept. Other assessments could be used where the students engage in tasks that require them to use their conceptual understanding. The emphasis of assessments is to have students work with examples of the concept, and to demonstrate their understanding of the critical attributes that are part of each example (and that are missing in nonexamples).

Each of the eight steps in the concept formation strategy guide the students in their understanding of the critical attributes. The main *classroom-management issues* involve ensuring that you are monitoring the students, guiding them through the steps, and providing ample opportunity for them to share their ideas. It is during the sharing that you can assess their learning, and that they can learn from each others' ideas. Therefore, concept formation requires the teacher to facilitate students' independent work and whole-class interactions.

The concept formation strategy is an effective tool for helping your students think through the critical characteristics of a concept. It should not be used to teach vocabulary words to your students, but should be used to explore a few important concepts that will provide a foundation for future learning. If understanding a complex idea is important for learning additional content in your course, then consider introducing the idea with the concept formation strategy.

NOTES

1. "Power, authority, and governance" is one of the ten national standards developed by the National Council for Social Studies (1994).
2. This procedure was developed by Parker (1987, 2005) and is based on the work of Taba (1967) and Ehrenberg (1981).
3. This is adapted from the work of Ehrenberg, 1981; Parker, 2005; and B. Weikel, personal communication, June 1995 and December 2005.

REFERENCES

Ehrenberg, S. D. (1981). Concept learning: How to make it happen in the classroom. *Educational Leadership, 39*(1), 36–43.

National Council for Social Studies (1994). *Curriculum standards for social studies: Expectations of excellence.* Washington, DC: Author.

Parker, W. C. (1987). Teaching thinking: The pervasive approach. *Journal of Teacher Education, 38*(3), 50–56.

Parker, W. C. (2005). *Social studies in elementary education* (12th ed.). New York: Prentice-Hall.

Parker, W. C., & Perez, S. (1987). Beyond the rattle of empty wagons. *Social Education, 52*(3), 164–166.

Taba, H. (1967). *Teacher's handbook.* Palo Alto, CA: Addison-Wesley.

Vygotsky, L. S. (1978). *Mind in society: The development of higher psychological processes.* Cambridge, MA: MIT Press.

CITED WEBSITE

Wikipedia:
    http://www.wikipedia.org

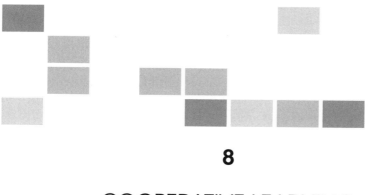

8

COOPERATIVE LEARNING

OVERVIEW

During lessons that use cooperative learning students work together in groups to help each other learn content and skills. Cooperation requires students to accomplish shared goals. During cooperative learning activities, students work to complete tasks that help them learn individually, and that help group members learn as well. In short, cooperative learning places students in groups to maximize their learning. In the process, students learn to use critical social skills. Cooperative learning groups typically range from three to seven students, with the ideal number being four or five. Keeping the size of the groups small encourages students to work together and to more actively participate. In this chapter we will help you understand the difference between cooperative group learning and conventional group projects. Many of the instructional strategies mentioned in section 2 of this book could employ cooperative learning groups. Cooperative learning, therefore, is an instructional strategy that involves placing students into groups, and helping them work together to complete a given task.

A DESCRIPTION OF COOPERATIVE LEARNING
AND RESEARCH FINDINGS

Educational researchers have examined cooperative learning extensively for several decades. Research studies consistently find that cooperative learning has positive effects on student achievement because the process of interacting with others promotes learning. Students in cooperative learning groups often learn more and learn more quickly when compared to students working alone, or not working in cooperative groups (Johnson, Johnson, & Holubec, 1994). Student achievement is highest when the cooperative learning activity requires group members to work together "to earn recognition, grades, rewards, and other indicators of group success" (Slavin, 1989–90, p. 52). Said another way, group goals and tasks requiring students to depend on each other and work together to attain group goals lead to higher levels of achievement. What causes this increase in achievement has been the focus of many years of research. Most research studies conclude that group goals and individual accountability decrease competition among students and motivate them to help one another learn and enhance their own learning. Cooperative learning has at its core the idea that students must both "pull their own weight" and work together to accomplish a task. The cooperative tasks are designed so that one person is not able to complete the group's assignment alone. By holding members individually accountable, the group is positioned so that members help each other, work interdependently (and not independently), and learn more. Individual students often complain about "working in groups" because they feel as though they have to do all the work, because they have had previous experiences in groups where partners "slack off" or "do nothing." This takes place because a teacher does not have a method in place for holding all the group members accountable. Often teachers assign a group grade. This is in conflict with cooperative learning research, because group grades will not promote individual achievement the way group goals and individual accountability will. Consider the following example of one approach for holding students individually accountable. A biology teacher places students in groups of three and assigns them the task of analyzing water samples from six different streams. The teacher then specifies that each student needs to analyze two samples, and that each student needs to compose a report comparing his/her two analyses with the other group members' analyses. The group must produce a PowerPoint presentation on the "state of water in our community," and the students each receive a grade for analysis and comparisons. The PowerPoint presentation is recorded as either satisfactory or unsatisfactory. The teacher grades in this fashion so that the students will analyze their samples and hold each other accountable for completing the analyses. The group is interdependent, but each member is assessed on her individual work. What other examples of group investigations can you come up with for your content area that have this mix of individual accountability and group rewards?

Findings from 164 research studies on cooperative learning specify that placing students in groups (as opposed to having students select their own groups), assigning a task where they must work together, and teaching specific social skills has a positive effect on student achievement (Johnson, Johnson, & Stanne, 2000). Research in these areas reveals that when students cooperate, and the emphasis on competition and individual achievement is decreased, student learning increases. For example, placing students in heterogeneous cooperative learning groups at least one time a week has a significantly positive effect on learning (Marzano, Pickering, & Pollock, 2001). Similarly, students spend more time "on task," are more motivated to complete assignments, and are more capable at transfering their learning to other contexts during cooperative group activities (Johnson & Johnson, 1999; Kohn, 1992). By contrast, when students with lower abilities are grouped together, their academic performance decreases (Kulik & Kulik, 1987, 1991), and when students are placed in groups *without* support structures that reduce competition and increase interdependence, they do not attain higher academic levels of achievement (Reder & Simon, 1997).

Cooperative learning has a positive impact on social interactions among students, because students learn how to interact with one another. When you teach you will model for your students how to work with others. One of the most consistent findings is that "when students of different racial or ethnic backgrounds work together toward a common goal, they gain in liking and respect for one another" (Slavin, 1989–90, p. 53). Why do you think this might be true?

Cooperative learning has also been shown to increase classmates' acceptance of students who are traditionally marginalized because of low academic ability (Cohen, 1994; Cohen & Lotan, 1997; Johnson & Johnson, 1989–90). Students are marginalized, or placed outside of the mainstream of the classroom, for reasons such as ability, ethnicity, wealth/poverty, or appearance. Cohen (1994) has examined how student "status" leads to different behaviors in groups, and leads to different treatment by peers; she notes,

> A status characteristic is an agreed upon social ranking where everyone feels it is better to have a high rank than a low rank. Examples of status characteristics are race, social class, sex, reading ability, and attractiveness…high status individuals are expected to be more competent than low status individuals across a wide range of tasks that are viewed as important. When a teacher assigns a task to a group of students, some of whom are higher and some lower on any of the status characteristics described above, these general expectations come into play…those who are higher status come to hold a high rank in the status order that emerges in the group interaction. Those who hold lower status come to hold a low rank on that status order. (p. 33)

No one formally assigns status to students, just as no one formally assigns status to people in society at large. It is one aspect of a diverse society that perpetuates the status quo and the current power structure in that society. High-status students are expected to be better (and they come to expect it of themselves), and low-status students are not expected to make important contributions to the group (and they begin to believe they have little to offer). Members of a group often promote some members to be active (high-status students), and some members to be subordinate (low-status students). If left to their own devices, most student groups will reiterate the existing status of students. Even when groups are changed, a students' status often follows him to the next setting (Cohen & Lotan, 1997). However, cooperative learning has been found to increase the status of marginalized students. By assigning students to groups; structuring tasks to require interdependence; reducing competition; and proactively teaching students how to divide the workload, understand group goals, listen, paraphrase ideas, and encourage each other, teachers can help students overcome the barriers of status and marginalization. Additionally, students increase friendships with group mates after working together in cooperative learning groups or teams, and over time students increase their abilities to listen to others, consider ideas from all members of a group, assign tasks equally, and have a greater sense of concern for the success of all members in the group. We often hear from people in a wide range of occupations (e.g., teachers, doctors, lawyers, contractors, retailers, small business owners, community service workers) that the ability to work with others cooperatively is a critical "job skill." We add to this idea that it is also a critical skill for citizens of a democracy. The research clearly suggests that cooperative learning promotes learning of skills and content. The idea that cooperative learning promotes prosocial behavior among students is an added value of using cooperative learning strategies.

The question that arises in the midst of this research support is, *What are these strategies?* Cooperative learning is much more than simply placing students in groups and assigning them a task. This simplistic approach fosters behavior where one or two capable students "take over" and complete the task. Students who are marginalized by peers and even by the larger community because of reputation, ethnicity, gender, lower ability, or other social factors are often further separated from the assignment. At its worst, group work becomes an activity in which students merely go through the motions of interacting with one another. Resentment is stirred up in the student who ends up completing the task on his own, and students who do not participate in class might even be pressured to contribute to a lesser degree. Groups, thus, can create resentment, reinforce stereotypes, and benefit some students to the detriment of others. The teacher must structure group work. We think that merely asking students to work in groups (even if you assigned them to the groups) can at times do more academic and social harm than good. Very specific attributes are needed to promote positive interdependence (which we believe is another name for cooperation). Johnson, Johnson, and Holubec (1994, p. 26) have developed the following five "essential elements" of cooperative learning that we believe will help you structure your future use of student groups:

1. positive interdependence
2. face-to-face interactions
3. group goals and individual accountability
4. interpersonal and small-group skills
5. group processing

The following overview of these elements is intended to help you clarify the importance of each when you plan to use cooperative learning.

Positive Interdependence

When people cooperate they have *positive interdependence* on each other. Students must see that they need each other to accomplish a task and to learn. Many techniques are available for teachers to use in promoting this. Teachers might request that students share resources, materials, and information so that the students genuinely need each others' ideas and information. For example, in a biology class, each group member might be responsible for learning a different example of a symbiotic relationship, but the group needs to use all the examples together. Each member informs group mates about the information she has gathered. The teacher could also have the group establish mutual goals about how members might help each other learn the content or skills. A group might have the goal that each member will complete her research about a symbiotic relationship in the next two days. Or, the group might set the goal that everyone will provide a paragraph description and a photo of the symbiotic relationship. Goals could also specify the role of each member during a class presentation.

Positive interdependence can also be fostered when the teacher provides group awards. This could be in the form of praise (e.g., applause and commendations after an effective presentation to the class), extra-credit points (e.g., points awarded if all members' test scores are above a certain percentile), or other incentives that the whole group receives other than a grade. Finally, interdependence is fostered by assigning roles within the group that are necessary for the group to progress. For example, students in a group might take on the following roles: (1) the *coordinator* (someone who allocates responsibilities and keeps the group on task); (2) the *checker* (someone who makes sure all members of the group are participating and understanding the content); (3) the *recorder* (someone who takes general notes for the group and organizes the final group solution); and (4) the *skeptic* (someone who keeps the group from leaping to premature conclusions) (Heller et al., 1992; Johnson & Johnson, 2004). These are simply suggested roles, and you will develop your own based on the needs of your students. These roles are assessed and monitored by the group and by the teacher. Students hold themselves accountable, and exhort or encourage each other to fully complete their roles. As the teacher you must remember that you are helping students learn content (e.g., symbiotic relationships) *and* that you are helping students learn interdependence. You must monitor student interactions with both in mind. We will discuss this in more detail in the assessment section of this chapter.

Face-to-Face Interactions

Many of the cognitive and social benefits of cooperative learning occur during face-to-face group interactions and discussions. Requiring students to meet and work as a group is essential. These meetings may occur during class so that you can monitor student interactions, or they may occur outside of the classroom if the group needs to complete tasks as homework. Students cannot work toward many of the interdependent elements listed above without meeting face to face. Likewise, these interactions require students to engage in higher-order thinking such as summarizing, explaining, elaborating ideas, and seeking clarification. The interactions promote content and skill learning. It is also during these interactions that students cooperate in earnest with others who may be "different" from themselves. As the teacher, you need to assess the degree of cooperation that occurred. We will explore this more in the assessment section of this chapter.

Your students will likely lack social skills that promote interdependence with others. Face-to-face interactions are a critical element for "developing harmonious interracial relations in desegregated classrooms" (Cohen, 1994, p. 17) that the research on cooperative learning suggests. At times you may need to stop a group project and work solely on interaction skills. The following experience of one student teacher serves as an example.

Jill placed students in heterogeneous groups, and assigned them to hypothesize about underlying causes of the Civil War. After the first day, she noticed that most of the groups were not working together. The assigned task required interdependence, but the ability and ethnic diversity of the groups seemed to hamper students' willingness to work together. Jill decided to work on the relationships of the students, and spent two days engaging in trust-building and team-building activities (e.g., leading a blindfolded partner around an obstacle course, identifying positive character traits of group members). She plainly told students that she placed them in groups with classmates they did not know well, and that she would be watching to see how well the groups worked together. She told them that she wanted little competition in the groups, and that each student would assess his own performance and his group members' performance in helping the group work together. After the two days, she resumed the Civil War assignment, and closely monitored student interactions. At least twice a week she had students turn in group and individual assessments of their progress. Jill used these assessments to teach specific social skills to the class. After working in the groups, every student received at least 85% of the total points possible for the project!

Group Goals and Individual Accountability

Cooperative learning groups all will have goals, such as completing a task/ assignment, working to accomplish a project by cooperating, and the mutual goals listed above (in the "Positive Interdependence" section). In addition, each student must be held individually accountable for her own learning. Cooperative groups have not met their goals until every member of the group has learned. Group members need to work hard at their own learning, and work to support each other. You may think of creative ideas for holding students accountable, but a few common ideas include:

dividing a large group project into smaller tasks that are divided among the group; that way the group is responsible for the larger project, and each member is responsible and held accountable for completing one or more critical tasks

quizzing/testing each member individually on material the group was learning together; this will keep students accountable for learning content and for teaching it to each other

having one member answer for the entire group; this way the students will prepare together so all members can provide answers effectively

Interpersonal and Small-Group Skills

Most people do not have adequate preparation to work cooperatively in a group, and your students will be no exception. Cooperative learning is dependent upon you helping your students learn effective interpersonal/social skills. These are taught in the context of the group project. Students need to learn trust, decision-making abilities, conflict management skills, and motivation techniques. For example, the ability to criticize an idea and not the person presenting the idea is difficult to learn. Learning this while working on a group project will allow students to develop this skill in an authentic setting. Similarly, confronting students who are not sharing the workload is difficult, but necessary, and a cooperative group becomes a powerful setting in which to learn how to do this. Many times the interpersonal and group skills are identified because a group is struggling to work together. Rather than fearing this, you need to take full advantage of "uncooperative" group work by identifying and helping students learn the social skills that will help the groups work together more effectively. More on how to do this follows later in this chapter in the section "Logistical Concerns."

Group Processing

You will eventually want your students to learn how to work cooperatively, assign roles, hold each other accountable, and promote group mates' learning. Therefore, you must allow students the time to analyze how well their groups are working, how well classmates are learning, and how well they are using social skills. Not only does it help you and your future students determine if they are learning, but it promotes effective relationships among the group members. The structure for facilitating group processing will vary, but generally it involves students reflecting on how well they are meeting goals, identifying any obstacles/problems that might prevent them from cooperating, and developing action plans for overcoming the problems. Some teachers observe their students during group tasks and provide written feedback about how well the groups have worked together and areas that need to be improved (some teachers may even have the students undertake these observations). We like to think of this as a debriefing period. It demonstrates to your students that you value group work, and that you are interested not only in the product; the process is important enough to discuss and improve on so that the next group project will be even better.

Implicit in all of these elements is the point that the teacher helps students learn the process of working together. Students are assigned to groups—on purpose—by the teacher in order to maximize their learning of content and social skills. Cooperative learning usually requires that students are placed in *heterogeneous* groups. In other words, the students do not form or select their own groups, but the teacher forms groups with mixed ability, mixed ethnicity, and mixed gender. Students will tend to choose to work with classmates who are similar to themselves in terms of culture and ability. This type of *homogeneous* grouping does not necessarily help strudents learn content more effectivley, and it does not promote the social benefits of cooperative learning. High-ability students do not have opportunities to deepen their understanding by helping group members learn key concepts, and lower-ability students do not have peers who can help them attain a deeper level of understanding (Slavin, 1993). Homogeneous groups have no positive effect on increasing students' understanding of culture or viewpoints different from their own (Mitchell, Rosemary, Bramwell, Solnosky, & Lilly, 2004); therefore teachers need to place students in groups purposefully (as opposed to randomly). We suggest grouping students as heterogeneously as possible. When placing students, consider the ethnicities, genders, and ability levels of your students, and try to group students in a way that cuts across these categories. Personalities of students, previous experiences working together, knowledge of the topic they are exploring, and the amount of time you are able to spend working on social skills will also impact your placement of students. We find that placing students in groups is a very difficult task, because so many variables interact. However, your thoughtful work in placing students will help promote the type of student achievement reported in the cooperative learning research and is well worth the effort. As you get to know your students better, you become more insightful at grouping them, and you begin to see how the group projects benefit your students.

The idea of cooperation is not new nor is the goal of having students work cooperatively in groups. What we want you to think about in this chapter is the intentional grouping of students so they are able to work effectively together to accomplish tasks. Cooperative learning is not easy to accomplish because time and effort are needed to place students in groups, assess their progress, and determine both the social and academic needs of your students. In chapter 3 we described three categories of learning objectives: *academic, intellectual,* and *social.* Cooperative learning will help students learn academic content, intellectual thinking skills as they research and complete assigned tasks, and social interaction skills as they learn to work interdependently with group members.

STEP-BY-STEP PROCEDURES FOR PLANNING AND IMPLEMENTING COOPERATIVE LEARNING

To take full advantage of the content learning and the social benefits of cooperative learning, you will need to make preparations before your students begin working.

Step 1: Forming Groups

You should usually plan on forming groups with three to five students. Groups of this size allow for the benefits of heterogeneity while still being small enough to promote interdependence and individual accountability. Often teachers will place students in groups randomly, or they will allow students to select their own groups. As we wrote above, cooperative learning research clearly suggests that the teacher places students in groups to serve a purpose. Usually, this means that each group is made up of students who are different from one another in several categories: ethnicity, ability, gender, and so on. We suggest that you think about the task you will have students complete, and place students in groups accordingly. Consider the following examples:

> A social studies teacher wants his students to create a policy recommendation to the local city government about developing a vacant lot. The space could become a park, shopping center, or community center. How might he place students in groups? He might be sure each group has a student who has some artistic skills so the group can provide a sketch of their recommended land use. He might decide that the perspective of boys and girls need to be considered, so the groups will be of mixed gender. He might also decide that groups with mixed ability will promote better learning of the issue for all the groups' members.

> A language arts teacher wants her students to write a team biography on the courage of Rosa Parks. Each team member is responsible for learning and writing about a different event in Parks's life that demonstrates her courage. The group will turn their individually written events into chapters and work to ensure that all the chapters flow together. The group will also develop a timeline of Parks's life, a cover page, and an introduction to the biography.[1] The teacher might decide to place students so that each group has a member with strong research

skills, and a member who needs help with research skills. She might also create groups of mixed ethnicity.

Students in a biology class are exploring cellular reproduction. The teacher worries that the students are socially immature. She might thus decide to create groups that are of mixed ability but of the same gender. The groups are comprised of all girls or all boys, but within each group the students' ability is diverse.

The point of these examples is to consider how the content will best be learned with groups, and how placing students purposefully in groups may best promote student learning. Remember, the research on cooperative learning clearly states that mixed groups promote student learning. Research studies consistently find that high- and low-ability students learn and benefit from working in mixed-ability groups. How you mix them will depend on how well you know your students, and on the task you are assigning.

Step 2: Conducting the Group Work

Any classroom activity using cooperative learning will follow the same general sequence: an introduction to the task; an invitation or request to work interdependently on the task; and a final product or performance by the group that is assessed. During the introduction, you will place students in groups and provide an overview of what you want the groups to accomplish by the end of their time working together. Following this you will assign the task(s) the groups will accomplish, help the groups get started with materials and resources, and assist them as they begin working together. The final part of the sequence involves the groups showing what they have accomplished, and while it is a group product, individual work in developing the final product should be clear.

We find it useful to consider cooperative learning activities as being informal or formal (Johnson, Johnson, & Holubec, 1998). *Informal cooperative learning* involves quickly formed groups that may work together for a few minutes or a whole class period. You might have these groups focus their attention on the content they are learning, talk through a problem, or clarify student understanding (InTime, 2004). If you use informal cooperative learning, you will likely place students in groups spontaneously without a lot of planning. The task may be quickly stated ("Please look at your answer to problem number 4 with the person sitting next to you," or, "I would like you to quickly form groups of three and recall two reasons in favor and two reasons against drilling for oil in wildlife preserves"). And though the task may require students to work together (cooperate), it does not necessarily possess all of the critical cooperative learning elements that researchers have identified.

An example of an informal cooperative learning strategy can be found in Kagan (1992). With this approach the teacher asks a question of the group. Each member of the group has a number (one through five, depending on the size of the group). The group members consult to make sure everyone knows the answer. The teacher then calls out one number and the students in each group who were assigned that number must produce the answer. This is an effective review strategy. Another example of a review strategy is "Think/Pair/Share" (see chapter 5). With this approach, the teacher poses a question, students pair with a classmate near them, and they share their ideas and thoughts about the question. A third example of informal cooperative learning is the use of "buzz groups." This is the equivalent of small-group brainstorming in which the teacher presents a topic or question to students in small groups and they then talk (or "buzz") with each other about the topic. For example, if you teach a social studies or an earth science class your students might form buzz groups to brainstorm answers to the question, "Where should we haul our community's garbage?" Students in a literature class could buzz about their predictions of what will happen next in a story they are reading. Buzz groups, like the Think/Pair/Share method, are also useful as a preparation for whole-class brainstorms or discussions. Students are more likely to talk in small groups (especially if they have worked with each other on previous projects), and after they have talked together in groups students may feel more comfortable sharing with the larger class.

Formal cooperative learning groups work together longer, usually from one class period to several weeks. You can structure almost any assignment to fit within formal cooperative learning (InTime, 2004). As Johnson, Johnson, and Holubec note, "Formal cooperative learning groups ensure that students are actively involved in the intellectual work of organizing material, explaining it, summarizing it, and integrating it into existing conceptual structures. They are the heart of using cooperative learning" (1998, p. 7).

Informal cooperative learning is useful for specific tasks that are completed fairly quickly. Not a lot of time is spent helping students learn "how to cooperate," but time is spent completing assigned tasks. If students lack cooperation and social skills, then informal cooperative learning may be difficult to use. Formal cooperative learning helps students learn content *and* social skills. It requires additional time to teach social skills. Teachers grade students more so during formal cooperative learning, because of the structure and time students spend together. We will address this more in the assessment section of this chapter.

Three Common Types of Cooperative Learning

In this section, we present three common formal cooperative learning strategies for you to consider:

1. student teams/achievement divisions
2. the jigsaw approach
3. group investigations

A fourth formal strategy, structured academic controversy, fits more appropriately as a discussion technique. In this strategy, students interact with one another to form an opinion about a controversial issue. We describe it in detail when examining classroom discussions in chapter 10. Obviously, many forms of cooperative learning exist, and you may develop your own forms that have all of the necessary critical elements. These four strategies are ones that many teachers and researchers consider to be the most common and effective to use. Each strategy involves the important elements listed above (teacher selected-groups, positive interdependence, face-to-face interactions, group goals and individual accountability, interpersonal and small-group skills, and group processing).

Student Teams/Achievement Divisions (STAD)

This method (Slavin, 1983, 1988, 1995) involves competition among groups, and is useful when reviewing information and preparing for a quiz or test. Competition *within* groups destroys cooperation because students become independent (and not interdependent), but competition *among* groups may actually draw members within a group closer. To use STAD you will follow three essential steps. First, you will present content to your students through lecture, reading assignments, or other instructional strategies. Second, you will place your students in mixed groups of three to five members and ask them to complete a series of worksheets and activities that review the content and help them master the information they just received. The students help teammates learn the content; those who need help learn from those who understand the content. The students who already understand the content increase their understanding as a result of explaining/teaching it to students needing assistance. The third step is the assessment. Each student takes quizzes on the information as individuals, and the team receives points based on the level of individual improvement over previous scores. The students are graded on their performances on the quiz, and the groups receive bonus points based on members' improvements.

STAD is appropriate for a variety of subjects that focus on material with specific "correct answers" (Newmann & Thompson, 1987). Consider the following example: A mathematics teacher wants students to review the use of trigonometry when working with right triangles. She could place students in teams, and provide a number of exercises using sine, cosine, and tangent for solving problems with right triangles. After a class session of the teams working together, the students take a quiz on using these principles. The teacher sets aside the next class session for the groups to meet and correct wrong answers and help each other clarify their conceptual understanding. This is followed by a final quiz over the material, and the group is rewarded for improved quiz scores.

The Jigsaw Approach

This cooperative learning method (Aronson, Blaney, Stephen, Sikes, & Snapp, 1978) effectively uses groups to examine information that the whole group is studying. Where STAD focuses students on specific facts, ideas, or skills, the jigsaw approach focuses students more on connections and relationships among the content. For example, each student in a five-member group is given information that comprises only one of five parts of the information. Each student in the group is responsible for a different piece of information. Students leave this original "home" group and join other students who have been given the same information. These are referred to as "expert groups"; all students with the same piece of information get together, study it, and decide how best to teach it to their peers in the original group. When the "experts" are finished, the students return to their home groups (which are now comprised of one expert on each of the five topics), and each teaches his portion of the lesson to the others in the group. Students work cooperatively in two different groups, their home group and the expert group, and are held individually accountable by the performance of their group on an assessment over all five parts. This strategy was later updated as "jigsaw 2" when it added the idea that all students are presented with all of the information first, and then they are separated into expert groups. This updated approach becomes one of clarifying and learning information that everyone has already seen at least one time.

The jigsaw approach is complicated until you have observed it in use, or tried teaching with it, so we offer a very simple example to help clarify the strategy: Students in a literature class are reading a novel. The teacher wants to be sure all students understand the first five chapters. After students read the first five chapters, he places students in home groups of five and assigns each student one of the five chapters. All of the students assigned to chapter 1 then meet together (as do all of the students assigned chapters 2, 3, 4, and 5) to clarify the characters, setting, and plot of their chapter. Their goal is to become experts on their assigned chapter. Students then return to their home group. Since each of the five chapters is again represented, the students each tell the group about the chapter on which they became experts, and collectively the group members receive an overview of the five chapters.

Group Investigation

This method (Sharan & Sharan, 1989–90) provides students with a significant amount of choice and control. Groups are mixed, but they are additionally formed to match students who share an interest about the same topic. For example, if the teacher wants students to examine stem cell research, some students may be interested in cloning, others in controversies surrounding cloning research, and others in stem cell potential. The group members help plan how they will research the topic and how they will present it, and divide the work among themselves. The teacher facilitates this task based on the needs of the group. Each member then carries out her part of the investigation, and the group summarizes the work and presents its findings to the class (Sharan & Sharan, 1989–90, p. 17). This strategy requires the teacher to act as a resource while providing direction and clarification as needed. The teacher's task is to create a stimulating work environment. Six specific stages comprise group investigation. To contextualize these stages, think through how each might help students in groups of four who are asked to work on a science fair project explaining how boats float (adapted from Blosser, 1992; Sharan & Sharan, 1989–90, pp. 17–20):

1. The teacher identifies the general topic and students identify subtopics.
2. Students work together to plan how they will carry out the investigation of their subtopic or set of questions, and they equally assign tasks.
3. Students investigate the topic, and work to complete their tasks.
4. In their groups students analyze and evaluate the information they have collected, and plan how to present this information to the rest of the class.
5. Each group presents a summary of the results of its investigation so that all students gain a broad perspective of the general topic. The students teach the class about their topic.
6. The teacher solicits feedback from the class about the presentations, and feedback from the group members about the topic, the process, and the presentation. The teacher also assesses each student's part of the investigation

CLASSROOM MANAGEMENT ISSUES

When students work in cooperative learning groups the classroom needs to be managed in a unique manner. In chapter 1 we mentioned that a characteristic of effective teachers is that they do not sit down while teaching. Instead, they monitor the classroom by interacting with students and assisting them (Doda, George, & McEwin, 1987). During cooperative learning activities you will need to actively monitor each group's progress to ensure that they are progressing according to your plan, that they understand the task and have appropriately divided the workload among themselves, that their questions are answered, and that you provide them with guidance for working together to complete their task.

When you monitor the groups, you are assessing both their group progress and each member's individual progress. Every member of a group should be able to explain both the group task and his individual part in accomplishing that task. When monitoring groups, a good question to ask students is, "How are you helping your group right now?" If they are cooperating, all students should be able to tell you their own progress and the group's progress. If a student is not working very hard, then you will refer him to his role as part of the group and request him to work on completing that task. For example, if a group is in the computer lab to locate different types of volcanic activity around the world, students may each be examining a different region for "hot spots." Each student should be able to tell you his progress in locating volcanoes, as well as how this fits into the group task. If you come across a student who is off task, you can easily determine what this student should be doing, and ask him a question such as, "What does your group expect you to be doing right now?" In this way, the student will need to answer to the group norms and expectations.

As we mentioned earlier in this chapter, placing students into groups does not guarantee cooperation. Even purposefully placing students into groups to create a mix of ability levels, ethnicities, skills, and genders does not necessarily result in interdependence and cooperation. As the teacher you will need to establish group norms and expectations. Using cooperative learning requires that you are willing to teach cooperative skills to your students. These skills may not be part of your content area, but they are critical if your students are to work interdependently. The first task is to help students recognize the need for a particular social skill. We have seen this need emerge when groups cannot get along, fail to complete a task, or come and complain to the teacher about a group mate. A less frustrating approach for students is for the teacher to communicate to the class before problems arise why different skills are important. You may use skits, video clips, examples from real-life experiences, or other strategies to help students recognize the importance of cooperation. As the teacher, you need to help students understand particular cooperative or social skills. One effective approach for this is to model the skill as the teacher and incorporate the use of a *T-chart*, or a *looks like/sounds like chart*. These charts help students identify behavioral expectations for specific cooperation skills. They are called *T-charts* because they have two columns and are shaped like the letter *T*. Consider this example (adapted from Johnson, Johnson, & Holubec, 1994, p. 72):

T-CHART FOR "WORKING TOGETHER IN A GROUP"

Looks Like	Sounds Like
Eye contact	"Good idea"
Facing group mates	"Have you thought about this?"
Interested/engaged in the talk	"What is your idea?"
Listening	"That is interesting"
One person speaking	"I don't agree, because . . ."

Adapted from Johnson, Johnson, and Holubec, 1994, p. 72.

The whole class, or each group, completes the T-chart. When they complete the first column, they consider what they would see when watching a group of peers working together in a group. For the second column, they come up with comments that they might hear (note that these exact phrases are not what it important, but the ideas behind the comments). We suggest posting these in the classroom as an additional form of accountability. This could be a type of rubric that students adhere to during group projects. We have seen teachers develop T-charts for cooperative skills such as "Criticizing Ideas and Not People," "Encouraging Group Members to Pull Their Own Weight," "Disagreeing with Someone's Idea," and "Coming to a Group Consensus." As we mentioned earlier, these often arise during the class interactions. For example, when groups are struggling to divide the workload evenly, it may be a good time for you to help them develop a T-chart for that skill. It is an effective tool for accountability because the students develop it, and because the expectations are clearly delineated. Other social skills that you should model to your students, and help them learn to use, include: setting goals, brainstorming with others, encouraging all members of the group to participate, dividing the workload equally, and solving problems together.

One of the key management tasks during group projects is to be aware of the progress each group is making. Just as students will finish at different times when they are working individually, groups will complete their tasks at different times. If it is important that all groups finish at approximately the same time, then you may need to modify the task so slower groups are able to finish on time, or add enhancements to the task so faster groups are able to continue learning while the other groups finish. Consider this example from a literature class: You want your students to think about the themes of seven Native American legends. You decide to place your 28 students into seven groups of four, and assign each group one of seven different legends. You plan to use the jigsaw approach, and ask the expert groups to take 15 minutes to identify the main characters in the legend, the plot, and possible themes. One group is struggling to complete these three tasks in the time you allotted, and two groups are close to finishing five minutes after starting. If you approach the "slower group" you may find they are not on task, not understanding the task, or some other reason for not moving along efficiently. Check with them shortly after they begin working on this assignment (recall that in chapter 1 we referred to the work of Jones, who suggested that teachers visit all groups quickly at the start of an assignment to ensure that all students understand the task given to them). An additional clarification of the task may be all they need to complete the work on time. However, you may identify other reasons for their delay, and you may need to modify the task. You might ask them to not worry about the characters, and focus only on the plot and the theme. This modification might be just enough for the group to finish with the others. As for the "fast group," often groups finish quickly because they do not fully complete the task. A group that has answered too superficially needs to recognize where they could have gone into more depth, and be asked to finish the original task more completely. If the group has completed your task adequately, then you have the opportunity to challenge them to explore new ideas or content. This group might consider how foreshadowing is used, or how their legend compares to myths they have read. These enhancements should be thought of ahead of time, and they should not be construed by students as "busy work." You should reward students for their efficiency, not punish hard work by assigning irrelevant extra work.

When we talk with teachers they often share a paradox of using student groups: students do not know how to work in groups, but they can only learn how by working in groups! As a result, you will find each successive group project may work more effectively then the previous ones. Many teachers have groups of students complete classroom tasks as a way to help them learn cooperative skills. For example, a group of four students may be assigned the task of designing a bulletin board for an upcoming unit; another group might serve as a teacher's steering committee that gives advice about upcoming projects or field trips. A third group might help the teacher update the class website. These duties are then rotated monthly so that all the groups are able to work on the different projects. The idea here is to provide opportunities for students to practice working interdependently, plan together, set group goals, and develop mutual trust. When the students are asked to work on a more academic task, they have had the chance to develop an initial cooperative skill set from the classroom tasks.

LOGISTICAL CONCERNS, INCLUDING BENEFITS AND OBSTACLES

Because cooperative learning requires students to work interdependently, you must set up the room in a manner that is conducive to group work. Desks and chairs should be positioned so that students can meet in their groups and interact face to face. The groups need to be far enough apart so that students are not distracted by other groups. If the physical space of your classroom is small, then be sure students talk with soft voices. As the groups start working together to accomplish tasks, individual students may need to leave your classroom for the computer lab, art room, library, and the like. Be sure you know school policies about allowing students out of the room. Similarly, think about the role of homework for projects that require several days of work. If you allow class time for the work, then you are able to closely monitor the groups and students do not need to coordinate their busy schedules. The drawback of this is that you must use class time. We find that a combination of class time and homework is effective. At the start of the task, provide time in class until the groups have identified how they will work interdependently. After that, you can offer short 10- to 15-minute "class meetings" for the groups to check progress and/or exhort one another. By providing class time for meetings, students can complete tasks on their own, and then bring their ideas and answers to the group during the next class meeting.

One of the largest concerns of cooperative learning has to do with group assignments. We examined this earlier in the chapter, but it is worthwhile to restate that students benefit from working in groups that are purposefully formed by the teacher, and are not self-selected. Often students have had negative experiences working in groups (and so have their parents), so it is important to provide a rationale for using cooperative teams for students or parents. We find that handing out a list of the group members, and telling each group where to meet and what their task should be, is a great help in helping groups get started working together. For example, if a group of students are meeting to explore American child labor practices in the early 1900s, you might hand out a sheet of paper that has each group numbered and that lists the names of each group member. You might say, "On this sheet of paper I have listed the group in which you will each be working. You will notice that each group has a number from 1 to 7. I would like all members of group 1 to meet at the table by the door, all members of group 2 meet by my desk . . . ," and so forth. "Move to these locations very quickly, so we do not waste time. When you have arrived, the first order of business is for each member to tell the group at least one idea about child labor in America during the early 1900's that you learned from your reading last night, and all of you should record these ideas in your notes." This type of script will get the groups into place quickly and help them get started. You could also prepare a handout with a series of procedures that you want the students to follow, and a timeline for the completion of each task. Rather than waiting for your direction, the worksheet provides structure for the groups' work.

If you plan to assign specific roles to students in the group (as we described earlier), you need to have the roles clearly described prior to the activity. You also need to think about how successful each student will be in an assigned role, and whether you are adequately serving traditionally marginalized students.

We described the jigsaw approach earlier, but here we revisit one logistical problem specific to this approach. Remember that during a jigsaw exercise students are in two groups: an "expert" group where they learn with others about specific information, and a home group where they share their newly formed expertise. If you are able to form groups that have the same number of students, then jigsaws work smoothly. When one or two groups have a different number of students than the others, logistic problems can arise. For example, a class with 30 students can be divided into five expert groups of six students each. When each of the six "experts" rejoin to make their home group, there will be six groups with five members in each group. Consider how you will move students from expert to home groups if you have 29 students. Thinking through this scenario will prepare you ahead of time for using the jigsaw method.

APPROPRIATE ASSESSMENT TECHNIQUES TO USE WITH COOPERATIVE LEARNING

Teachers need to assess the content learning that is taking place, and they need to assess the social interactions and relationships of the students in the group. Many times teachers will need to intervene with a group to help reestablish expectations for interactions during group work, to assist in the division of the workload and tasks, and to facilitate students in understanding the content. The T-charts described in the section on classroom management can be used as a rubric for expected student behavior, and students can be held individually accountable for how closely they meet the expectations described in the chart. You could even assign a grade on how well the students met the criteria stated on particular T-charts.

Self-assessment and group assessments are effective tools for determining how effectively the groups worked together, and for having students reflect on their contributions to the group goals. The following rubric is one example for eliciting students to reflect on the process of working in groups.

In addition to a self-assessment tool, you can also provide the groups with a document that outlines all of the components of the group task. For example, the Group Biography Planning Sheet on page 202 is a tool that could be used if students are working in cooperative groups to produce a group biography. Each member writes her own chapter, and the group works interdependently to complete several additional components of the biography (this example is adapted from Parker, 2005).

This document is helpful at the beginning of the task, because students can use it to identify all of the tasks that need to be completed. This follows the idea (described in chapter 3) of making expectations clear to students at the start of a project (Wiggins, 1990). This document is also useful as an assessment tool, because you will be able to connect different aspects of the task to particular students. The group needs to promote excellent achievement from all of the members, but sometimes not all students perform up to this

---

GROUP- AND SELF-EVALUATION

Please award each member of your project/presentation group a score reflecting their effort in the group work. Score each of the six categories on a scale of 0 to 2, and enter the total score in the space next to each name. A "2" means you/they were excellent. A "1" means you/they were adequate. A "0" means you/they did not meet expectations. Under each name/score, please provide a succinct explanation for the score that you gave. Write these in clear phrases/sentences/statements.

- Interaction in group meetings (0, 1, 2)
- Contributions to group discussions (0, 1, 2)
- Attendance at group meetings (0, 1, 2)
- Contributions to presentation (0, 1, 2)
- Contributions to packet (0, 1, 2)
- Preparation of materials (0, 1, 2)

_____ / 12 _____
              (Your name)
_____ / 12 _____
              (Teammate name)
_____ / 12 _____
              (Teammate name)
_____ / 12 _____
              (Teammate name)

GROUP BIOGRAPHY PLANNING SHEET

Please complete this with your team members and hand in *before* the end of class today. You will be assessed on how well you complete the task(s) you have signed up to complete for the group.

Group Members: _____

_____

Critical Events/Chapters and Illustrations:

Title of Chapter 1: _____ by: _____
Title of Chapter 2: _____ by: _____
Title of Chapter 3: _____ by: _____
Title of Chapter 4: _____ by: _____

Give the name(s) of those who will be responsible for completing the following:

Foreword: _____
Introduction: _____
Map: _____
Timeline: _____
Bibliography: _____
"About the Authors" page: _____
Cover page: _____
Formatting: _____

Adapted from Parker, W.C. (2005)

expectation. A form that identifies each student's task allows you to hold students accountable.

You will also develop rubrics for grading the overall quality of student work. Again, the group does not receive a grade, but each student does. You will assess students on their contribution to the group goals, and on their individual contributions to the end task/product. When you have determined a project for your students, you may want to refer to chapter 3 and reread the section on designing valid assessment tools and developing rubrics.

GUIDELINES FOR DECIDING IF COOPERATIVE LEARNING IS APPROPRIATE FOR THE CONTENT OF A LESSON

We believe that cooperative learning can be used to teach in most content areas. However, it is important for you to consider the following five factors when determining its usefulness for your classroom.

Time

Cooperative learning is a time-demanding instructional strategy. It takes time for students to think about content together, to work together, and to teach/practice using the social skills that are necessary for working together. Cooperative learning promotes content learning and social skill development. If you have enough time to work with students in both of these areas, then cooperative learning will be effective.

Group Formation

Do you have enough information about your students to place them in mixed groups that will promote learning? You may want to wait a week or more into the school year before using cooperative learning so that you are able to get to know your students. You also want to consider if the cooperative learning will be formal or informal. Informal cooperative learning groups are formed with convenience in mind to allow for quick assignments (e.g., four students are grouped because they are sitting near each other, or a group is formed because the teacher has them count off by fours).

Social Skills Development

As we mentioned above, cooperative learning is based on you placing students into groups. Often groups have conflicts until they learn to cooperate with one another. This will require you to motivate and facilitate students to work together as a group. Consider if you are willing and able to help students respect differences and interact with peers who are from different cultures, religions, ethnicities, or socioeconomic groups.

Clear Task Expectations

If you have a clearly stated task for students to perform, consider why working in groups will benefit the students more than working independently. How will a group project enhance student learning of this content? How will it enhance student satisfaction with their learning experience? Formal cooperative learning strategies serve specific purposes. STAD is best used when you want students to learn specific answers to questions. It is an effective review task. The jigsaw approach allows you to efficiently examine a complex topic by dividing the information among the group and having the group members teach each other. Group investigations, unlike STAD, allow groups freedom in completing their tasks. It is an effective approach for inquiry and student-led research projects.

Assessment

Can you separate the task so that students are able to be held individually accountable? Could you create a rubric that clearly states the group goal/task (for example, to make a presentation on the formation of the National Park System) and that assesses students' individual work in the group (for example, each student is assessed on her contribution to the research and presentation on the National Park System).

MAKING IT WORK IN YOUR CONTENT AREA

Select a topic that you believe students will be able to learn about while working in groups. From the list of three "formal cooperative learning" approaches (STAD, the jigsaw approach, group investigations), select the one that will be effective for helping students learn the content. If you are working with a group of students, consider how you might divide them into smaller groups of four or five. Since you must know your students before you are able to effectively place them in groups, you may not be able to consider the formation of the groups at this time; that will come when you begin teaching. Next, consider the following:

List the topic students will work on together. Develop a clear question or statement such as, "How does the Columbian Exchange still impact us today?" or "Determine the defining attributes of the following geometric figures."

Write out lesson objectives:

Social objectives dealing with what students are to learn about working together.

Academic objectives dealing with the knowledge base to be explored

Forming Groups: Describe the rationale for choosing the cooperative learning strategy and for placing students in mixed groups.

In addition to ability, gender, and ethnicity, what are other attributes to consider when placing students in groups for this project?

What makes this a good issue to explore in groups?

How does it fit with the curriculum?

Lesson Procedures for Conducting Cooperative Group Work

Student preparation and helping the groups work: What needs to take place before the groups work together? Will students learn new material during the group project, or will they work with material already introduced? What social skills do you think need to be learned before the project begins? How will you teach those to students (e.g., with a T-chart? role-play?). Also, write down what you will do while the groups work. How will you monitor their progress? What will you do with groups that finish early? What might you do with groups that are moving at a slower pace?

If you are using STAD, how will you present the material to your students? What handouts or supplements will the groups need when working together to review and learn the information? Have you designed the quiz or quizzes that you will need at the end of the group work? How much time will the groups need to learn the content?

If you are using Jigsaw, what preparation will the students need before the group work? How will you divide the task so students can become experts on one part of the material? What information will they use to build their expertise (e.g., handouts, Internet, books, etc.), and how will you facilitate their learning? How much time should you allow for the expert groups to work?

If you are using a Group Investigation, how will you present the general idea of the project so the students are interested in the topic? Have you posed the task in a clear statement that the students can understand? How can you facilitate the students as they divide the workload among the group members? How will they learn the information? Do you need to reserve a computer lab, library, telephone for interviews, etc.? How will the groups present their information?

Assessment

Reread the section on assessing cooperative learning, and determine how you might assess student learning. Consider how to assess their "social skills" and/or their understanding of the content.

CHAPTER REVIEW

Cooperative learning has at its core the idea that students must "pull their own weight" and work together to accomplish a task. The cooperative tasks are designed so that one person is not able to complete the group's task alone. By having the members individually accountable, the group members are positioned to help each other, work interdependently (and not independently), and learn more. Much of the research on cooperative learning has examined specific ideas for placing students in groups, assigning a task where they must work together, and promoting student learning in the process. Research in these areas reveals that when students cooperate together, and the emphasis on competition and individual achievement is decreased, student learning increases. One of the most consistent findings is that students of different racial or ethnic backgrounds gain in liking and respect for one another after working in cooperative teams. Cooperative learning has also been shown to increase classmates' acceptance of students who are traditionally marginalized because of low academic ability. Five "essential elements" of cooperative learning are:

1. positive interdependence
2. face-to-face interactions
3. group goals and individual accountability
4. interpersonal and small-group skills
5. group processing

Informal cooperative learning involves quickly formed groups that may work together for a few minutes or a whole class period. *Formal cooperative learning* groups work together from one class period to several weeks.

In this chapter, we have presented three common formal cooperative learning strategies for you to consider. Each strategy involves the important elements listed above (teacher-selected groups, positive interdependence, face-to-face interactions, group goals and individual accountability, interpersonal and small-group skills, and group processing):

1. student teams/achievement divisions
2. the jigsaw approach
3. group investigations

When students work in cooperative learning groups the classroom needs to be managed in a unique manner. When you monitor the groups, you are assessing both their group progress and each member's individual progress. Every member of a group should be able to explain both the group task and his individual part in accomplishing that task. As the teacher you will need to establish group norms and expectations. Using cooperative learning requires that you are willing to teach cooperative skills to your students. These skills may not be part of your content area, but they are critical if your students are to work interdependently.

Teachers need to assess the content learning that is taking place and they need to assess the social interactions and relationships of the students in the group. Many times teachers will need to intervene with a group to help reestablish expectations for interactions during group work, to assist in the division of the workload and tasks, and to facilitate students in understanding the content. *Group- and self-assessment* are effective tools for determining how effectively the groups worked together, and for having students reflect on their contributions to the group goals.

We believe that cooperative learning can be used to teach almost any content area. However, it is important for you to consider the following five factors when determining its usefulness for your classroom:

1. time
2. group formation
3. social skills development
4. clear task expectations
5. assessment

NOTE

1. This idea is adapted from the work of Zarnowski, 2003.

REFERENCES

Aronson, E., Blaney, N., Stephen, C., Sikes, J., & Snapp, M. (1978). *The jigsaw classroom.* Beverly Hills, CA: Sage.

Blosser, P. E. (1992). Using cooperative learning in science education. ERIC Bulletin, SE 053 432. Retrieved February 3, 2006 from http://www.stemworks.org/Bulletins/SEB92-1.html.

Cohen, E. G. (1994). *Designing groupwork: Strategies for the heterogeneous classroom.* New York: Teachers College Press.

Cohen, E., & Lotan, R. (1997). *Working for equity in heterogeneous classrooms: Sociological theory in practice.* New York: Teachers College Press.

Doda, N., George, P., & McEwin, K. (1987). 10 current truths about effective schools. *Middle School Journal, 18*(3), 3–5.

Heller, P., Keith, R., & Anderson, S. (1992). Teaching problem solving through cooperative grouping. Part 1: Group versus individual problem solving. *American Journal of Physics, 60*(7), 627–636.

InTime (2004). *Chapter one: Cooperative learning overview.* Retrieved February 8, 2006 from http://www.intime.uni.edu/coop_learning/ch1/types.htm.

Johnson, D. W., & Johnson, R. T. (1989, December–1990, January). Social skills for successful group work. *Educational Leadership, 47*(4), 29–33.

Johnson, D. W., & Johnson, R. T. (1991). What cooperative learning has to offer the gifted. *Cooperative Learning, 11*(3), 24–27.

Johnson, D. W., & Johnson, R. T. (1999). *Learning together and alone: Cooperative, competitive, and individualistic learning.* Boston: Allyn and Bacon.

Johnson, D. W., & Johnson, R. T. (2004). *Assessing students in groups: Promoting group responsibility and individual accountability.* Thousand Oaks, CA: Corwin.

Johnson, D. W., Johnson, R. T., & Holubec, E. J. (1994). *The nuts and bolts of cooperative learning.* Edina, MN: Interaction.

Johnson, D. W., Johnson, R. T., & Holubec, E. (1998). *Cooperation in the classroom.* Boston: Allyn and Bacon.

Johnson, D. W., Johnson, R. T., & Stanne, M. B. (2000, May). *Cooperative learning methods: A meta-analysis.* Retrieved April 6, 2006 from http://clcrc.com/pages/cl=methods.html.

Kagan, S. (1992). *Cooperative learning.* San Juan Capistrano, CA: Resources for Teachers.

Kohn, A. (1993). *Punished by rewards: The trouble with gold stars, incentive plans, A's, praise, and other bribes.* Boston, MA: Houghton Mifflin.

Kulik, J. A., & Kulik, C. L. C. (1987). Effects of ability grouping on student achievement. *Equity and Excellence, 23*, 22–30.

Kulik, J. A., & Kulik, C. L. C. (1991). Research on ability grouping: Historical and contemporary perspectives. Storrs, CT: University of Connecticut, National Research Center on the Gifted and Talented. (ERIC Document Reproduction Service No. ED 350 777).

Marzano, R. J., Pickering, D. J., & Pollock, J. E. (2001). *Classroom instruction that works: Research-based strategies for increasing student achievement.* Alexandria, VA: Association for Supervision and Curriculum Development.

Mitchell, S. N., Rosemary, R., Bramwell, F. G., Solnosky, A., & Lilly, F. (2004). Friendship and choosing groupmates: Preferences for teacher-selected vs. student-selected groupings in high school science classes. *Journal of Instructional Psychology.* Retrieved April 8, 2006 from http://www.findarticles.com/p/articles/mi_m0FCG/is_1_31/ai_n6073185.

Newmann, F. M., & Thompson, J. A. (1987, September). *Effects of cooperative learning on achievement in secondary schools: A summary of research*. (ERIC Document Reproduction Service No. ED 288 853).

Parker, W. C. (2005). *Social studies in elementary education*. (12th ed.). Upper Saddle River, NJ: Merrill/Prentice-Hall.

Sharan, Y., & Sharan, S. (1989, December–1990, January). Group investigation expands cooperative learning. *Educational Leadership, 47*(4), 17–19.

Slavin, R. (1993). Ability grouping in the middle grades: Achievement effects and alternatives. *Elementary School Journal, 93*, 535–552.

Slavin, R. E. (1983). *Cooperative learning*. New York: Longman.

Slavin, R. E. (1988, June). *Student team learning: An overview and practical guide*. Washington, DC: National Education Association.

Slavin, R. E. (1989, December–1990, January). Research on cooperative learning: Consensus and controversy. *Educational Leadership, 47*(4), 52–54.

Slavin, R. E. (1995). A model of effective instruction. *Educational Forum, 59*, 166–176.

Wiggins, G. (1990). The case for authentic assessment. *Practical Assessment, Research and Evaluation, 2*(2). Retrieved December 6, 2004 from http://PAREonline.net/getvn.asp?v=2&n=2.

Zarnowski, M. (2003). *History makers: A questioning approach to reading and writing biographies*. Portsmouth, NH: Heinemann.

9

SIMULATIONS, ROLE-PLAY, AND DRAMATIZATION

OVERVIEW

Pierre Cauchon, Bishop of Beauvais, waited anxiously for the jury to return with the verdict. He had been overseeing the trial of Joan of Arc for two days and was sure the verdict would be rendered soon. He wondered if the riveting testimony given by Nicolas Loiseieur would convince the jury that she was guilty of heresy or if they would be convinced by those that testified in her defense. As the jury filed in, the murmur in the courtroom dissolved into silence. "Have you reached a verdict?" Bishop Cauchon asked the jury foreman.

"We have sir. We find Joan of Arc to be ..."

About a week prior to "the verdict," Mr. Johnson had assigned each student in his world history class a role in the trial of Joan of Arc. A student jury was to decide if she was freed or burned at the stake. He explained that this was part of the culminating project for their unit on medieval Europe. Some students were assigned key roles because they had shown they were up to the challenge and responsible for the preparation. Others were selected for major roles randomly. Several were selected for the jury because they had a history of poor attendance and the role-play could continue if they were absent. He found detailed role responsibilities in a curriculum guide, but decided to include an essay at the end of role-play to better assess student learning. Now, as he looked at his classroom filled with students dressed in thrift-store medieval wear, he knew they had had fun—but he would wait for the essays to determine if the role-play was effective.

Using a simulation, role-play, or dramatization *can* be a fantastic experience. Students have fun and are engaged in learning. Teachers see a learning environment develop, just as they had hoped. Unfortunately, using highly participatory strategies like these can have a downside. Using an instructional strategy that involves a high degree of student interaction, participation, and autonomy can be frustrating. If you ask practicing teachers about using these strategies you will probably find mixed responses from both the weary and the excited. Some of the risks associated with this strategy include: students who see it as "dumb" and refuse to participate; students who feel uncomfortable performing anything seriously and will play the clown to be disruptive; classes that become out of control; students who fully participate and have fun but are uncertain if they learned anything. Of course, the rewards of enthusiastic, energetic, and effective teaching and learning are possible as well. It is also possible that this might just be *the* unique way to interest several hard-to-reach students in your class. As in many worthwhile endeavors there is a high degree of risk. Of course, we think the risk of trying is worth it, and so have included these strategies for you to investigate.

In this chapter we introduce three theatric strategies: *simulation, role-play*, and *dramatization*. These instructional strategies involve some aspect of the stage—a scene change, a particular role, or the use of scripted material. We will offer a description of these theatric strategies, propose procedures for planning and implementation, and discuss logistical concerns, classroom management, and assessment issues. Finally, we will propose guidelines to help you decide if these strategies are appropriate for the content of a lesson.

DEFINING THEATRIC STRATEGIES

If you have attended a play recently you will have noted the set designs, the performed roles by the actors, and the oral interpretation of scripts. These three aspects of stage communication are key to understanding and utilizing instructional theatric strategies. Fortunately for most of us, we don't need to become professional Shakespearian actors to be able to use these strategies in the classroom. Simulations, role-play, and dramatization that effectively create sets, establish roles, and utilize scripting can be important elements of learning in your classroom. Many times it may not be important to precisely determine if an activity is a simulation, role-play, or dramatization; there certainly can be overlap among these methods. However, an understanding of how these strategies are similar and different may help you choose one that best fits your objectives. A simple way to distinguish among the three is to remember that *simulation* focuses on the set design (change in environment), *role-play* focuses on the actor's role, and *dramatization* focuses on scripted dialogue.

Simulations allow students to experience simulated phenomena and then debrief about their reactions. They are more concerned with students reacting to the environment in which they find themselves than taking on a particular role or personality. Much like the creation of a set to establish a scene in a play, a simulation establishes an alternative environment within the classroom that reflects another scene of life. Part of the classroom may be turned into a space-craft or a covered wagon, for example. This environment may be reflective of something they could encounter in the real world (the stock market) or it may not (a colony on another planet). Students are asked to engage and interact with the alternative environment or with others situated within that environment. As you will see, this physical set change in itself does not necessarily make an activity a simulation.

A simulation will ask students to take on a functioning part within the alternative environment (a president, a farmer, an engineer, a waiter) and will give the student enough information (news reports, documents, maps, expert advice) about a specific issue or problem to be able to make appropriate deci-sions or interact with others. A simulation will not ask a student to change her personality but will ask her to deal with the responsibilities of her job or task within the situation or environment in which she finds herself. A person might become the president of a country but will not be asked to take on the values or attitudes of another person. She may be responsible for a particular part but will always keep her own personality. For example, a student may be asked to take the part of a school board member deciding a controversial curricular issue but will not be asked to play the personality of a particular member of the local school board.

In role-play students learn about and act as someone (or something) dif-ferent from themselves. This involves taking on the personality of a person in order to empathize, understand, or explore feelings, attitudes, conflicts, or values. Others may ask students to assume the characteristics of some type of matter (e.g., an atom) in order to learn about its structure or relationship with outside influences (e.g., heat). Role-play is more concerned with acting a part or imitation than it is with exploring an environment or situation. Role-play, as opposed to simulation, is usually brief and performed in front of an audience of classmates. Typically, the information provided to students would be related to the role to be played rather than the situation in which students find themselves. Simple examples of role-play would include having students act like atoms under extreme temperature changes, asking students to play various European leaders (such as Neville Chamberlain) during the Sudetenland crisis prior to World War II, or having students explore attitudes or values by choosing roles related to an instance of interpersonal conflict.

At times teachers will combine simulations and role play so that students experience a phenomenon as they are acting in a particular role or so that roles played by some students will impact the environment of the other students. For example, during a civil-rights lesson related to Harper Lee's *To Kill a Mocking-bird*, several members of the class might be asked to play the role of "enforcer" so that only boys can sharpen their pencils during class time. Another common example is that of a middle school classroom turned into a medieval feudal system: students are assigned roles (queen, jester, peasant, knight) in the feudal hierarchy.

Dramatization takes students one step closer to the stage. During this strategy, students act in a given role, during a scene, and often with a script. Using this technique can involve professionally written scripts or those written by the students themselves. Dramatization can be as simple as having volunteers do an oral interpretation of a text selection from a magazine, as involved as a culminating research project that scripts a historical event, as innovative as a pantomime, or as elaborate as a full-class play including props, costumes, and purchased scripts. Usually, this technique is used to help students empathize with a particular viewpoint or better understand an event, but it can also be effectively used to help improve student communication skills.

A DESCRIPTION OF THEATRIC STRATEGIES AND RESEARCH FINDINGS

Classroom teachers choose to use these strategies for several reasons, but primarily because they require a high degree of student participation in a somewhat atypical activity. For many this could lead to increased motivation and engagement. Simulation can be a particularly stimulating strategy since it requires complex thinking that involves difficult moral choices based upon values and beliefs (Bransford, Brown, & Cocking, 2000; Greenblat, 1987). These dramatic strategies can help create an environment in which to examine a variety of perspectives and develop empathy for those from different cultures (Fisher & Vander Laan, 2002). Teachers at times want to have their students become more physically involved in a lesson, and these strategies certainly discourage passivity. Many see the somewhat unusual nature of these activities as helpful in creating an environment to practice communication skills. Partly because of this, these strategies are particularly popular with students speaking English as a second language (ESL) and in world languages classrooms. While there are many possible reasons for using these strategies, the research literature suggests that the strengths of theatric strategies are important to student learning.

One of the strengths of these strategies is student engagement. While many find these strategies *fun,* the real goal is to get well beyond mere enjoyment. An activity that is "just for fun" is not a learning activity; it may be important for establishing a positive environment, but something more is needed to make it a learning activity. Most educators would agree that an important aspect of learning is engagement. An engaging strategy would be part of a lesson that is thought provoking, interesting, and energizing. In feedback from teacher workshops conducted by Wiggins and McTighe (2005) it was found that learners are engaged when work:

- is hands-on
- involves mysteries or problems
- provides variety
- offers opportunity to adapt, modify, or somehow personalize the challenge
- balances cooperation and competition, self and others
- is built on real-world or meaningful challenge
- uses provocative interactive approaches such as case studies, mock trials, and other types of simulated challenges
- involves real audiences or other forms of "authentic" accountability for the results (p. 195)

It is easily noted that theatric strategies encourage most if not all of these findings in one way or another. Each strategy will have its own unique strengths for developing an engaging lesson.

Role-play and simulation, especially, are highly interactive strategies that usually require authentic intellectual work—that is, work that requires application of knowledge and skills that go beyond a routine use of facts and procedures. This type of work moves a student from learning about an ecosystem, for example, toward learning to apply information to protect the environment while considering the concerns of other interest groups. This involves students using their own ideas to make decisions and solve problems. Researchers have found that interactivity and authentic intellectual work have a positive impact on student achievement. One study examined the link between different forms of instruction and learning. This study of elementary and middle school students and teachers in Chicago showed that interactive teaching methods were factors in increased learning in reading and math (Smith, Lee, & Newmann, 2001). Another study of middle school students examined the relationship between the type of assignment given in class and the quality of student work and achievement on standardized tests. Assignments were rated according to how "authentically" the students were asked to perform work. These researchers concluded that students from a variety of socioeconomic backgrounds benefit from assignments calling for more authentic intellectual work as shown by both classroom assessments and standardized tests (Newmann, Bryk, & Nagaoka, 2001). Several recently published reports on the use of theatric strategies by classroom teachers suggest that students benefit from the unique way in which they focus on analysis in a contextualized learning environment (Houser, 2005; Leonard, Davis, & Sidler, 2005; Steinbrink & Helmer, 2004).

Theatric strategies in general, but especially dramatization, make use of physical activity during the lesson. As you have seen in chapter 1, Gardner (1999) has developed a theory of multiple intelligences. This theory suggests that society tends to value those with linguistic or logical abilities while overlooking those with other skills. To the degree that school is a reflection of society at large this would imply that students with acting, musical, dancing, or other artistic skills are being overlooked in the classroom. Theatric strategies are particularly strong in the areas of bodily kinesthetic, musical, interpersonal, and intrapersonal intelligences. The use of strategies that utilize these intelligences would be beneficial to a diverse group of learners—which, of course, includes those from all classes. When Gardner refers to *intelligences* he is thinking of aptitude, not learning styles (Gardner, 2003). However, even if a learning style or preference isn't an intelligence, it could still be important to consider for the variety of students in your classroom. Learning preferences may very well include one of the theatric strategies.

Another benefit often associated with theatric strategies is improved communication skills and confidence building. These strategies not only offer an opportunity for practice, but, as Jones suggests, the "power of a simulation arises from the reality of the communication skills" (1995, p. 7). Learning about communication can also be achieved through drama. Scenes with scripts have a communication component that is very different from communication in a simulation or role-play. As we have noted, many times teachers use dramatization in connection with learning about, empathizing with, or understanding a person or event. At other times, the lesson objectives deal primarily with communication or preparing students to communicate their learning. In these instances teachers have found dramatization to be useful (Farris & Parke, 1993; Heathcote, 1992; Johnson, 1998).

CLASSROOM APPLICATION

Exercises that Improve Communication Skills

Theater games can be useful when focusing participants on one aspect of communication. One component of effective communication is the use of visuals. Gestures, facial expressions, and other visuals can help a speaker communicate more effectively. Another aspect is the use of verbals—variety in tone, rate, and volume help a person give meaning to words.

Consider this common scenario: A student is asked to present the results of an inquiry project to the class. His research is wonderful but the presentation is painful as the student stands in the front of the room glued to one spot on the floor, looking like his body has been stuck in an Ice Age glacier while never looking up from his papers and speaking in a monotone. The class loses interest. What can a teacher do?

Classroom Activity   One theater exercise that helps students practice visuals and verbals in communication is *dialogue*. Partners or groups of students are given one of the following dialogues:

1: Do you like them?
2: Well . . .
1: You *do* like them!
2: They're blue.
1: I love blue, don't you?
2: Blue is the color of the sky.
1: What's your point?
2: It's blue.
1: You're blue.
2: What are you implying?
1: Do you like them?

1: Oh! Look at that!
2: So cute.
1: Hi baby!
2: I don't think she's smiling at you.
1: How would you know?
2: I know these things.
1: Oh, please.
2: I'm serious!

Two students are asked to read (orally interpret) a dialogue while two other students use gestures and expressions to visually interpret it. Next, the partners switch so the readers try to visually interpret, and vice versa. However, this time the group tries to give the dialogue an alternative meaning. Try this exercise with students in your class.

Extension   Most teachers don't have a background in theater and may be a bit apprehensive to try or may not be aware of exercises that can help in this area. Three areas vital to effective communication are the use of visuals, vocals, and verbals. Oftentimes there are several people in class who have some theater background and can be used as "experts." Through personal class experience or by looking through resource materials, brainstorm theater exercises that might be helpful for your future class in developing communication skills.[1]

STEP-BY-STEP PROCEDURES FOR PLANNING AND IMPLEMENTATION

Theatric strategies vary widely in terms of purposes for the classroom. As we have indicated, a simulation would most likely serve a different purpose from that of a dramatization or role-play. We have discussed the distinct characteristics of these strategies to help you understand which might fit your purposes. In this section we discuss ways to effectively implement each of these strategies so that you can learn from the experiences of others who have been successful. Remember, using these strategies can be risky. Some teachers have been frightened off because they have had less-than-successful experiences. However, there is no reason to think you will not become one of the many who successfully use and enjoy these strategies regularly. Teaching adolescents isn't hard—it just isn't easy.

Simulation

The way the facilitator talks about the simulation can lead participants to have expectations and behaviors that do not reflect the simulated environment. One simulation expert suggests "appropriate" and "inappropriate" terminology for use during a simulation (Jones, 1995). You'll note that, in general, Jones is promoting language that helps communicate that the event is not play or game time, but instead an opportunity to participate as oneself (not play a role) in a unique situation that requires thoughtfulness and problem solving. The suggested language helps others understand that someone views the simulation as a way to interact with others in the way they would in the "real world." A participant wouldn't try to "win" unless the simulation environment caused her to think that was important in some way. She wouldn't act like another person unless the simulated environment required it. For example, if the simulation asks groups of students to give advice to the U.S. president and the Soviet premier during the Cuban Missile Crisis, they would not be told they were going to play a game where they will role-play political advisors. Nor would they be told that the team that gives the best advice will win.

While use of a specific word may not sabotage your simulation, the words do reflect underlying attitudes about what you are trying to accomplish and can be important. Below is a list of terms (adapted from Jones, 1995, p. 14) for your consideration:

Appropriate Terms	Inappropriate Terms
simulation, activity, event	game, drama, role-play, exercise
participant	player, actor, puzzler, trainee, student
facilitator, organizer	teacher, trainer, instructor
behavior, function, profession	playing, acting, staging
role (functional)	role (acting a part)
real-world responsible behavior	winning (losing) the game
real-world responsible ethics	point scoring, just for fun
professional conduct	performing the game or exercise

From Jones, 1995, p. 14.

When implementing simulation it is important for you, the future teacher, to recognize that your role has changed. No longer are you the know-it-all behind the desk with all the correct answers. During a simulation the teacher will likely have four facilitating roles (Joyce, Weil, & Calhoun, 2000):

1. *Explainer.* At the outset the class will need to know how to participate in the simulation. Students need to know the general goals, context, and environmental particulars that make up the simulation. Students won't need to know everything about the experience, as much will occur that cannot be predicted. There will be plenty of questions to answer, however.

2. *Referee.* During the simulation, someone will need to help negotiate disputes or make decisions about the simulation that involve the group. This should already be built into the simulation but nonetheless such intervention may be necessary. This should be done in as limited and nonintrusive a way as possible.

3. *Coach.* According to Joyce, Weil, and Calhoun (2000) the teacher should be prepared to intercede as coach to assist participants when necessary. This supportive component would assist the learning during the simulation. However, Jones (1995) argues that a teacher should not intrude into the simulation as coach. There would be no "coach" at a business meeting, or at a United Nations meeting, or at most real-world events. Coaching would disrupt the student "ownership" of the simulation and be counterproductive. We pass this information on to you along with the reminder that a simulation is an *untaught event*, and adolescents may need some prompting.

4. *Discussion leader.* At the completion of the simulation it is important to have a debriefing time. The teacher will need to be prepared to facilitate this discussion.

Most simulations come with clear instructions and step-by-step procedures. There are at least four common phases that each simulation should go through (Joyce, Weil, & Calhoun, 2000). The first phase is *orientation*, during which the teacher presents the simulation overview and explains the learning objectives for the simulation. The second phase involves *organizing* the simulation; in this phase the teacher establishes the simulated environment by explaining rules, assigning roles, and explaining the type of decisions that may need to be made. Some teachers will hold an abbreviated practice session if they feel some students may not completely understand. During the third phase the simulation is *operational* and there may be opportunities for feedback or time for metacognitive reflection. The final phase, *debriefing*, is one that is sometimes overlooked but is essential for effective simulation; during this phase students are given the opportunity to summarize and analyze events and offer insights while comparing their perceptions with those of other students. Students are also asked to discuss how the simulation compared to the real world. Finally, students are brought back to the learning objectives to discuss how the simulation helped them learn. This would also be a good time to discuss ways the simulation could be improved for future classes.

Key Concepts for Simulation Procedure Allow for and expect mistakes or errors of fact made by students. These can be recorded and dealt with during the debriefing if they are not addressed by others within the simulation. Also keep in mind the following:

A simulation is an untaught event.

The teacher should let the simulation run its course, even if it is heading in an unintended direction. Again, this can be dealt with at the debriefing.

Resist the temptation to become involved or to intercede. Sometimes, of course, it is necessary to intercede, but try to stay out of things.

A debriefing time at the end is vital.

A metacognitive time is helpful during or after a simulation.

Simulation is not a game and not about winning or losing. It is possible that winning or losing might be a natural part of the simulated environment (i.e., the stock market or an election), but winning should not be a fixation of students during the simulation.

A simulation strategy involves the reproduction of a simulated environment not a reproduction of characters as in a role-play.

Role-Play

As we have noted, role-play takes us one step closer to theater. Because this strategy isn't quite as free-flowing as a simulation it probably isn't as complicated. It does, however, have its own set of issues and should be considered carefully. Shaftel and Shaftel (1967) suggest nine phases for conducting role-play for learning about personal and social dimensions of education. For example, this model would be good if you wanted students to explore their feelings or attitudes about an interpersonal conflict at school. These phases can also be of benefit for teachers choosing to use role-play for other types of objectives but may need to be modified:

1. *Warming up.* A problem is identified or introduced and questions posed to the class that help focus students on key issues.
2. *Selecting participants*: The roles are analyzed and volunteers are selected.
3. *Setting the stage:* The participants show they understand their roles and ask questions.
4. *Preparing the observers:* The peer observers and the teacher decide what to observe and assign focused tasks.
5. *Enacting:* Role-play is executed.
6. *Discussion and evaluation:* The class or small group reviews the action of the role-play, discusses major focus areas with observers, and develops modification ideas for next phase.
7. *Reenactment:* Participants play modified roles or extend role-play to suggested alterations.

8. *Discussion and evaluation:* Repeat phase 6.
9. *Sharing and generalizing the experience:* The class or small group relates the role-play exercise to the real world and explores principles of behavior.

Dramatization

Unless you plan to be a theater teacher, you will be less concerned about the quality of the acting and more about what students are learning about your subject. When planning for dramatization we suggest you consider the following guidelines.

Objectives   The reason you are asking students to perform should be very clear to you and stated in your objectives. Why are you using this strategy?

Class Environment   Creating an environment in class that supports and enhances this strategy is key. This is discussed further in the "Classroom Management Issues" section of this chapter.

Time   It is usually best to think of this strategy in terms of skits rather than plays. Your curricular schedule will probably limit your time, but you will also need to consider the attention and interest level of the students you have in class.

Props   Use limited props as needed, but don't become overwhelmed by this detail, as students can easily use imaginative props. Keep an eye out at garage sales for odd looking props and have students bring props from home. Simple props such as a hat or umbrella can add a lot and may be all that is needed.

Scripts   You can find scripts on the Internet, from creatively like-minded teachers, or from published sources; or you can use scripts written by you or your students. Also, remember that oral interpretation, a form of dramatization, makes use of any text such as scenes from novels, magazine or newspaper articles, diaries, or movie scripts.

Casting   It is probably best to ask for volunteers for the various available roles. Assign key parts to those who are motivated and interested and not necessarily to those who are the best actors. More limited roles can go to those who are less interested or less willing. It is usually not in the interest of all involved to require a student to participate in dramatization, but keep in mind that many adolescents will need encouragement to try.

Rehearsal   Make it as serious or as light-hearted as you think is warranted for the script and the particular students involved. Be sure that if it is a group project all the students are interpreting the script and the expectations for the assignment in the same way. Hurt feelings occur when several in a group see this presentation as meaningful and personal and one person wants to make a joke out of it.

Performance Be sure to give the audience the expectations for the dramatization. Is it a spoof? Is it about a serious personal issue? The classroom audience should know your behavioral expectations in advance based upon your expectations for the dramatization.

Debriefing Consider taking some time following the drama for a large group debriefing. It may help to have a guided, written, individual reflection time prior to the debriefing time.

CLASSROOM APPLICATION

Examining a Theatric Idea

Decide if the following medieval fair—adapted from an idea created by middle school core (English/social studies) teachers at Fairhaven Middle School in Bellingham, Washington—is a simulation, a role-play exercise, a dramatization, or a combination of these; explain why. What ideas do you really like? What ideas do you have that might improve this idea or add your unique twist to the idea? (How would you select the king? How much time would you give students to prepare and participate? Can you describe any other contest ideas?) Can you think of an idea similar to this one for your content area or for high school?

THE MEDIEVAL FAIR

Kingdoms:

Each seventh grade teacher will have her two core classes choose:
    a name for their kingdom
    a symbol for their kingdom
    royalty for their kingdom: a queen, a king (royalty must also meet qualifications for knighthood)

Knighthood:

Knighthood will be open to both girls and boys. Requirements for knighthood are:
        all assignments for a three-week period in core classes must be turned in
        a 3.0 grade point average
        demonstration of knightly conduct: respect, courtesy, and promptness

Heraldry:

Each kingdom will have its own symbol for its own coat of arms. Each kingdom will be responsible for making a banner displaying its coat of arms. In addition, each knight and each student will have his own coat of arms, which must include the symbol of the kingdom.

Activities:

1. *Jousting Contest (Outside)*
   One must qualify as a knight to participate in the jousting contest.
   Equipment for jousting:
   Steeds: big wheels
   Swords: rubber bats
   Armor: football helmets, shields
   Target: egg
   Shield: to be provided by participants, made of cardboard only!
   It should be 18″ x 24″ and decorated with the knight's own coat of arms.
   Jousters will make two passes on big wheels; then may engage in open combat until one breaks the egg of the opponent. Jousting contest will be an elimination contest until we are down to three people. At this time, the kings and queens may challenge one of the knights to a jousting contest until there is but one unvanquished foe.

2. *Magic Acts*

3. *Juggling: Exhibition*

4. *Riddles and Court Jesters: Exhibition*

5. *Music*
   Gregorian Chants, instrumental, vocal (a cappella)

6. *Plays*
   Romeo and Juliet
   Pyramus and Thisbe

7. *Poetry*
   Selections to be read by students, including medieval poetry. Selections include:
   Shakespearean sonnets
   Beowoulf
   Chaucer's *Canterbury Tales*
   The Song of Roland
   Tales of 1001 Arabian Nights

8. *Chess/Checker/Backgammon Tournaments*
   To be held in the kingdoms at the teacher's discretion.

9. *Excalibur*
   Costumes: knight, lady, jester/minstrel, monk, nun, beggar, wizard (Merlin), squire

Also consider non-European costumes of the period: Japanese feudal period costumes (daimyo, samurai), Arabian

The Excalibur event: Split the log and gain royalty. To qualify for a
chance to swing the ax and split the log, the royal adzman will require
five push-ups. Each qualifying contestant will have just one chance.

Learning Stations:

Each classroom has learning stations that relate to at least one of the fol-
lowing topics:
Castles
Siege weapons
Catapult competitions
The Church
Cathedrals
Monasteries
Stained glass
Village life
Manor life
City life
Knights
Feudalism
Music
The Plague
Dress and food
The Islamic world
The Byzantine world
Crusades
Guilds
Torture
Merchants
Chivalry
Gregorian and Julian calendars
Medieval names
Education
Science
Entertainment
Medieval holidays
Falconry
Heraldry
Architecture
Monk Day
The medieval banquet*

---

* Created by teachers at Fairhaven Middle School, Bellingham, WA.

LOGISTICAL CONCERNS FOR THEATRIC STRATEGIES

Probably the biggest logistical concern about using these strategies is the ability to acquire appropriate and interesting ideas. Below we offer resources for ideas related to simulation, role-play, and dramatization that have been used by classroom teachers. There are many websites online that contain helpful ideas. We have listed several that allow you to search by the name of the theatric strategy—you will find hundreds of ideas. We have also listed one example of a developer and publisher of educational curriculum, Scholastic's Tom Snyder Productions, which has a good reputation for producing computerized simulations and role-play exercises. You could search online for other educational production companies that produce high quality simulations, role-play exercises, and dramatizations for a price. These products often have a free trial period after which they must be purchased.

Educational Production Company:

Tom Snyder Productions (http://www.tomsnyder.com)

Social Studies or Language Arts: Decisions, Decisions 5.0
Ancient Empires
Feudalism
Building a Nation
The Constitution
Immigration
Colonization
Revolutionary Wars
The Environment
The Cold War
Prejudice
Lying, Cheating, Stealing
On the Campaign Trail
Town Government
Substance Abuse
Violence in the Media
Mathematics
Adrift!
Cliffbound!
Fire!
Lost!
Emergency!
Stakeout!
Prime Time Math: Grades 4–7 Collection
Prime Time Math: Grades 6–9 Collection

Science
    Endangered Species
    Hidden in Rocks
    Safe Water
    Rainforest Researchers
    Great Solar System Rescue
    Great Ocean Rescue
    Nature: Virtual Serengeti

Free Online Resources

Teaching English as a Second Language
    http://iteslj.org/links/TESL/Lessons/Role_Plays/

Reluctant Writers
    http://www.readwritethink.org/lessons/lesson_view.asp?id=217

Free Databases That Can Be Searched by Theatric Strategy

    http://www.learnnc.org/lessons
    http://www.lessonplanspage.com
    http://www.eduref.org/Virtual/Lessons
    http://teachers.net/

CLASSROOM MANAGEMENT ISSUES

The environment of your classroom is key to using theatric strategies successfully. You do not need to be a drama coach; you do not need to be able to recite the major themes of any of Shakespeare's plays; but you do need to have an environment established in your classroom that encourages creativity, active learning, student responsibility, and experimentation. In this section we will discuss this type of environment in connection with simulation, role-play, and dramatization.

One of the reasons to use these strategies is to promote a lesson-design philosophy that encourages intrinsic rather than extrinsic motivation. Theatric strategies have natural attributes that encourage student-generated enthusiasm and interest. A classroom in which students have been passive and consistently motivated by external factors will have a difficult time instantaneously transforming itself for a simulation. Warning: student interns may be set up for failure if trying these strategies in this type of a classroom environment. In classes where students are used to passive learning it is a good idea to bring students along with smaller activities. For example, before using a full role-play try a series of theater games such as that suggested in the "Classroom Application" section above. Take the time to thoughtfully build the commonplace of *milieu* as described in chapter 4.

A classroom in which these strategies will thrive will be one where a climate of trust and support has been established. This is important, as students are taking a risk and may be made to feel uncomfortable. A classroom climate that is energized, fun, and supports risk takers is necessary. Students need an environment where they know it is okay to make mistakes and learn from them. Theatric strategies will thrive in an environment where creativity has been encouraged and supported—where it would not be seen as unusual or strange to play a quick theater game or do some other unusual activity as a lesson "hook." This would be an environment in which students' original work is proudly displayed or presented at parent nights.

Theatric strategies are active strategies. Sometimes students get a bit feisty and noisy. Other teachers may wonder what is going on in your room, and if you are able to "control" your students. You will need to come to peace with that. As with test pilots flying at supersonic speeds, you will at times "push the envelope." This will require you to have acquired skill in efficiently dealing with off-track behaviors and helping students understand what behaviors are acceptable during a simulation but not in other classroom settings. You will need to clearly and consistently let students know behavioral expectations during a theatric strategy. They will probably need to be reminded what you want them to accomplish and what type of behavior is appropriate and inappropriate. New teachers sometimes have difficulty with this consistency and send mixed messages. This causes an increase in inappropriate behavior and the "tiger-by-the-tail" syndrome.

Clearly stated expectations are important to maintaining a positive environment. During an early phase of each of these strategies students should be told the purpose of using the strategy as well as expectations during certain events. For example, hurt feelings or misunderstandings will occur if some students are operating in a simulation mode (not playing another personality) and other students are operating in role-play mode (pretending they are someone else and acting with another's values or beliefs). During dramatization, some students will want to be comedians while others will want to be dramatic. These differences will need to be resolved early to avoid conflict and withdrawal.

When using theatric strategies it will be important for you to consider effective ways to form and work with groups. In chapter 8, "Cooperative Learning," we discussed strategies for holding individuals within a group accountable as well as considerations for group formation. Individuals within the group that have special needs such as ESL students will need to be given careful consideration. This might include an evaluation of levels of English proficiency before assigning roles or tasks in a simulation or role-play exercise. Students having special needs with reading English may need additional time in advance to look through scripts or other directions that are not usually given to other students. This is especially important if it avoids awkward or embarrassing situations for these students in front of the class.

We will now turn your attention to techniques to use while assessing these strategies. A scoring guide can also include criteria from the area of classroom management. You should consider including credit for these process learnings, as described in the next section.

APPROPRIATE ASSESSMENT TECHNIQUES TO USE WITH SIMULATION, ROLE-PLAY, AND DRAMATIZATION

Assessing theatric strategies presents its own set of unique issues, but we can also draw from general assessment ideas that are common to other instructional strategies. If you have well-thought-out objectives in mind they will help with assessment focus, just as they do with other strategies. For example, if the purpose of using a dramatization is to help students learn to *empathize* with different perspectives during a conflict the assessment should focus on whether students learned to empathize. Can they share the thoughts, feelings, or emotions of several different people after the dramatization? Can they say, "Oh, this is why that was such a terribly difficult decision"? Sometimes, however, when using unique teaching strategies the process of learning, rather than the intended learning, is evaluated. In other words, should how well a person acts during a dramatization be included in a rubric if acting skill is not the intended learning? It would depend upon where the objectives are guiding the lesson.

This is not to say these process learnings (performance, participation, responsibility) can't be included in an assessment in some minor way, but they should not be a focus of the assessment unless they are part of the lesson objectives. The process could be assessed to the degree that you are assessing participation or responsible behavior in the class as a whole. Most classroom teachers aren't as concerned with how a student performs during simulation, role-play, or dramatization. It is likely that knowledge or skills associated with the course content are the focus of the lesson objective. Because of this it would follow that a well-thought-out assessment design would probably include a simple rubric related to process objectives (performance, participation, responsibility) as well as another means of collecting assessment data related to the lesson objectives. For example, a U.S. history teacher has an objective that states, *After participating in a simulation students will be able to evaluate, according to the rubic provided, three perspectives on the dropping of the Bomb at the close of World War II.* To assess the *process* the teacher designs a simple rubric that is to be completed first by the students and then completed by the teacher. He does this to hold students accountable for their individual work within the groups and because the course syllabus states that participation is expected. An example follows.

SIMULATION RUBRIC

Student Name: _____

1 = Poor
2 = Average
3 = Good
4 = Excellent

Performance

Performed duties of assigned team role.

Participation

Communicated with others to enhance the simulation.

Responsibility

Work was completed and presented on schedule.
Total _____/12

To assess the *lesson objective* the teacher requires a persuasive paper, accompanied by the following rubric:

PERSUASIVE PAPER RUBRIC

Criteria	1	2	3	4
Position and perspectives	Position and perspectives unclear	Position stated, poorly maintained, missing viewpoints	Position clearly stated and maintained, missing other viewpoints	Position clearly stated and maintained while showing understanding of two other perspectives
Supporting evidence	Unrelated or unreliable evidence	Limited or questionable sources	Clearly related and reliable but limited	Clearly supportive and sufficient evidence
The six traits of writing[2]	Need for revision outweighs strengths	Strengths and need for revision about equal	Strengths outweigh weaknesses; minor revisions	Shows control and skill

As we have shown, theatric strategies are a way that teachers can reach students that may be hard to reach. It would follow that the assessment techniques used with these strategies would be unique and address what students are learning from multiple perspectives. Often, teachers will look at products from the experience to help assess student learning. For example, at one high school as part of a simulation students made tools that Native Americans were using at a given time period. The rubric used by the teacher required students to show an understanding of techniques (drying a deer skin), needs (making a fish hook), and materials of the period (bone or rock), appropriate artistic symbols (what anthropologists have discovered), as well as a certain amount of creativity (making a basket). Another teacher had students choose the type of product from the simulation they would like to create to show their learning as guided by a rubric. This can be a good opportunity for student involvement in choosing how they would like to show what they are learning.

GUIDELINES FOR DECIDING IF THEATRIC STRATEGIES ARE APPROPRIATE

As we have noted, there are a number of reasons that theatric strategies are thought to be useful. They are thought to be interesting and motivating strategies that require a high degree of student participation in a way that is uncommon. Simulations, in particular, can be intellectually stimulating, as they require complex thinking that involves difficult moral choices based upon values and beliefs.

These strategies can help create an environment in which to examine a variety of perspectives while encouraging active, physical involvement. Many teachers see these as helpful in creating an environment conducive to practicing communication skills. As with all instructional strategies, the theatric strategy a teacher chooses should reflect the purpose of the lesson—the objectives— because one strategy will be better suited to certain purposes than another. For example, in general, while simulation may require a high degree of analysis or evaluative skills, dramatization may not. As you look at your objectives, see if any of the above strengths of theatric strategies align with what you are trying to accomplish. As you revisit the understanding by design model (Wiggins & McTighe, 2005) in chapter 3 you will recall that the model calls for this type of "backward design."

Simulations, role-play, and dramatization are some of the most effective strategies available to ESL and world language teachers. Based upon the *total physical response* premise that students learn best when they become physically involved in learning a new language, theatric strategies provide an ideal way to accomplish this. They encourage thinking and creativity as they enable students to develop and practice a new language in a fun way. However, many ESL students come from backgrounds where they are used to direct instruction.

They may be uncomfortable trying these strategies at first because of this and their perceived English language deficiencies.

Sensitive issues can cause unique difficulties for theatric strategies. Many teachers will avoid a student performance about a sensitive issue for fear that some students will react in immature and insensitive ways. For example, middle school students with the "giggles" may embarrass themselves and others by unthinking, innocent laughing at friends during a performance about the Holocaust. It would be wise to consider the maturity level of your class before using these strategies with sensitive issues. For example, it would probably be better to use dramatization rather than simulation with a group of immature students if the subject were civil rights—or to choose a different strategy altogether.

MAKING IT WORK IN YOUR CONTENT AREA

With a partner, create an outline for a theatric strategy lesson for your future classroom. If possible, work on a lesson that is related to a unit you are developing. The lesson might be symbolic, or an attempt to re-create/simulate an actual event or occurrence. You need to be prepared to do this by fully thinking through the process yourself. (Note: you could do this activity by gathering a specific simulation, role-play, or dramatization exercise from resources available to you, or this can be done in a more general way without a specific simulation/role-play/dramatization in hand.) The following items should be included in your lesson plan:

1. Lesson Objectives
2. Simulation Preparation
   Your preparation: Based on the objectives listed above, what needs to be done before the simulation/role-play/dramatization exercise? Consider the roles of students and teacher, the procedures that will be followed, the rules of the activity, background information that you will need, handouts, and "stuff" that will be used during the activity. Some of this is material preparation; some is thinking through the logistics.
   Student preparation: Within what unit of study will this fit? What background do the students need? How will they learn/gain this background information? What will precede this lesson? What will follow? How will students learn their roles, context of the activity, procedures?
3. Initiation and Direction
   Describe how you will begin the lesson. Set up the activity for the students, direct them to the proper spots, initiate the day/activity so the students know what is necessary for this to be a successful simulation/role-play/dramatization.
4. Describing the Scenario
   How will you explain to the students the scenario in which they will be operating? You have already told them what they will be doing (simulation/role-play/dramatization), but now you tell them about the specifics.

5. Assigning Roles

Describe, briefly, how students will be assigned to different roles. Consider doing these assignments "on purpose" rather than randomly, and having the purpose be to enhance student learning in some way (e.g., mixing students by gender, or across ability levels, etc.). How will the students know the part(s) to which they are assigned?

6. Enactment

Describe what should happen during the simulation/role-play/dramatization. What will the students be doing? What will YOUR duties be to ensure that it goes as planned?

7. Debriefing

Describe how you plan to examine what happened, examine emotions, draw parallels, and connect the simulation/role-play/dramatization to the content/curriculum and, of course, to life outside of the classroom. Script a good portion of this—at least scripting the questions you could ask after the activity ends.

CHAPTER REVIEW

Simulation, role-play, and dramatization involve some aspect of the theater—a scene change, a particular role, or the use of scripted material. *Simulation* allows students to experience a simulated environment. In *role-play* students learn about and act as someone (or something) different from themselves. *Dramatization* gives students an opportunity to act in a given role, during a scene, and often with a script.

Educators have found that strengths of theatric strategies include student engagement, interactivity, the requirement of application of knowledge and skills, and complex thinking that involves difficult moral choices based upon values and beliefs. Theatric strategies can also be motivating, create environments in which to examine a variety of perspectives, encourage physical involvement, and allow for the practice of communication skills.

In this chapter we have presented models for effective implementation of these strategies, as well as resources from which to glean ideas for your classroom. This chapter has given suggestions about classroom management issues that are unique or have an impact on implementing these strategies as well as suggested assessment techniques associated with simulation, role-play, and dramatization.

NOTES

1. This is adapted from the ideas of Robert Keiper, Assistant Professor of Secondary Education at Western Washington University.
2. The six traits of writing are ideas, organization, word choice, sentence fluency, conventions, and presentation, and they can be found at the Northwest Regional Education Library website (http://www.nwrel.org; retrieved March 10, 2006).

REFERENCES

Bransford, J. D., Brown, A. L., & Cocking, R. R. (Eds.). (2000). *How people learn: Brain, mind, experience, and school*. Washington, DC: National Academy Press.

Farris, P. J., & Parke, J. (1993). To be or not to be: What students think about drama. *Clearinghouse, 66*(4), 231–234.

Fisher, J., & Vander Laan, S. (2002). Improving approaches to multicultural education: Teaching empathy through role-playing. *Multicultural Education, 9*, 25–27.

Gardner, H. (1999). *Intelligence reframed: Multiple intelligences for the twenty-first century*. New York: Basic Books.

Greenblat, C. S. (1987). *Designing games and simulations*. Beverly Hills, CA: Sage.

Heathcote, D. (1992). Excellence in teaching: What it takes to do things well. *Teaching Theatre, 4*(1), 3–6.

Johnson, A. P. (1998). How to use creative dramatics in the classroom. *Childhood Education, 75*(1), 2–82.

Jones, K. (1995). *Simulations: A handbook for teachers and trainers* (3rd ed.). East Brunswick, NJ: Nichols.

Joyce, B., Weil, M., & Calhoun, E. (2000). *Models of teaching* (6th ed.). Boston: Allyn and Bacon.

Newmann, F., Bryk, A., & Nagaoka, J. (2001). *Authentic intellectual work and standardized tests: Conflicts or coexistence?* Chicago: Consortium on Chicago School Research. Retrieved March 1, 2006 from http://www.consortium-chicago.org/.

Smith, J., Lee, V., & Newmann, F. (2001). *Instruction and achievement in Chicago elementary schools*. Chicago: Consortium on Chicago School Research. Retrieved March 1, 2006 from http://www.consortium-chicago.org/.

Shaftel, F., & Shaftel, G. (1967). *Role playing of social values*. Englewood Cliffs, NJ: Prentice-Hall.

Wiggins, G., & McTighe, J. (2005). *Understanding by design* (2nd ed.). Alexandra, VA: Association for Supervision and Curriculum Development.

10

CLASSROOM DISCUSSION AND DEBATE

OVERVIEW

During discussions, students and teacher interact with one another by listening, thinking, and sharing. As the participants discuss a topic, they think about different points of view and new information. Although discussion is a useful instructional strategy to help students learn in any content area, its dependence on social interactions and participation also encourages students to "learn how to talk" with others. This is a powerful skill for citizens in a democracy, where one of the many roles is a willingness and ability to interact with others on matters of common concern (Engle & Ochoa, 1988; Gross & Zeleny, 1958; Hess, 2000; Parker, 1996). Contradicting this positive view of discussion, however, are research findings that suggest it is rarely used in America's classrooms. Recitation persists in classrooms, despite its frequent criticisms (Cazden, 1988; Goodlad, 1984; Hoetker & Ahlbrand, 1969; Stodolsky, Ferguson, & Wimpelberg, 1981), and despite the fact that teachers claim to use discussion frequently. As an example, researchers have observed that a teacher talked for 87.8% of the class period during the portion of the lesson he claimed used discussion (Swift & Gooding, 1983). Before exploring discussion further, it is important to briefly clarify the difference between classroom discussion and recitation. Recitation and discussion are two methods of instruction with different characteristics. *Recitation* is characterized (Bellack, Kliebard, Hyman, & Smith, 1966; Gall & Gall, 1990; Wilen & White, 1991) as a teacher-dominated classroom activity, typically entailing an interaction pattern between teacher and student similar to:

teacher-initiated statement/question → student response → teacher feedback/evaluation

Good (1983) defines recitation as a "traditional learning exercise and teaching procedure in which students repeat orally or explain material learned by individual study or previously presented by the teacher and in response to questions raised by the teacher" (p. 478). In contrast to this, Wilen and White (1991) define *discussion* as a "structured conversation in which participants work cooperatively to present, examine, compare, and understand often diverse views about an academic topic or issue" (p. 492).

A DESCRIPTION OF THE STRATEGY AND RESEARCH FINDINGS

Classroom discussion serves several educational purposes because it is a unique form of classroom talk. Discussion requires students and teacher to talk back and forth at a highly cognitive and affective level. Dillon (1994) has examined classroom discussion, and notes that what students and teachers talk about is "an issue, some topic that is in question for them. Their talk consists of advancing and examining different proposals over the issue" (p. 7).

In a summary of literature about the use of discussion in instruction, Gall (1985) has reported that discussion is an effective way to promote higher-level thinking, develop student attitudes, and advance student capability for moral reasoning. In short, discussion provides opportunities for student thoughtfulness about a chosen topic or issue. Attempts to suggest the necessary and sufficient conditions for discussion have been made (Bridges, 1979, 1987; Haroutunian-Gordon, 1991; Miller, 1992), as have characteristics of different types of discussions (Alvermann, O'Brien, & Dillon, 1990; Gall & Gall, 1990; Larson, 1997; Roby, 1988), and the influence of teacher questions on classroom discussion (Dillon, 1994; Hunkins, 1995; Roby, 1988). These attempts characterize discussion as a structured activity in which the process of discussing encourages students to pool ideas and information and to illuminate alternative perspectives. Students develop skills and abilities in civil discourse, criticism, and argument. These skills are extremely important for two reasons. First, democratic life requires citizens to interact using civil, critical discourse to make policies about important public issues (Barber, 1989; Parker, 1996). The classroom holds the potential for students of different race, gender, social status, and ability to learn how to engage one another in discussions about issues of common concern (Dewey, 1916/1985). Second, discussion requires students to learn the content so that they can talk about it.

Teachers who do use discussion, however, use it as a label for many types of teacher-student interactions (Dillon, 1984, Hess, 2000; Larson, 1997, 2000, 2003; Roby, 1988). Regardless of the type of discussion, certain attributes must be apparent if a discussion is to promote student learning. Bridges has examined the use of classroom discussion (1979, 1987) and established a list of conditions that are necessary if people are to learn from a discussion. Bridges (1987, p. 34) has theorized that there are three defining guidelines or conditions for discussion. Each is presented below with a parenthetical rephrasing to help clarify his points:

1. Discussion involves a general disposition on behalf of members of the group to listen, to consider, and to be responsive to what others are saying. (You cannot have a discussion if the members of the group are unwilling or unable to listen.)
2. Discussion involves members of the group contributing from their different perspectives, opinions or understanding. (You cannot have a discussion if everybody is saying the same thing or nobody is saying anything.)
3. Discussion is guided by the central purpose of developing the group's knowledge, understanding and/or judgment on the matter under discussion. (It is different from group talk, from negotiation of power, from debate aimed at winning votes or defeating one's adversary, from group therapy—none of which has this central purpose.)

According to Bridges, discussion must be a rule-governed, structured activity so that it encourages collaborative and exploratory development of hypotheses, the pooling of ideas and information, and the illumination of alternative perspectives. It also develops students' skills in criticism and argument. Thought of in this manner, the three necessary and sufficient conditions for discussion provide a disposition, a set of general rules, and a structure to classroom discussion. Bridges suggests that discussions contribute to discussants' understanding of topics by expanding each discussant's information on a topic with information from other discussants; fostering different perspectives on a topic; providing opportunities for discussants to present alternative ideas about a topic; providing opportunities for other discussants to criticize, accept, or refute these alternative ideas; and encouraging mutual modifications among discussants' opinions to produce a group decision or consensus. Group interaction is the important component for each of these as it shapes and directs the exploration of a topic.

STEP-BY-STEP PROCEDURES FOR PLANNING AND IMPLEMENTING THE STRATEGY

Teachers use different forms of discussion to serve different purposes in the classroom (Larson, 2000). Whole-class discussions will serve a different learning objective than will small-group discussions. Classroom discussions will vary according to the purpose of the discussion, use of questions, and the issue being discussed. This chapter examines six effective types of discussion. While each serves different purposes, each is appropriate for examining current, controversial, and/or perennial issues. Teachers report that simply planning to have a whole-class discussion with students often is too vague an aspiration. Very few students actually talk, and valuable class time is often wasted with irrelevant comments and student behavior problems. The six types of discussion described below are "tried and true" ways to promote student involvement in classroom discussions. They will be effective in both middle school and high school classrooms. They provide specific structure for engaging students in small-group and whole-class discussions. The six types are:

1. taking a stand
2. the issues/values continuum
3. the future's wheel discussion
4. the fishbowl discussion
5. the structured academic controversy
6. the electronic threaded discussion

While debate has completely different learning objectives than discussion, it is also examined at the end of this chapter. It is important for you to know how to use this strategy as well. By identifying seven different strategies for helping students talk with each other about course content (six types of discussion and debate) you can better ensure that the strategy is aligned with your learning objectives.

Taking a Stand

This type of discussion is useful with large classes (Larson, 1997; Oliver & Newmann, 1972). It is best used when teachers want students to consider opposing viewpoints around a controversial issue. The primary focus is to clearly and systematically discuss public policy issues in the classroom by aiming conversations "at *persuasion*, *problem solving* and *clarification* when discussants take a stand on public issues" (Oliver & Newmann, 1972, p. 6; emphasis in the original). Students consider the pros and cons of an issue, devise solutions to problems, and determine a specific policy or action to implement. During policy discussions, the teacher continues to pose questions that encourage students to follow a rational process, consider multiple points of view, and decide on a course of action that the class advocates as a group. Discussants have to think on two levels. First, they must choose a position about an issue and think of reasons to defend it; second, they must reflect on the discussion process itself (the process of verbally interacting with classmates). A *taking a stand* discussion has five steps:

Present an Overview of the Issue, and the Opposing Sides   Begin the discussion by presenting an overview of the issue. For example, provide a handout describing the predominant reasons for the controversy, without detailing specifics of the controversy. Phrase the issue as a question requiring a choice or a decision for action so students form an opinion on the issue by responding to the question. Following this, present two opposing sides of the issue in a *point/counterpoint* format. After the overview, point, and counterpoint, encourage the students to ask questions and clarify their understanding.

Divide the Class in Half, Assigning Each Half One of the Two Sides of the Issue   Divide the class in half randomly. One half moves to one side of the classroom and assumes the *point* side, while the other half moves to the opposite side and considers the *counterpoint*. Be quick to acknowledge to the students that they were assigned these perspectives. Later, they will have the opportunity to stand on the side they truly support. Once in their groups students pair with someone standing near them, and share in their own words the most compelling points on their side of the issue. This puts each student in a position to talk face to face with someone about the one side of the issue. Select students from each side to tell the class these compelling points. By doing so, the issue is described in students' words, and students' understanding can be informally assessed.

Encourage Students to "Go with Their Own Beliefs"   With the two sides of the issue restated in their own words, ask students to take a stand based on their own belief about the issue, and move to one of three locations in the room: one side supports the *point*, one the *counterpoint*, and a location in the middle represents the *undecided*. Once the class is divided, have each student consider why he moved, and explain the reasoning behind his move to someone standing in the same location. These three locations are to represent students' current thinking only. Encourage them to move freely among these locations, based on the ensuing discussion. Occasionally, one side of the room may be left empty; no students have moved to that position. If this happens you may ask students why they did not move there, or you, yourself, may need to represent that side of the issue. Your preparation needs to be such that you know how to articulate the main points of the point and counterpoint positions.

Encourage Student Interactions and Descriptions   To begin the large-group discussion, ask three or four students on the *point* side of the room to explain their strongest arguments for deciding to stand on that side. After *each* explanation, ask the students on the opposite side of the room (the *counterpoint* side) to respond *only to the comments* they heard from their classmates. The interactions proceed in this manner until both the point and counterpoint sides have presented what they believe are the most significant arguments for their side of the issue. The teacher's role during this initial voicing of opinions is to keep the responses focused on specific lines of reasoning and commentary. When no additional information or ideas are contributed to the discussion, each group gathers in a circle and begins to develop an answer to the question, "What is a solution to this issue/problem?" Students must consider the pros and cons they have heard on *both sides* of the issue, and determine an appropriate policy decision. With three policy options/solutions roughed out (one each from the point, the counterpoint, and the undecided), come back together as a large class and explore together, via discussion, these options. Ask the students to try to combine the three so the class can reach a consensus. Often, students will request more information about the issue, and you should allow time for research at home, in the library, and/or on the Internet.

Dialogical Reasoning on Paper   Since the purpose for this activity is to encourage students to deliberate about public issues, focus them away from winning an argument or defending a particular side of an issue. Instead, you want the students to consider competing positions as well as their own, and be able to represent the arguments each might make. After the class discussion about an acceptable policy, students write a four-paragraph essay (Parker, McDaniel, & Valencia, 1991):

Paragraph 1. Introduce the issue by providing an overview of the main points and major areas of controversy.

Paragraph 2. Describe the primary arguments presented by the "point" side.

Paragraph 3. Describe the primary arguments presented by the "counter-point" side.

Paragraph 4. Conclude the paper by suggesting a policy that might meet the interests of the two sides.

The Issues/Values Continuum

This technique allows the teacher and students to assess the diversity of opinions in the classroom while requiring students to think about their own positions on issues. This strategy also allows students to describe perspectives to their peers, and explore their own opinions and ideas. You can use this strategy with historical issues by placing students in a specific time period or use it to let them reflect on current or controversial issues. These can be in-depth discussions if students are able to research and prepare before the class meeting; they will be brief discussions if students rely only on knowledge they bring to class without any chance to prepare. This type of discussion has four steps:

Making the Continuum   Draw a line from one side of the chalkboard to the other. The end points of the line represent extreme points of view. Label the end points to represent dichotomous positions of the issue. Common points on the continuum are: "strongly agree"; "agree"; "disagree"; and "strongly disagree."

Moving on the Continuum   Select an issue that is related to your course content. Pose a solution to a problem to the class. These might be current events, such as *Gun control laws need to be stricter* or *Casinos should be allowed on American Indian reservations*. These issues can also examine specific opinions about course topics, such as *Hemingway has a clear theme in* The Old Man and the Sea, or *Farmers should be encouraged to grow genetically altered vegetables*. Students indicate their positions by moving to the point on the line that reflects their view.

Explain Placement   Allow students from each end and the middle to explain their views; allow students to change their placement if they hear persuasive arguments.

Follow-Up Activity   For an ongoing exploration of an issue, you might tape a paper continuum to a wall. Have students write their names on pieces of paper and tape them onto the continuum. As they gain new knowledge or insights they—literally—change their positions by moving their name along the continuum. At the end of your exploration of the issue, debrief with students about when and why they may have changed their opinions.

The Future's Wheel Discussion

This technique focuses classroom discussions in a way that leads to decision making. Students think through the implications of potential outcomes on any issue, and begin to think about the future, and the implications of decisions on future decisions, actions, and policies. This activity can be completed in small or large group discussion settings, and is comprised of the following five steps:

Describe the Issue   Draw a circle on the chalkboard with a clearly articulated problem or issue in the middle of the circle. Have students think about this problem, and come up with possible solutions.

Brainstorm   As students brainstorm possible solutions, place their ideas on the board in circles surrounding the main issue/problem and attach them with arrows (like the spokes from the center of a wheel). The more ideas students can generate, the better.

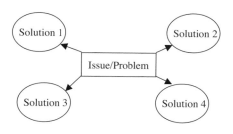

Look to the Future   Extend the wheel one step farther and examine possible results of each solution, and write them on the board. For example, if we decided to solve the problem with solution number 3, then what consequences would result? This can be done as a whole class, or in small groups. These "second generation" outcomes are attached with arrows as well. These steps can be repeated to the third, fourth, and even fifth generations.

Figure 10.1

Analysis   Students analyze the "future's wheel" to determine *desirable* outcomes—those can be marked with a *D*. Students also identify what they think will be the most *probable* outcomes with a *P*. Have students consider:

Which outcomes are probable and desirable?
Which outcomes are probable but not desirable?
What can be done to make these less probable or more desirable?
Which consequences are desirable but not probable?
What could be done to make these more probable?

Consequences　Students consider how consequences imply relationships between factors they might not always think about, such as technological, economic, political, sociological, or psychological factors.

Extension　Have students make a decision/choose a solution to the initial problem and write about why they chose their solution, considering all the implications of their choice.

The Fishbowl Discussion

This technique is used to help students develop effective group skills of participation and observation (Gorman, 1969; Hoover, 1976; Mail, 1968; Priles, 1993). While fishbowl discussions follow a wide variety of formats, they all are used so that discussants learn about the topic of discussion *and* develop the requisite skills and attitudes needed to listen and talk during a discussion. It is a technique that helps teachers navigate between using discussion as a method of instruction, and having discussion ability be a curriculum outcome. Fishbowl discussions place one small group of discussants within a larger circle of observers. The smaller group is "in the fishbowl," and as they discuss they are observed and critiqued by classmates outside of the "bowl." A fishbowl discussion has six basic steps:

Grouping the Students　The class is divided into three equal groups. Members of group 1 and group 2 are paired. Group 1 sits in a close circle. Group 2 sits in a circle outside of group 1. Members of group 2 position themselves to see the face of their counterparts in group 1. Members of group 3 form the outer circle, and sit outside of the second group in no particular order.

Engaging in a Discussion　Select an issue related to the curriculum that has some degree of controversy. It does not need to be highly controversial, just an issue that will promote some differences of opinion. The students in the inner circle (group 1) begin to discuss

Figure 10.2

the controversy. To promote participation by all of the students in group 1, the teacher may limit the speaking of students until all have shared. For example, the teacher may allow each student to share one time until all others in the group have spoken, unless the student asks a question of another student. If a student wants to speak a second time but others in the group have not spoken for the first time, she can only speak to ask a question of someone who has not talked. In that way, all students are limited in their sharing, but all students also serve to encourage each other to share during the discussion. Let the discussion run for 15 minutes, unless the talk drops off before that.

Observations   During the fishbowl discussion, members of group 2 observe their partners and take notes on how they interacted with others. The goal of group 2 is to create an accurate recollection of the participation in the discussion. While members of group 2 observe their partners in group 1, members of group 3 observe and take notes on the interaction patterns of group 1. They do not critique individuals, but observe the whole process to identify how the discussion flows, who the leaders are, what behaviors were observed, and how cooperative/cohesive the group appeared to be.

Debriefing   After the 15-minute discussion, student pairs in groups 1 and 2 meet. The pairs talk about the discussion, and critique the role of the group 1 member in the discussion. Ideas and suggestions are made that might improve the interactions and enhance the discussion. Members in group 3 meet with the teacher and talk about the process they observed. They address the notes that group 3 took during the observation. At this point the teacher may want to share with the large class some observations about the process.

Reassembling   The groups reassemble and continue to discuss the original issue. Each class member assumes his original role, and discussion lasts for 10 minutes. At the end, students are asked to write their responses to the discussion, what they learned about the issue being discussed, and what they learned about discussion.

Switching Roles   At the next class session, group 1 moves to observe the whole discussion, group 2 moves into the fishbowl, and members in group 3 observe an assigned partner in group 2 (i.e., all the groups rotate through the roles. The first four steps are now repeated. Now, switch again; the roles are rotated a final time, and the first four steps are repeated once again.

The Structured Academic Controversy

Using academic conflicts for instructional purposes is a powerful approach to discussing controversial issues in the classroom. The structured academic controversy allows for an organized approach that enhances cognitive and affective learning. This strategy is often considered to be a type of cooperative learning (chapter 8 examines cooperative learning in more depth), because students work together to understand a controversial issue. It also requires students to discuss the issue, and provides excellent structure for small-group discussions (Johnson & Johnson, 1988). The purpose for using this approach is similar to the *taking a stand* discussion, with the difference that the interactions take place in small groups and not with the entire class. The "structure" in a structured academic controversy (SAC) holds all students to a high level of accountability. Students are required to talk in their groups, and to examine different sides of a controversial issue. The format for organizing controversies consists of four steps:

Choosing the Discussion Topic   The choice of the topic depends on the interests of the instructor/students and the purposes of the course. Two well-documented positions need to be prepared, and the topic needs to be age appropriate, so select a topic that has information available.

Preparing Instructional Materials   The following materials are needed for each position:

    a clear overview of the controversy
    a definition of the position to be advocated with a summary of the key
        arguments supporting the position
    resource materials that provide evidence and support for the arguments

Guiding the Controversy   To guide the controversy, the teacher gives students specific instructions in five phases:

Learning the Positions   Students plan with a partner how to advocate the position effectively. They read the materials supporting their position, and plan a persuasive presentation. They attempt to master the information supporting their assigned position and present it in a way that will ensure the opposing pair will comprehend and learn the information.

Presenting Positions   As a pair, students present their position forcefully and persuasively to the opposing pair. Each pair listens to the other and attempts to learn the opposing position. Students take notes and clarify anything that is unclear.

Discussing the Issue   Students argue forcefully and persuasively for their position, presenting as many facts as they can to support their point of view. Students listen critically to the opposing pair's position, asking them for the facts that support their viewpoint. Each pair presents counterarguments.

Reversing Perspectives   Working as a pair, students present the opposing pair's position. The goal is to be as sincere and forceful about this position as possible. This is also a good formative assessment of how well the pairs listened to each other during the previous steps. Any new insights and facts should be added to this presentation. Students elaborate on this perspective by relating it to other information they learned previously.

Reaching a Decision   At this phase, the students "leave their allegiance" to a particular point of view, and together the two pairs summarize and synthesize the best arguments for both points of view. They then attempt to reach a consensus on a position that is supported by the facts. Follow a format, perhaps, similar to that of the fifth step of the *taking a stand* discussion.

Debriefing   Debrief as a class about the decisions, the process, and the dynamics of SAC. Ask such questions as:

Did you understand all sides of the issue?
What are the strongest points of your decision?
What are the weak points of your decision?
Describe the benefits and difficulties of building a consensus.
What insights do you now have about committee work?
What insights do you now have about public policy making?
What are questions or issues for future discussion?

The Electronic Threaded Discussion

During electronic threaded discussions, students "talk" with one another electronically and asynchronously via computer. Discussions are typically referred to as "forums," and comments made by students are called "posts." Thus, when students engage in the threaded discussion they enter a discussion forum and either post a new response to the initial question (known as beginning a new thread), or respond to a classmate's message (known as adding to an existing thread). Merryfield's (2000) description of what such a forum looks like is helpful:

> The "threads" develop as an outline of message headings and grow longer and more complex as people post messages on new topics or respond to messages already posted. Threads can be ... only one message or quite long with 10–15 messages. (p. 507)

By clicking on the thread, the full message is opened for the reader.

A threaded discussion forum is useful for students in interacting about public and controversial issues. Students' responses demonstrate that threaded discussions allow for solid academic interactions with others. Not all quiet students will add to discussion boards, but those students that are quiet thinkers may benefit from sharing their ideas with classmates if they perceive an electronic format to be more conducive for them to "talk." Threaded discussion does not replace classroom discussion. The face-to-face talking that occurs in the latter provides students with a powerful opportunity to interact about an issue and practice using the social skills needed by participatory citizens in a democracy. However, the threaded discussion supplements classroom discussion in the same way that a follow-up writing assignment supplements a face-to-face discussion (Larson, 2003). In addition, the teacher is able to formatively assess students' understanding of the topic under discussion. Complete, accurate records of what was "said" during the discussion are posted at the forum. While it takes a considerable amount of time for students and teachers to read these, it is a very accurate approach for determining who is participating, and to assess the quality of the interactions. Threaded discussions follow four steps:

Establishing a Discussion Forum   Teachers who manage and edit their own website using Microsoft FrontPage can create threaded discussion areas on their website.[1] Your school district may also have licenses to use web-based threaded discussion software such as Blackboard (http://www.blackboard.com), or DiscusWare (http://www.discusware.com). Such a forum might look like the example screen shot in figure 10.3.

Figure 10.3

Posting the Initial Thread   Once the site for threaded discussion is established, a topic is posted to the electronic discussion board, and the students are asked to respond. An example of a posted question might be, "Almost all communities have people who are poor and/or homeless. What responsibility to the poor or homeless do the 'not poor' or 'not homeless' have? Does local/state/national government have a responsibility to aid the poor/homeless? Why?"

Student and Teacher Responses   This is where the discussion takes place. Students respond at least two times: once to the initial question and once to another classmate's comment. You may decide to reply to your students' postings, or you may decide to let them interact with each other. The time that is needed for these discussions is significant, because students must read classmates' comments, select the appropriate comment(s) to respond to, and compose a written response. More details about this third step are addressed in the "Logistical Concerns" section below. While the other discussion techniques involve skill in listening and speaking, threaded discussions do not. Instead, they require skill in reading and writing.

Optional Debriefing   Students may respond to the following prompt: "What do you think about your participation in the threaded discussions?"

STRUCTURED DEBATE

By strictly timing a debate and establishing a sequence for who speaks when, you can ensure wide participation in classroom debates. These debates can be planned for 30 students or fewer, depending on the availability of teacher assistants/parents who will help with the supervision of the process. This strategy works best with issues that have two dominant sides (e.g., a point and a counterpoint). Debate is more competitive than the six discussion approaches, because it has the strongest emphasis on a "winner" of the debate. Learning about the issue occurs as your students research and prepare for their side of the issue, and prepare responses to arguments from the opposing side. The structure of a debate promotes learning about an issue and thinking logically, but does not provide students with experience at "everyday conversations" about public issues.

Selecting an Issue and Assigning Groups

Choose an issue with clearly opposing views. Place students into groups of six to eight. These groups need to be divided in half. In other words, each group of six will be two groups of three; each group of eight will be two groups of four. These two groups will represent the opposing sides of the debate. You can assign students to these groups randomly, or have students choose the side that reflects their own opinion—the goal is to end up with two groups of equal size. Depending on the number of students in your class you may have three or four groups of students ready to debate an issue. A class of 32 will have four groups of eight. If this is the case, you might have them all debate the same issue, or each group could investigate a different issue.

Preparation and Background

Preparation is important: provide students with readings (or access to readings, and have them do a predebate inquiry) that will help them establish the main arguments for each side of the issue.

Establishing the Rules for Debate

Observe the following rules:

Flip a coin to see which side starts.
Allow a three-minute opening statement from each side.
Allow each side to present supporting one- or two-minute speeches.
Each student on each side must speak before anyone can speak a second time.
No one can talk but the recognized speaker.

Regrouping

After everyone on each side has had a chance to speak, give each side five minutes to regroup and discuss their arguments. Continue the debate, this time cutting speaking time to 30 seconds. You can continue to alternate sides, but recognize students at random.

Switching Positions (Optional)

After an additional 8–10 minutes of debate, make the groups switch and argue the other side of the issue. This is similar to the "Reversing Perspectives" step in a *structured academic controversy*.

Variation Possibilities

Allow some students to start out undecided and join sides as they decide; have groups list the main points they have made when they regroup; have a panel of student judges who record the most persuasive arguments for each side.

LOGISTICAL CONCERNS, INCLUDING BENEFITS AND OBSTACLES WHEN USING THESE STRATEGIES

If you have ever been part of a classroom discussion in a lecture hall, you know the importance of room size and layout. It is difficult to talk with classmates when seated in rows facing the front of the room (and looking at the back of the head of the person in front of you). The layout of the classroom is important. Moving student desks or tables into groups of four or six or seating students in a semicircle are easy ways to encourage more face-to-face interactions. Some of the discussion approaches described above specify student location. For example, the *taking a stand* and *issues/values continuum* discussions have students stand up and move about the room. Chairs and desks might be pushed to the side of the room. Fishbowl discussions require students to sit in a series of concentric circles. Many teachers design seating charts in the shape of a square or semicircle so they do not have to rearrange the classroom whenever they want to plan a discussion. If you engage all your students in a whole-class discussion be sure to monitor all your students' levels of engagement.

Good discussions depend on knowledgeable discussants. You will need to allow your students some time to gather information prior to a classroom discussion. This is often called *prior knowledge*—knowledge that students have before an activity begins. Not only will student participation increase when they know about the topic, but opportunities to expand on their prior knowledge will occur during the interactions with classmates. Before you lead a discussion you need to determine your students' prior knowledge. If the topic is new to them, then you will plan for a discussion after students learn pertinent information. If you determine that students' prior knowledge is adequate, then the discussion will allow for deeper understandings. For these reasons, classroom discussions are excellent activities immediately following a research project, class reading, or homework. The discussion allows students to talk about what they have learned and in the process think about the information anew. They are also useful when examining current events or controversial issues about which students have some prior understanding.

Sometimes discussions will give students the false impression that issues are dichotomous—that only two points of view revolve around a topic. For example, dichotomizing the issue of cloning results in two points: (1) scientists should clone; or (2) scientists should not clone. Obviously, cloning is a more complex issue, and it oversimplifies the topic to think of it this way. Consider the *taking a stand* discussion approach. It begins by dichotomizing an issue into two sides, point and counterpoint. However, at the end, the students are asked to develop a policy statement about the issue, and multiple points of view are incorporated. In other words, structuring the discussion as a point/counterpoint initially oversimplifies the issue, but ends by promoting students to think outside these two positions.

How you present the issue to your students is also a very important part of a discussion. Consider this issue: A city's drinking water supply is a nearby lake. This lake also is a recreation center for fishing, waterskiing, and other water sports. In addition, the lake is ringed with houses. The drinking water supply is becoming increasingly polluted. Depending on your content area, you may ask a number of questions. A biology teacher might explore water quality, pollutants, and/or bacteria in lakes from recreational use. A mathematics teacher might encourage students to calculate the flow of water, or whether the amount of water in the lake will effectively dilute the contaminants. A social studies teacher might consider the history of the city's water supply, and historical uses of the lake, or she could have students develop a policy recommendation for the city council about future use of the lake. Finally, an English teacher might have students write an editorial letter to the city paper, where they argue in favor of a particular use of the lake. In each of these cases, the teacher must be careful about posing the question so that a maximum of thinking and talking is encouraged. A poorly formed question will dichotomize the issue. For example, posing the question as "Should this city outlaw the use of outboard motors on the lake?" limits answers to *yes* or *no*. A better question is, "What might the city do about its drinking water problem?" Posed this way, the problem has a wide range of possible solutions, including but not limited to outlawing outboard motors. The point of these examples is that the issues and questions provided to the students need to be carefully designed ahead of time so that maximum thinking is encouraged through the discussions.

CLASSROOM MANAGEMENT AND STUDENT MOTIVATION ISSUES

Discussion strategies depend on students talking. From the above examples of discussion you may notice that students may speak to the whole class, to a small group, or even to a single partner. During whole-class discussions you can easily step in and control the interactions; you can correct errors, challenge student comments, instruct students to respect classmates, and even help them understand that the goal of discussion is not to win but to understand the topic better. However, many students are able to "slip through the cracks" and not participate. They can rely on the more verbal students to carry the conversations. This is problematic for a couple of reasons. First, students who do not engage in a class activity are not able to meet the learning objectives. If a student is able to avoid talking during the whole class discussion, he may not be learning from the talk. Second, students may feel inhibited from talking to the whole class because of their gender, race, or status in the classroom. As Parker states the second problem, "discussion may appear open and democratic while masking domination" (2001, p. 111). Moving students into groups encourages more participation, and usually is more engaging for a larger number of students. However, groups limit the control you have over the discussions; instead of monitoring one discussion, you will need to oversee several. Discussions, therefore, require management strategies for whole-class discussions and small-group discussions. Both will be examined in this section. However, a set of guidelines for student behavior is helpful to ensure that the behavior is conducive to learning. For example, the following ideas could be presented via an overhead projector or classroom poster:

EXPECTED BEHAVIORS

Discussants are to ask themselves:

- Am I listening to what other people are saying or did I miss an important point?
- Am I clearly making claims and supporting claims with facts?
- Am I critiquing ideas and not individuals (keeping a high respect for human dignity)?
- Are we developing together a shared understanding of the problem or issue?[2]

Whole-Class Discussions

As mentioned above, during whole-class discussions you have control over the interactions, but participation by all of the students is often limited. For example, if your class has 30 students, and you have one hour for a discussion, each student will be able to talk for two minutes. In all likelihood only about ten students will talk, and the others will listen to them. The *think/pair/share* strategy (see chapter 5) is a simple yet powerful approach for promoting student engagement and helping move a discussion along. You pose a question and ask the students to *think* about a possible solution, *pair* with a partner (or somebody sitting next to them), and *share* their thoughts about the question. By following this with a whole-class discussion of the same question, students may feel more at ease "going public" with the thoughts they have just given to their partner. Thought of in terms of writing, *think/pair/share* is their rough draft, and the whole-class discussion is their second draft. Some students may have difficulty pairing with someone near them. It is a good idea to place them with partners (for example by simply saying, "You two will be a pair," or "You three will talk together"). This is also helpful to ensure that no one is left out, and that the groupings are not too large. During whole-class discussions it is imperative that all your students are listening to the person talking. Equally important, however, is for you to ensure that one student is not dominating the conversation. In other words, you want to make certain that all students are listening, and that no one is talking too much. This is a difficult task. Many teachers have students raise their hand so that they can call on students and help spread out participation. Others teachers do not want to play this gatekeeper role, and want students to direct their comments to each other and not the teacher. Teachers often move to the back or to one side of the room as a way to encourage more student-to-student interaction. You still must monitor student comments to be sure that they are representing their ideas clearly and factually.

Small-Group Discussions

Cohen, a sociologist who studies student interactions, has suggested that the size of a group impacts participation. Groups larger than seven encourage many students to not participate. If students are in a group with seven or fewer classmates, greater participation by all students occurs (Cohen, 1994). Most of the discussion approaches mentioned above require having students in smaller groups. As with the *think/pair/share* activity during the whole-class discussions, students often need help forming these groups. Again, the most straightforward approach is to group students that are near each other. If you know of students who do not work well together, then you will want to form the groups to maximize the learning. Students can form their own groups, but you need to monitor closely that all students are included. Most of the research on group work suggests that the teacher should place students in groups for a purpose. You may want to mix the groups so they are heterogeneous in regard to areas such as experience, communication skills, gender, ethnicity, or other categories that will enhance student learning. You may even want to group students in homogeneous groups. For example, middle school students often benefit by talking about controversial issues in same-sex groups. Once they are in the small groups, monitor the students to be sure they understand the task, know of any time limits, and are engaged in the project. The key at this point is to move continually among your students as they interact. Do not engage in lengthy conversations with your students; rather, encourage them to talk with their partners/group mates about the topics. If you talk in depth with students, they will not develop their own understanding of the topics, and you will not be able to observe all of your students. Your primary tasks during large groups discussions are to be sure students understand the question you have asked them to discuss (e.g., "What are the strongest points on your side of the issue?"), that they are discussing this with their partners, and that these discussions are not taking up too much class time. By reminding them to focus on the question and topic, you can help keep them engaged.

Electronic Threaded Discussions

Electronic threaded discussions posit a management issue slightly different from the other discussion strategies. Often students read the initial question(s) put forth by the teacher, and respond to that prompt with a lengthy statement. Reading and responding to classmates' postings seems to occur less frequently as the discussion continues. Somehow the energy that is present at the beginning of the discussion needs to be perpetuated. Clearly, as students post more messages, the reading task becomes more burdensome. Changing the discussion topic, or attempting to post "refocusing questions" periodically helps reduce the backlog of unread messages. As with face-to-face discussion, students need instruction about "how to" discuss electronically. Identifying a structure that allows the teacher's voice to be "heard" is important. While classroom discussions typically take one or two hours, threaded discussions can last an entire semester because the Internet allows the interactions to transcend the time-and-place restrictions of meeting in a classroom. When the students are together in a computer lab, momentum is not a concern; when students post on their own time, it is. Experienced teachers who use threaded discussions put limits on how long students can post to a given forum. For example, you may limit the threaded discussions to three days. Since students interact over a short period of time, they know their comments will be read, and responses will be posted quickly. Students' interest in visiting the discussion forum is heightened when they know that new comments will be posted frequently.

APPROPRIATE ASSESSMENT TECHNIQUES TO USE WITH THESE STRATEGIES

Assessing classroom discussions create unique challenges. Once you decide the purpose for a discussion, assessment becomes much easier. Consider these two purposes:

> Discussion is used as an instructional strategy, where the purpose is to have students engage in verbal interactions so they learn the content.
> Skill in discussing becomes the desired outcome of this strategy.

If you solely have the first purpose, then you may not want to assess students' participation during verbal interactions. A report, presentation, and/or written response will allow you to adequately assess learning (for example, the *dialogical reasoning on paper* step of the *taking a stand* discussion). However, if you solely have the second purpose, then you assess much more of the process during the discussions. For example, during a fishbowl discussion, students are assessed on their skill in explaining their ideas and thoughts rather than merely recounting memorized facts and details.

Formative assessments of discussions help students listen and respond to each other appropriately. By teaching students how to discuss, the benefits for using discussion in the classroom can be extended to all areas of students' lives. Most teachers believe that discussion skills need to be taught, that students left to their own will not engage in fruitful discussions. Certain notions—such as supporting opinions with facts, and criticizing an idea rather than the person suggesting the idea—require skill. As such, they need to be learned by the students and assessed by the teacher. Once these are learned, however, the very process of discussing a topic may facilitate abstract learning processes (Bridges, 1979, 1987). Usually, you will assess both your students' engagement in the discussion and how well they learned the content. Below is one type of rubric that will help you assess both.

CLIPBOARD CHECKLIST FOR CLASSROOM DISCUSSIONS													
Date of Observation:													
Activity													
C = Consistent E = Emerging N = Not seen/observed													
Student	*CLASSROOM OBSERVATION*	*Describes issue clearly*	*Elaborates with relevant examples*	*Asks thoughtful questions regarding issue*	*Restates arguments, then counters*	*Gives relevant support*	*Notes gaps in logic*	*INDIVIDUAL WRITTEN WORK*	*Summarizes others' ideas*	*Develops on thesis*	*Gives arguments to support thesis*	*Examples strengthen argument*	*Organizes main points to build argument*	*Strong closing*

Use this checklist on a clipboard to keep track of students on a daily basis. You can assess students' discussion skills on a three-point "scale:" (1) consistent; (2) emerging; (3) not seen/not observed. Five to eight students can be targeted for observation each day, taking care to vary the days each student is observed. After several weeks, several clipboard checklists can be combined to complete individual rating scales for each student. This allows for more accurate generalizations about students. This rubric has two sections. The first section, labeled "Classroom Observation," assesses students during the discussions. The second section, labeled "Individual Written Work" assesses student learning through a presentation, written paper, or some activity after the discussion ends.

Allowing the students to self-assess their participation allows you to compare your perceptions with theirs. The figure 10.4 rubric might be given to students to complete, and then be completed by you.

This rubric requires that you and your students decide the gradations between a score of 0 and 6. In other words, you decide before the discussion what scores of 1, 3, or 6 might be. Often this is a helpful rubric when using a fishbowl discussion, a threaded discussion, or a debate.

Both of these rubrics are appropriate for formative and summative assessments. Formative assessments are very important in helping students learn the skills needed to engage in discussion. Formative assessments of student understanding also occurs during the *think/pair/share* segments of discussions, and as the students talk about the compelling points of the issue. You assess their comments for accuracy. A threaded discussion has the comments in text for review. You and your students can refer to the postings to assess their contributions and/or complete a rubric.

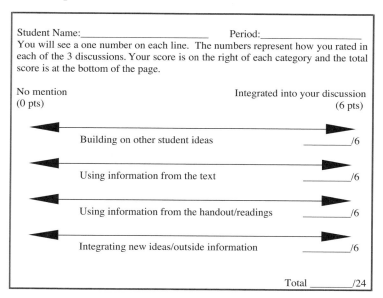

Figure 10.4.

You will have students who are disinclined to talk. A student who is shy may not feel comfortable speaking, and will require opportunities to talk in smaller groups. Gender has been shown to influence speaking in classrooms. Some studies suggest that girls may talk less frequently than boys, especially if the conversations are perceived as combative. Culture is also an influence on student talk. Some cultures promote talking out loud, while others view excessive talking as disrespectful. In any of these cases, it is imperative that you are aware of your objectives and your students' needs. You can work with your students (and talk with their families) to help negotiate how they might engage in meaningful classroom discussions.

GUIDELINES FOR DECIDING IF A STRATEGY IS APPROPRIATE FOR THE CONTENT OF A LESSON

Each discussion strategy listed herein serves specific purposes. Those purposes were identified as part of the discussion for each strategy. This section, however, suggests general guidelines for determining the appropriateness of using discussion in helping students learn. While the majority of all classroom talk is synonymous with recitation-style approaches, significant social and cognitive changes have been reported to occur in students when classroom talk shifts more toward adult "conversations" (Cazden, 1988). As Cazden explains this move away from recitation and toward discussion,

> One important shift is from recitation to something closer to a "real discussion" ... talk in which ideas are explored rather than answers to teacher's test questions are provided and evaluated; in which teachers talk less ... and students talk correspondingly more; in which students themselves decide when to speak; and in which students address each other directly. (p. 55)

Discussion is thought to be a useful teaching technique for developing higher-order thinking skills that enable students to interpret, analyze, and manipulate information. Students explain their ideas and thoughts rather than merely recount, or recite, memorized facts and details. During discussion, learners are not passive recipients of information that is transmitted from a teacher but are active participants. Their active involvement with each other and the course content helps them construct a deeper and more flexible understanding of the topic (Johnston, Anderman, Milne, & Harris, 1994; Tharp & Gallimore, 1988).

When students interact during discussions and debates, they need to have a deep and flexible understanding of the content, and they need to have skill in discussion itself. The following questions should help you consider whether or not classroom discussion will be an appropriate activity to plan for your students.

Are Resources Available to Help Learn Differing Points of View? Will the Discussion Help Students Learn About the Issue/Topic?

For discussions to educate students, they should be serious interactions through which students "support their ideas with evidence, where their opinions are subject to challenge by their peers as well as the teacher, and where the teacher's ideas are equally open to criticism" (Engle & Ochoa, 1988, p. 47). The purpose of probing questions and discrepant viewpoints is to encourage interactions and to encourage students to respond with the most powerful evidence available to them.

Can Your Students Discuss Issues?

Teachers think of discussion as a skill that requires practice sessions. As such, they often preteach discussion skills to their students in an attempt to front-load behaviors, attitudes, and interactions they consider critical for classroom discussions. They set time aside to prepare students for discussions; some begin this preparation the first day of school. Teachers tell students about courtesy, respect, and manners for talking—and possibly disagreeing—with classmates. They tell students to view the class as a community to encourage more interaction. This is something that does not happen without effort on the part of the teacher and willingness on the part of the students. Teachers make efforts to earn students' trust, and students are held accountable to respect their classmates. One teacher we know reported this as a training process: "I train them from the beginning to become a learning community ... there is an atmosphere of trust."

What Types of Interactions Do You Want During the Discussion?

Parker (2001) theorizes that discussions can have the "look and feel" of a seminar or of a deliberation. The purpose of a seminar is to improve understanding about a topic, book, and/or idea. He suggests that seminars start with a question such as, "What does (the topic of the discussion) mean?" and proceed in a way that is conducive to improving everyone's understanding. Deliberations start with a question such as "What should we do?" As such, deliberations intend not only to improve the discussant's understanding, but also to reach a decision about a shared problem (Parker, 2001, p. 114). Consensus building and compromise are more prevalent in deliberations. With any discussion, however, the emphasis needs to be taken off "winning an argument." Classroom discussions need to value the learning that comes from the process of interacting.

MAKING IT WORK IN YOUR CONTENT AREA

Consider the courses you will be certified to teach at the middle school or high school level. Select a topic that you believe will engage students in a discussion. Productive discussions are a result of careful planning. Consider the following:

Identify the topic students will discuss.
Write out lesson objectives:
  Objectives dealing with what students are to learn about discussion.
  Objectives dealing with the knowledge base to be explored.
Describe the rationale for choosing the issue.
  What makes this a good issue to discuss?
  How does it fit with the curriculum?
Decide what type of discussion will best help students learn the issues.

Lesson procedures: Explain why you chose the type of discussion technique you did and how it will help students learn. Consider the following:
Student preparation:
  How will you prepare students to engage in a discussion on this topic? What experiences, readings, and information will they need ahead of time?
Discussion questions:
  Write out actual questions you would pose to your class. Come up with some opening questions (to help students recall information and establish facts), interpretive questions (to help students draw relationships and compare/contrast information), and opinion questions (to encourage your students to draw their own conclusions and articulate them).
Assessment:
  Reread the section on assessing classroom discussion, and determine how you might assess student learning. Consider whether you want to assess their "discussion skill" and/or their understanding of the discussion topic.

CHAPTER REVIEW

Whole-class discussions will serve a different learning objective than will small-group discussions. Classroom discussions will vary according to the purpose of the discussion, use of questions, and the issue being discussed. This chapter helped you consider six effective types of discussion, as well as structured debate. Each is briefly summarized below:

1. *Taking a stand* is best used when teachers want students to consider opposing viewpoints around a controversial issue.
2. *The issues/values continuum* allows the teacher and students to assess the diversity of opinions in the classroom, while requiring students to think about their own positions on issues.
3. *The future's wheel* focuses classroom discussions in a way that leads to decision-making.

4. *The fishbowl discussion* is used to help discussants develop the requisite skills and attitudes needed to listen and talk during a discussion, *and* to help them learn about the topic being discussed.
5. *Structured academic controversy* is often considered to be a type of cooperative learning because students work together to understand a controversial issue. It also requires students to discuss the issue, and provides excellent structure for small-group discussions.
6. *The electronic threaded discussion* does not replace classroom discussion, but supplements face-to-face interactions—especially about controversial issues.
7. *Structured debate* is more competitive than the six discussion approaches because it has the strongest emphasis on a "winner." It works best with issues that have two dominant sides (e.g., point and counterpoint).

When you use discussion you will need to be aware of logistics such as moving chairs, placing students in groups, student preparation, and establishing a classroom environment that is conducive to talking. Students need to be clear of the goals of the discussion, and they must know that their ideas are an important part of the learning. One of the ways you can help is to develop a set of guidelines for the students to follow and hold students accountable to them.

You may assess student participation, or you may decide only to assess what students have learned from the discussion itself. Rubrics help you focus on the pertinent parts of the discussion in order to better assess students. These rubrics need to be developed with the students, and/or distributed to them before the discussion takes place. As with any assessment, the objectives for the discussion need to match the assessment. Formative assessments of discussions help students listen and respond to each other appropriately. Certain notions—such as supporting opinions with facts, and criticizing an idea and not the person suggesting the idea—require skill; they need to be learned by students and assessed by the teacher.

The following questions help you consider whether or not classroom discussion will be an appropriate activity to plan for your students:

Are resources available to help learn differing points of view, and will the discussion help students learn about the issue/topic?
Can your students discuss issues?
What types of interactions do you want during the discussion?

NOTES

1. Use the Discussion Web Wizard. Instructions for setting up a discussion web will vary depending on your version of FrontPage, so use the help window of the program, or online tutorials at Microsoft's FrontPage website.
2. These guidelines are developed from work done by Barber, 1989; Larson, 1997; and Parker, 1996.

REFERENCES

Alvermann, D. E., O'Brien, D. G., & Dillon, D. R. (1990). What teachers do when they say they are having discussions of content area reading assignments: A qualitative analysis. *Reading Research Quarterly, 25*(4), 296–322.

Barber, B. (1989). Public talk and civic action: Education for participation in a strong democracy. *Social Education, 53*(6), 355–356, 370.

Bellack, A. A., Kliebard, H. M., Hyman, R. T., & Smith, E. L., Jr. (1966). *The language of the classroom.* New York: Teachers College Press.

Bridges, D. (1979). *Education, democracy and discussion.* Windsor, England: National Foundation for Educational Research.

Bridges, D. (1987). Discussion and questioning. *Questioning Exchange, 1*, 34–37.

Cazden, C. (1988). *Classroom discourse.* Portsmouth, NH: Heinemann.

Cohen, E. G. (1994). *Designing groupwork: Strategies for heterogeneous classrooms,* New York: Teachers College Press.

Dewey, J. (1916/1985). Democracy and education. In J. A. Boylston (Ed.), *Democracy and education: The middle works of John Dewey, 1899–1924* (Vol. 9). Carbondale, IL: Southern University Press.

Dillon, J. T. (1984). Research on questioning and discussion. *Educational Leadership, 41*(3), 51–56.

Dillon, J. T. (1994). *Using discussion in the classroom.* Philadelphia: Open University Press.

Engle, S., & Ochoa, A. (1988). *Education for democratic citizenship: Decision making in the social studies.* New York: Teachers College Press.

Gall, M. D. (1985). Discussion methods of teaching. In T. Husen & T. N. Postlethwaite (Eds.), *International encyclopedia of education* (Vol. 3, pp. 1423–1427). Oxford: Pergamon.

Gall, M. D., & Gall, J. P. (1990). Outcomes of the discussion method. In W. W. Wilen (Ed.), *Teaching and learning through discussion: The theory, research and practice of the discussion method* (pp. 25–44). Springfield, IL: Charles C Thomas.

Good, C. V. (Ed.). (1983). *Dictionary of education.* New York: McGraw-Hill.

Goodlad, J. I. (1984). *A place called school.* New York: McGraw-Hill.

Gorman, A. H. (1969). *Teachers and learners: The interactive process.* Boston: Allyn and Bacon.

Gross, R. E., & Zeleny, L. D. (1958). *Educating citizens for democracy: Curriculum and instruction in secondary social studies.* New York: Oxford University Press.

Haroutunian-Gordon, S. (1991). *Turning the soul: Teaching through conversation in the high school.* Chicago: University of Chicago Press.

Hess, D. (2000). Developing strong voters through democratic deliberation. *Social Education, 64*(5), 193–196.

Hoetker, J., & Ahlbrand, W. P., Jr. (1969). The persistence of recitation. *American Educational Research Journal, 6*, 145–167.

Hoover, K. H. (1976). *The professional teacher's handbook: A guide for improving instruction in today's middle and secondary schools* (2nd ed.). Boston: Allyn and Bacon.

Hunkins, F. P. (1995). *Teaching thinking through effective questioning* (2nd ed.). Boston: Christopher-Gorden.

Johnston, J., Anderman, L., Milne, L., & Harris, D. (1994). *Improving civic discourse in the classroom: Taking the measure of Channel One.* Research Report 4. Ann Arbor, MI: Institute for Social Research, University of Michigan.

Johnson, D. W., & Johnson, R. T. (1988). Critical thinking through structured controversy. *Educational Leadership, 45*(8), 58–64.

Larson, B. E. (2000). Thinking about classroom discussion as a method of instruction and a curriculum outcome. *Teaching and Teacher Education, 16*, 661–677.

Larson, B. E. (2003). Comparing face-to-face discussion and electronic discussion: A case study from high school social studies. *Theory and Research in Social Education, 31*(3), 348–366.

Mail, D. J. (1968). The fishbowl: Design for discussion. *Today's Education, 57*, 27–29.

Merryfield, M. M. (2000). How can electronic technologies promote equity and cultural diversity? Using threaded discussion in graduate courses in social studies and global education. *Theory and Research in Social Education, 28*(4), 502–526.

Miller, S. (1992). *Creating change: Towards a dialogic pedagogy.* (Report Series 2.18). Albany, NY: National Research Center on Literature Teaching and Learning (ERIC Document Reproduction Service No. ED 349 582).

Oliver, D. W., & Newmann, F. M. 1972). *Taking a stand: A guide to clear discussion of public issues* (rev. ed.). Middletown, CT: Xerox/American Education Publications.

Parker, W. C. (1996). Curriculum for democracy. In R. Soder (Ed.), *Democracy, education and schooling* (pp. 182–210). San Francisco: Jossey-Bass.

Parker, W. C. (2001). Classroom discussion: Models for leading seminars and deliberations. *Social Education, 65*(2), 111–115.

Parker, W. C., McDaniel, J. E., & Valencia, S. W. (1991). Helping students think about public issues: Instruction versus prompting, *Social Education, 55*(1), 41–44.

Priles, M. A. (1993). The fishbowl discussion: A strategy for large honors classes. *English Journal, 82*(6), 49–50.

Roby, T. W. (1988). Models of discussion. In J. T. Dillon (Ed.), *Questioning and discussion: A multidisciplinary study* (pp. 163–191). Norwood, NJ: Ablex.

Schwab, J. J. (1954). Eros and education: A discussion of one aspect of discussion. *Journal of General Education, 8*, 54–71.

Stodolsky, S., Ferguson, T., & Wimpelberg, K. (1981). The recitation persists, but what does it look like? *Journal of Curriculum Studies, 13*(2), 121–130.

Swift, J. N., & Gooding, C. T. (1983). Interaction of wait time feedback and questioning instruction on middle school science teaching. *Journal of Research in Science Teaching, 20*(8), 721–730.

Tharp, R. G., & Gallimore, R. (1988). *Rousing minds to life: Teaching, learning, and schooling in social context.* Cambridge: Cambridge University Press.

Wilen, W. W., & White, J. J. (1991). Interaction and discourse in social studies classrooms. In J. P. Shaver (Ed.), *Handbook of research on social studies teaching and learning* (pp. 483–495). New York: Macmillan.

CITED WEBSITES

Blackboard Inc.:
        http://www.blackboard.com
DiscusWare:
        http://www.discusware.com

11

STUDENT-DIRECTED INVESTIGATION

OVERVIEW

If an outsider walked into Heather Brown's English classroom conducting a student-directed investigation it might appear somewhat chaotic. Some of her primarily Native American students would be taking notes while viewing a documentary in the back corner. Other students would be asking for permission to go to the library. Others would be working on computers together as they analyzed data and researched statistics on bullying. One might be giving a fellow classmate a survey. Several would be deciding how to divide their responsibilities for a project on Native American boarding schools. Another student would be composing interview questions about traditional customs she will ask a tribal elder (Brown, 2004).

In some ways these students are very different from their adolescent peers in suburbia or the inner city, but they are also similar. They want learning to be engaging. According to Tomlinson (2003) there are three trends that strike at the core of effective teaching and learning in today's schools:

1. Classrooms are more diverse than at any time in our past and this trend will continue.
2. Due to this trend in diverse classrooms, teachers are looking to teach in more flexible, personalized ways.
3. There is an escalating demand that students acquire high-level knowledge and skills.

Increasingly, teachers are using the term *differentiated instruction* when they design plans that address these trends. One of the ways to meet the educational needs of all the students in the classroom is to focus on curriculum that both *promotes understanding* and *engages* students. *Student-directed investigation* is an important component of a classroom that accomplishes this. After considering this approach, you will be able to better evaluate the curriculum you develop using the criteria for high quality curriculum in the "Making It Work" section at the end of this chapter.

Defining Student-Directed Investigation

You may have heard the old proverb, "Tell me and I forget, show me and I remember, involve me and I understand." The strategies that you have been exploring through this text have varying degrees of student involvement. No teaching approach has greater potential for student involvement and engagement than student-directed investigation. This approach includes several varieties of investigation that share certain critical attributes. Different types of student-directed investigation would include inquiry learning, discovery learning, problem-based learning, project-based learning, experiential learning, and service learning. Student-directed investigation offers an opportunity to learn through experience in an environment that:

- involves the "real world" and offers meaningful, personally interesting challenges
- requires active learning
- provides opportunities to solve problems, answer questions, or address real needs
- allows for student ownership, responsibility, and choices
- offers students an opportunity to perform as experts or professionals

Precise definitions of the various types of investigation are difficult and somewhat nebulous. However, when you hear these terms used at a school you can assume that they include the characteristics referred to above as well as the following variations:

Inquiry learning: A focus on asking and investigating personally relevant questions.

Discovery learning: A focus on discovery and exploration that could potentially lead in any curricular direction. *Guided discovery* would be more structured and probably synonymous with inquiry learning or problem-based learning.

Problem-based learning: A focus on the process of solving a problem. This would be considered inquiry oriented when students are involved with identifying the problem.

Project-based learning: A focus on the process used to develop a product or other creation. This may or may not be problem based or inquiry based.

Experiential learning: A focus on learning through an experience usually not associated with a traditional classroom environment.

Service learning: A focus on learning through an experience of service to the community usually outside of the classroom or school.

A DESCRIPTION OF STUDENT-DIRECTED INVESTIGATION, AND RESEARCH FINDINGS

As you may have noted, student-directed investigation is grounded in constructivist learning theory. With this in mind, now is a good time to quickly review the basics of two predominant approaches to learning as described in chapter 1—*behaviorism* and *constructivism*. Much of the experimental data that serves as the basis for the behaviorist view was first generated by Skinner (1968). This view suggests that knowledge is universal, objective, and independent of the student. The behaviorist teaching approach is primarily focused on direct instruction because knowledge is transmitted to the student and received through the senses. The primary role of the teacher would be to break information and skills into meaningful packages, build them back together through a series of presentations or activities and, when finished, test to see if students have learned. Behaviorist classrooms tend to focus on teaching skill sequences, stress individualized rather than group work, and emphasize methods such as lecture, teacher-directed questioning, skill worksheets, teacher-led activities, and objective tests.

Constructivist theory has a different view of knowledge and therefore holds a different view of approaches to learning. While proponents of this theory hold a variety of opinions about knowledge and learning, they would agree with the underlying belief that knowledge is constructed by people through their personal prism of experiences. Constructivists believe that what a person knows is not a function of detached observation but created through interaction with the world and that knowledge and reality are subjective (Fosnot, 1989). Those holding this view give attention to the social context in which learning occurs. Learning environments similar to those in the "real world" are best suited to enhance learning. Constructivists support learning that focuses on the use of authentic tasks—that is, the every day practices of a particular group such as scientists, historians, or filmmakers. These tasks would be similar to on-the-job experiences or apprenticeships (Cognition and Technology Group at Vanderbilt, 1990; Collins, Brown, & Newman, 1994). Proponents of this view would have classrooms focus on problem solving, independent investigation, the pursuit of personal interests, and the utilization of higher-order thinking skills.

A brief overview makes these two perspectives appear to be mutually exclusive, and to some they are just that. In practice, however, perspectives fall on a wide continuum somewhere between two poles (Duffy and Johnson, 1992; Scheurman, 1998). For example, some teachers may not agree with the idea that reality is created by the individual but are still proponents of student-centered approaches to learning. However, through this discussion you can see how what you believe about the way students learn has a profound impact on the instructional choices you make in the classroom. This can be reviewed further by revisiting chapter 1.

Many teachers of adolescents have noticed that the naturally inquisitive nature of children seems to slowly fade. Sadly, our traditional system of education has not always encouraged the pursuit of independent inquiry. Instead, too often, students use almost all of their time in a required pursuit of the test answers. The facts, of course, are important, but so also are understanding and the use of information. Research in cognition, authentic learning, and student engagement support claims that student-directed investigation is a beneficial strategy for developing these attributes (Brooks & Brooks, 1993; Brown, Collins, & Duguid, 1989; Scheurman & Newmann, 1998). Others have described environmental approaches associated with this strategy such as independent inquiry and self-regulation to be advantageous approaches for developing understanding and application of knowledge (Boekaerts, 1997; Wisker & Brown, 1996). According to a summary of research on learning conducted by Bransford, Brown, and Cocking (2000) there are three implications for classroom teachers that are components of student-directed investigation. First, students should be placed in settings that prepare them for flexible adaptation to new problems and settings; second, students should organize information into the main ideas that structure a discipline—its most important theories or concepts and their interrelationships; third, students show understanding when they know how and when to put knowledge to use.

STEP-BY-STEP PROCEDURES FOR PLANNING AND IMPLEMENTATION

The various types of student-directed investigation will serve different purposes, and because of this, one type may be a better match for a learning objective than another. We have found these strategies to be equally effective at both the high school and middle school levels even though students' maturity levels vary drastically. Teachers will consider other variables such as time constraints, community resources and contacts, transportation, and the course schedule when determining which type of investigation to pursue. The following common types of student-directed investigation share the commonalities we describe in the preceding sections of this text and are very similar in many ways. However, they are unique in emphasis and require different considerations in planning because they are different procedurally.

Problem-Based Learning

Problem-based learning was originally designed for medical school programs when concerns were raised that students knew the medical information but lacked critical reasoning skills to use the information wisely. Some see this approach as a type of (or synonymous with) inquiry learning, as the two are very closely related. There are three primary features of problem-based learning: "initiating learning with a problem; exclusive use of ill-structured problems; and using the instructor as a metacognitive coach" (Gallagher, Sher, Stepien, & Workman, 1995, p. 137). In other words, from the outset the students are presented with a complex problem that has many variables and likely has several solutions. Students will be supported by a teacher to help them as needed but will not be given a process to follow. Many times students who are confronted with problems to solve do so only as an extension to a teacher-directed lesson; it is viewed as an activity to reinforce what the teacher has presented. Granted, this would be an effective way to extend a teacher-centered lesson; however, often the students do not know why they are learning the material. At the same time, they *do* learn to assume that in the real world all the information needed will be at hand in order for them to proceed. Problem-based learning confronts students with an ill-structured problem at the onset, allowing for problem solving through information resources and scaffolding. Ill-structured problems are an important aspect because they are, well, *messy*. This mirrors problems that people face regularly in life outside of school. During this approach, students are encouraged to consider problems that need considerable exploration and careful consideration, that can lead students along several different paths or alternate solution routes. These are problems that may have more than one correct answer or unclear solutions, and often require the use of key course concepts that can be readily transferred to other problems.

Many times teachers will substitute actual problems that face students with interesting generated problems that reflect the real world. One chemistry classroom used the following problem for a lesson on the effects of industrial pollution: "Richard, who is 15 years old, lives near an oil refinery. His family, which includes three children, one only a month old, has been living there for three years. His mother has noticed that since they moved to that house, her silver teaspoons became tarnished quickly" (West, 1992). The class then began with the problem (silver teaspoons becoming tarnished) and began looking for the solution. Of course, the teacher encouraged them to begin thinking about a solution that involves chemistry. In another class a middle school math teacher wanted to get students thinking beyond routine application of formulas and avoid the confusion surrounding area and perimeter. After using some preproblem warm-ups to garner interest, the teacher introduced a problem related to pizza pricing. Students were given a menu with prices for various individual slices from different sized pizzas (9-inch, 12-inch, and 15-inch). The students used various techniques (string, making grids, etc.) to determine circumference, radius, and area of each pizza. The students were then asked to explain why one of these measurements was most closely related to price and to determine which pizza they considered to have the best value. To follow this, students were asked to extend their learning by investigating the relationship between diameter and circumference by measuring other objects in the classroom and making tables and graphs to share their findings. Finally, students had the more challenging task of using the same techniques to compare radius and the area of circles (Harris, Marcus, McLaren, & Fey, 2001).

One procedure, of many, for the implementation of problem-based learning would be to include the following steps. These steps can be easily modified depending upon the requirements of the discipline or if the problem is to be worked on by the class, small groups, or individuals:

- The teacher frames the learning objectives, essential questions, and desired results.
- The teacher discusses objectives and assessment methods with students.
- Begin by identifying a problem that relates to a significant course concept. This could be student- or teacher-generated.
- Brainstorm what students know, what students need to know, and the process they can use to find out unknowns.
- Students collect and test data.
- Students manage and analyze the data.
- Students generate a plan or solution and test it.
- Students reassess their plan or solution and retest.
- Students present or publish their findings.
- The teacher facilitates debriefing to summarize learning and assess process.
- The teacher assesses student learning and teacher (self-)facilitation, and evaluates overall process.

Inquiry Learning

Another common approach that encourages students to think like professionals in the field (i.e., to think scientifically, like a literary critic, or to "do geography") is inquiry learning. Again, this approach is similar to problem-based learning in many ways, but we separate the two here to help illuminate the different emphases and forms of implementation. With inquiry learning the emphasis is on the pursuit of questions, making hypotheses, investigating, forming theories, and the possibility of taking action based upon evaluative judgments.

There are three basic types of inquiry that teachers use depending upon their objectives and other limiting factors. First is *structured inquiry*, in which students are given a research question or direction, a method, and materials, but not expected outcomes. Another type is *guided inquiry*. Here students are given a research direction and materials but need to determine the research method themselves. A third is *open inquiry*, in which students determine the research question, methods, and necessary resources.

You will be ready to begin the written phase of planning after determining what type of inquiry is most appropriate for your classroom. Some teachers have found that inquiry-oriented lessons are improved if there is a clear focus and direction for students. Students are not productive learners if they are unclear about what they are trying to accomplish or become frustrated by a lack of direction. The following planning template, adapted from the work of Exline (2004), is helpful with the development of an inquiry plan that gives focus and direction. It is useful for planning in any content area but may need to be modified depending upon the short-range (one hour?) or long-range (one month?) nature of your lesson idea. Some would use this template to help organize their thoughts prior to completing a more formal lesson plan as shown in chapter 4.

PLANNING TEMPLATE FOR INQUIRY LEARNING LESSON

Learning Objectives and Expected Outcome

What is the skills development focus (e.g., research, observation, synthesis skills)?

Habits of Mind/Ground Rules Being Emphasized

What are the rules of the discipline being studied that you wish to reinforce (e.g., aspects of the scientific method; literary ideas and ideals)?

Conceptual Theme Most Important to This Lesson

What are the themes that connect the lesson to previous lessons and the important ideas in the framework of the discipline (e.g., the way the discipline explores change, the way it makes connections between one idea and another, or the way theories or ideas can be applied to different levels of analysis)?

Specific Content

What is the content that your students need to know by the end of the lesson?

Sources and Resources Needed/Available

What sources and resources are needed (e.g., libraries, professional journals, local colleges/universities, the Internet, experts, materials)?

Potential Roadblocks to Learning

What problems do you see that may hinder student learning? What plan do you have to deal with these roadblocks?

Inquiry Attributes Already Possessed by Learners

What are the skill levels of the learners? What nurtured habits of mind do the learners possess? What are the levels of conceptual understanding of the learners? What are the levels of content understanding of the learners? How will you plan for enhancement and appropriate scaffolding?

<u>*Questions and Types of Questions to Be Raised and Explored*</u>

What are the main questions that you hope learners will explore, bearing in mind the various types of questions (inference, questions about hypotheses, etc.)?

<u>*Ongoing Assessment*</u>

How will you formatively assess student progress throughout the lesson?

<u>*Appropriate Sources and Resources to Effectively Monitor Progress*</u>

How will you summatively assess student learning?

<u>*Professional Preparation*</u>

What do you, as a teacher, need to find out before starting this lesson?

<u>*Plans to Help Advanced Learners Become Facilitators for*
Learners Needing Additional Help</u>

In what ways can advanced students work with others as the project progresses?

Inquiry lessons will loosely follow a process of inquiry similar to that shown in figure 11.1.

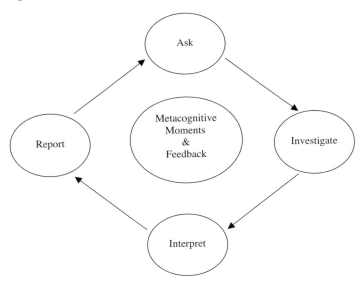

Figure 11.1

In general, the inquiry process begins with the questioning stage and proceeds to other stages as shown. Opportunities for metacognition and feedback occur throughout the process. While figure 11.1 may be of use as an overview of the process of inquiry, it is also misleading in that rarely is a high-quality inquiry lesson so neatly packaged. Many think of inquiry as more of a web. For example, after interpreting information, students may need to form another hypothesis and reinvestigate or ask a different question. Teachers using inquiry techniques would need to have an understanding of the basic process before they could confidently modify plans as circumstances in a fluid classroom would demand. The following suggestions for this process would need to be modified depending upon these circumstances as well as the type of inquiry (structured, guided, or open) that the teacher has chosen.

Stage 1: Asking   Most students will need assistance posing an appropriate question that is both interesting and challenging. Encourage students to consider what really interests them about a topic. Is the question under consideration one that can be answered with little effort or is it challenging and worthwhile? How will pursuing the question give them deeper insight into the overall lesson theme or objective? Students should be encouraged to avoid questions with simple answers, or yes/no questions, unless they need to do in-depth exploration to come to a decision. For example, *Should the Makah be allowed to hunt whales?* could be a poor question choice if students are not asked to provide in-depth supporting information from various perspectives. Care should also be given to guide students away from questions that are too broad—for example, the question, *What should be done about overpopulation?* After speaking with the students about their interest, this could be refocused to read, *What impact does the Mexican economy have on migration patterns?* Students could be asked to form conclusions or take a position after they have answered the question.   Once an appropriate question has been determined, a *need-to-know* chart can be used to help focus students. On a large visual the teacher would write headings for three columns:

What do we know?
What do we need to know?
How do we find out?

If the class is pursuing one question together this could be a large-group brainstorming session; if students are pursuing questions in small groups this could be done with teacher facilitation. This step is as important as any of the others since, commonly, students that have poor inquiry experiences can trace it back to the question formulation stage.

At this early stage students should be encouraged to formulate an investigation plan in which they meet with the teacher to determine direction and form a work schedule.

Stage 2: Investigating   Each discipline will have established techniques for investigating a question. For example, obviously using the scientific method is vital in a biology class, while a history class would have its own methods. For example, the scientific method most commonly used would include the following steps:

1. Form the question.
2. Make observations.
3. Form a hypothesis.
4. Do the experiment.
5. Draw a conclusion.

Historical methods would include techniques by which historians examine primary sources and other evidence to research and write about history. Guidelines for historical inquiry would require consideration of internal and external criticism prior to forming hypotheses through a process of historical reasoning. Investigating social issues would involve a perspective gathering component. The steps involved may be similar to the scientific method but this discipline, like all others, has its own investigative methods.

One source of information common to all fields is text-based resources. The teachers will need to be prepared to give suggestions and guidance for the selection of appropriate resources. This is especially true of the use of Internet resources, as evaluating online information can be confusing and difficult for students. How does a middle school or high school student know if information is reliable? Students should be made aware that consideration of authorship, publisher, currency, perspectives, coverage, and accuracy can help determine the reliability of a source. Many students will be familiar with the online resource Wikipedia; it may be a good starting point for research and be helpful in determining related topics or other guidance to find other resources. However, students should be taught the importance of finding multiple resources and that because there is usually no author to cite in Wiki, it should be seen only as a starting point.

CLASSROOM APPLICATION

Evaluating Online Information

Take a look at the following websites with one other member of your class.[1] View each site together while you discuss the criteria for evaluating online information listed below; these criteria were adapted from various library websites by Struthers (2005). You should use the questions below each major heading as a guide to consider the major points, as these subquestions are general aids to thinking critically about the site and may or may not be appropriate for each site listed. Complete this task by discussing your findings with the whole class. (Note: Care was taken to obtain sites from a variety of source types that appeared to be stable. If any of these web addresses become inactive this task can be completed with the remaining websites.)

The Cuban Missile Crisis
   http://www.gwu.edu/~nsarchiv/nsa/cuba_mis_cri/

Commemoration of the Holocaust
   http://www.ihr.org/other/tehrantimesdec05.html

Mankato, Minnesota
   http://city-mankato.us

Criteria for Evaluating Online Information
Authorship
   Is the author identifiable? Never use a source whose author you cannot
      identify. If the author is not clearly listed within the site, use the fol-
      lowing techniques to locate the author's name:
      • link back to the site's home page
      • ask the web development team or sponsoring organization to iden-
        tify the author
   Is the author a professional in the field?
   If the author's name is unfamiliar, is the site linked to an established
      authority on the subject?
   Has this author been referred to favorably by respected professionals in
      the field or by a respectable website? Does the document contain links
      to these professionals or to the respected websites? Are there also links
      from these sources that go back to the site you're assessing?
   Does the author include his/her e-mail address or a postal address so that
      you can contact the author directly from the site?
   Does the website belong to an individual, or is it part of a site maintained
      by an organization, academic institution, or other group? Does it list
      the author's position within this group?

Publishing Body/Publisher
   Is the type of material appropriate for the assignment? Professional
      sources from the web include professional home pages or online pro-
      fessional journals. Non-professional sources include personal home
      pages or online general audience magazines.
   Are you able to contact the webmaster or sponsoring organization from
      within the site?

Currency
   Does the site include information on when it was created or how often
      the site is updated?

Perspectives

Can you identify the goals of the site?

Are these goals clearly stated?

Does the focus of the text relate to the graphics in the site?

Is the perspective appropriate for your paper?

Are all sides of the issue fairly presented?

Coverage

Is there an in-depth understanding of the related issues that shows the author's familiarity with the subject?

Does the site acknowledge other sources within the text itself? Are there also links to these sources if they exist online?

Is the bibliography complete and thorough?

Are the appropriate theories, schools of thought, or techniques used in the discussion of the material standard in the field?

If the material is based on a new theory, is coverage of the new approach detailed? Does the site cover the advantages and disadvantages of the method compared to other current methods in the field?

Accuracy or Verifiability

Is the material comparable to related sources? The home page of an authority in the field will provide a good base of sources to use as a comparison for other sources.

Is the methodology given so that the author's work can be replicated or evaluated?

Do many mechanical errors (e.g., grammatical errors, typos, etc.) appear in the text? Errors suggest the author might be careless in presenting information.

Did you discover the site via a search engine? If so, how does the search engine you used look for information and, if relevant, rate the sites it retrieves?

The use of face-to-face or online experts is also a good way to make resource information available. During this investigative stage students could use the teacher for mini-lessons for small groups on an "as needed" basis. In addition, during this stage there may be opportunities to have student experts or community experts available as resources.

Stage 3: Interpreting   Students are encouraged to analyze information they have collected and to draw conclusions. To do this they will need to reflect on *what* information is relevant to the question under consideration and *how* it can help them answer the question satisfactorily. Both middle school and high school students will need assistance with the thinking skills needed to draw logical conclusions from the information they have collected. Some computer software—spreadsheets used to create graphs, for example—can be helpful to teach students to analyze and interpret information. This example would be especially helpful for those learners with a more visual orientation. Students can record both their interpretation notes along with investigative notes in an inquiry journal. A journal like this could be used as an assessment tool by the teacher as well as be a way for students to track their learning. After the interpretation of results is completed, students can record their conclusions and begin preparing for a report of their findings.

Stage 4: Reporting   Give students an opportunity to present their findings to an audience. This audience (small group of classmates, the School Board, PTA) should reflect the amount of time and effort students invested in the inquiry. For example, one middle school classroom used sophisticated computer software on loan from a university to investigate a question posed by the local city council: Should we—and if so, *where* should we—place a city park for our fast-growing town? The students took several months to investigate information and analyze data until they were prepared to make a recommendation. Their teacher, to her credit, saw this as a wonderful opportunity to have community leaders involved as part of the presentation audience. Naturally, this is not always possible nor advisable. Some inquiry projects are small, in-class affairs where informal reports are appropriate. It is important to provide a forum for students to present findings and field questions. This could be an audience of peers, the teacher, or the larger community. A presentation with a written document is a natural and oft-used form of report for an inquiry based lesson. However, it is not unusual to find classrooms that take a form of social action as a result of their inquiry. This might involve writing letters to the influential, making video reports that are sent to television stations, creating websites or blogs, or other ways the class desires to draw attention to their findings.

Stage 5: Metacognitive Moments   This stage should be thought of as an integrated part of the process. Create times throughout the inquiry that allow for student self-reflection, assessment, and adjustment. For example, take a few minutes along the way to hold a questioning seminar to explore what the students are concluding up to that point or what remains to be resolved. Use *think/pair/share* activities, exit cards ("On a card, write two specific things you learned today"), or one-minute papers ("Write for one minute about a prediction you can make based upon your experiment today"). Students could also use their inquiry journals to record questions about the process or for future pursuit and other reflective internal "talk" that may be helpful.

CLASSROOM APPLICATION

Technology-Enhanced Inquiry   One of the most popular formats for online inquiry-oriented lessons is called a *webquest*. The best webquests are not just scavenger hunts, but adhere to principles of inquiry we have discussed in this chapter. Information about the creation of webquests along with many teacher- and student-created examples can be found at the San Diego State University Webquest Homepage (webquest.org). Webquests have six key elements:

1. *Introduction:* Provides background information
2. *Task:* Includes either a question or task
3. *Resources:* Provide links to helpful resources to give direction
4. *Process:* Provides step-by-step guidance for completion
5. *Evaluation:* Outlines expectations through a scoring guide
6. *Conclusion:* Summarizes learning goals

After looking through the Webquest examples in your discipline:

• with a partner choose one example and decide what type of inquiry (structured, guided, open) is proposed and discuss why you would or would not use it in your class
• using the QuestGarden portion of the website create or modify a Web- quest for your future class using the principles of student-directed instruction set forth in this chapter

LOGISTICAL CONCERNS AND OBSTACLES

The attitudes of stakeholders can make the implementation of student-directed investigation challenging for some. Many educators, parents, and community members use their own experiences of school to judge what is appropriate for adolescents to learn and how they should learn it. This is commonly referred to as the impact of the *historic curriculum*. An inquiry-oriented approach may be at odds with a district that valued the memorization of content and recita- tion above the practical use of content through inquiry. Many of the statewide standardized tests attempt to assess student ability to think critically by hav- ing them show their thought process. However, critics argue that standardized testing is a poor format for assessing these important thinking skills. In either case, the perception of many is that inquiry-oriented approaches take time away from preparing students for "the test" and are seen by some as "fluff." Teachers using student-directed investigation should be prepared to share their rationale for its use.

Time constraints are viewed by many as the single greatest obstacle to the implementation of this strategy. These constraints involve both the lack of time for the teacher to implement a lesson of this sort and the lack of time in the cur- ricular schedule. Teachers are pressed for time on all sides. Some have found that collaborative techniques are helpful in the planning and implementation of lessons. Sharing ideas, plans, and resources with a small group of like-minded teachers can be tremendously helpful. Technology can be used to join or cre- ate collaborative support systems that will help save time. Additionally, many websites have lessons and other ideas available so that teachers can save time by modifying investigative ideas rather than trying to create from scratch. (See, for example, http://www.sciencenetlinks.com or http://smithsonianeducation.org.)

There will be many time pressures as you schedule lessons for your course calendar. This will create tension between "covering" the material and using additional portions of the schedule to go deeper. Many assume that because of the pressure of state testing there is no choice but to attempt to cover material in survey-course fashion. However, according to one extensive study that examined middle schools over a three-year period, this may not be the case. The authors concluded that "assignments calling for more authentic intellectual work actually improve student scores on conventional tests" (Newmann, Bryk, & Nagaoka, 2001, p. 29). You will need to be realistic about how you balance "coverage" and "authentic intellectual work," but the question really isn't *Should you do it?* but *How can you* best *do it?*

You should be aware that some challenges will involve student factors. Saye and Brush (1999) identify three of these challenges as student lack of engagement; student failure to consider a variety of competing perspectives; and student lack of content knowledge or the thinking skills necessary to apply the knowledge they possess. We have stressed the importance of teacher involvement in the process of engagement and perspective gathering. It is also important to prepare students through preinquiry activities. These can be thought of as practicing skills in order to get your class ready for true inquiry. By learning these skills independently, students are helped to overcome some of the challenges associated with this type of learning. Two examples provided by Wilke and Straits (2005) include giving students an article with an important section (e.g., the conclusion) missing and asking them to draw conclusions from the information remaining or posing an ethical question and asking students to discuss opinions, solutions, and opposing perspectives.

Students can be confronted with simple (but not immediately obvious) curiosities that arouse interest but also give opportunity for learning thinking skills. For example, one high school teacher wanted her students to learn about creating a hypothesis. At the beginning of class she stood a lit candle in a pan of water and placed a jar over the top. The students noticed that as the candle flickered lower and lower the water was pulled up inside the jar. When the flame went out, the water inside the jar was raised partway up the candle. The students were given 5–10 minutes during several class periods to create and test hypotheses using a variety of candles and jars available as resources. After several days the students, who worked in teams, were asked to share their hypotheses with the large group. The teacher was using this preinquiry technique to teach students about the process of scientific inquiry that she would use in other labs throughout the term.

CLASSROOM MANAGEMENT ISSUES

From a distance student-directed investigation looks as if students do everything and it runs on its own. This is far from the case. For every successful student-directed investigation, you will find masterful work by a behind-the-scenes teacher. So, in the case of Heather Brown's classroom described at the beginning of the chapter, what may appear to be "chaos" is actually a well-thought-out, planned system of learning.

A great deal of attention will need to be given to the classroom learning environment. You will need to create and nurture a "community of learners." This is a common concept for classrooms involved with student-centered approaches to learning. The development of a learning community is at the heart of this approach to learning (McGrath, 2003). According to Brown (1997) there are five critical pieces that work together to create a community of learners:

1. *Active, purposeful learning.* The design of a student-directed investigation will give opportunity for active purposeful learning.
2. *A learning setting that pays attention to multiple zones of proximal development.* Brown bases this component on the work of Vygotsky, who promoted the idea that through collaborative work on important topics learners will accomplish what they would not have been able to do alone. For specifics about collaborative learning, see chapter 8.
3. *The legitimization of differences.* Students should be encouraged to develop their individual areas of expertise for the good of the community of learners.
4. *A community of discourse.* A community is developed in which learners value methods for civil and worthwhile discussion.
5. *A community of practice.* Members of the learning community (which includes the teacher) value and respect each other and take responsibility for each other's learning through collaboration.

These five components of a healthy learning community could be explained to the class and perhaps acknowledged on paper and signed by students and the teacher as a way to show commitment to the principles.

You will notice that the roles for the teachers and students in a community of learners are somewhat unique. Teachers are thought of as colearners, coaches, facilitators, and sometime experts. Realistically, teachers can immerse themselves in the community only to a degree due to their responsibilities with evaluation and facilitation. These responsibilities naturally will affect student-teacher relationships even in the most dynamic of learning communities. Student roles will include assuming responsibility for learning, making process decisions, taking the initiative to determine direction, self-initiating, and participation as expert or coach at times.

One of the challenges for facilitating a successful student-directed investigation is to give students the responsibility for their learning while helping them stay on a pathway to success. It is important for teacher to help monitor self-directed work time by helping students consider their work schedule and set deadlines. It would be a mistake to assume that most students could, without assistance, create a work plan and stick to it. Here are a couple of suggestions that may be helpful:

Create a work plan together. Sit down with each student (or group) and help them create their schedule. Your role is not to give them a schedule but to help them understand what needs to done and when it needs to be completed—to help them learn to take responsibility on their own.

Monitor the students' schedule. After a schedule is created, a series of deadlines is helpful. These deadlines can be created by the students themselves or provided by the teacher. This again could be thought of as taking the responsibility of learning back from the students; however, this is a way to help students assume responsibility with the support needed for them to be successful. This series of deadlines could be part of a scoring guide or a part of a procedure with which students receive feedback. (For example, "You will need to turn in your first reflection for our service learning project on Tuesday so that I can give you feedback before our next site visit." Some use "research accountability receipts," citation forms, or similar forms to keep track of what students accomplish with their time at the library or at home in order to assist them with their schedule. Part of the learning beyond the content is related to making and keeping a schedule to accomplish a task on time. Students will probably need your help.

APPROPRIATE ASSESSMENT TECHNIQUES

Assessment can be difficult during student-directed investigation because the purpose of the strategy deals with thinking skills practice and the use of content. This focus requires techniques that are different from those associated with traditional testing for knowledge acquisition. Performance assessment, or authentic assessment, is a natural fit for this type of strategy because they ask students to demonstrate their thinking. This form of assessment is detailed in chapter 3.

There is a logical process to follow as you plan for assessment. As we discuss the assessment process we are assuming that you will have aligned your goals and objectives and thus have identified desired outcomes for the lesson. We assume these objectives will have guided you into deciding that a student-directed investigation is an appropriate strategy to use in helping students learn. The objectives will also help you create a scoring guide that reflects your thinking on the valued outcomes. In other words, the criteria you select for your scoring guide should be aligned with the objectives you have selected for the lesson. There are many valuable lessons your students will learn during their investigation; however, they need to know what in particular you will be assessing at the end of the day. A good way to do this is by sharing the scoring guide with the students "up front."

In a performance assessment the scoring guide is often a rubric or a checklist. This gives the teacher the opportunity to reduce (although not eliminate) the subjective aspects of this type of assessment. However, using student-directed investigation allows ample opportunity to use a variety of assessment techniques to collect multiple perspectives of student learning.

The Checklist

A checklist is similar to an analytic rubric, but without the descriptors and with more criteria it typically is a list of criteria that can be checked off as the teacher sees evidence of students' meeting expectations. Here is an example:[2]

CHECKLIST FOR ORAL PRESENTATIONS

Student Name: _____ Date: _____

Reviewer Name: _____

Project:

Category	Responsibilities
Content	❏ The information I gave was interesting or important to others.
	❏ I was well informed about my topic.
	❏ I used vocabulary that the audience could understand or defined unfamiliar terms.
	❏ I used an effective and appropriate attention-getting device.
	❏ Logical appeals included reliable, factual information.
	❏ I used emotional or persuasive appeals where appropriate.
	❏ I added supportive detail to the main point(s).
Delivery	❏ I maintained eye contact most of the time.
	❏ I spoke to the entire audience, not just one or two people.
	❏ My enunciation was clear and easy to understand.
	❏ My rate of speech was not too fast or too slow.
	❏ My voice could be heard easily by the entire audience.
	❏ My voice varied in pitch; it was not monotone.
	❏ I did not use filler words (e.g., "um," "uh," "ah," "mm," "like," etc.).
	❏ My body language was not too tense or too relaxed.
	❏ I didn't fidget, rock back and forth, or pace.
	❏ I used notes sparingly; I did not read from them.

(continued)

Category	*Responsibilities*
Organization	❏ I organized ideas in a meaningful way.
	❏ The information and arguments/details were easy to follow.
	❏ I stayed focused and did not stray off topic.
	❏ The introduction included a clear statement of the main point(s).
	❏ I included necessary background information about the topic.
	❏ The body of the presentation contained support for, or details about, the main point(s).
	❏ The audience could distinguish the introduction, body, and conclusion.
Presentation Aids	❏ Presentation aids were used during the speech.
	❏ Presentation aids were relevant to the speech.
	❏ Presentation aids improved the presentation or reinforced main points.
Resources	❏ I used resources that addressed the topic thoroughly.
	❏ I used credible print resources.
	❏ I used credible electronic resources.
	❏ I cited my sources using the required format.
	❏ A bibliography was available.

The Conference
By talking with the teacher in conference the student explains what was learned and provides evidence. The teacher has an opportunity to ask questions or probe for understanding.

The Portfolio
A portfolio is a collection of samples of student work and reflective notes from the student and others that show progress.

The Rubric
The rubric is a matrix that provides criteria and descriptors for rating students at various levels. *Holistic* rubrics provide criteria that look at the overall quality of the task, while *analytic* rubrics breakdown the most important aspects of the task.

Here is an example of a holistic rubric:[3]

HOLISTIC RUBRIC FOR FICTION WRITING

5—The plot, setting, and characters are developed fully and organized well. The *who, what, where, when,* and *why* are explained using interesting language and sufficient detail.

4—Most parts of the story mentioned in the score of 5 above are developed and organized well. A couple of aspects may need to be more fully or more interestingly developed.

3—Some aspects of the story are developed and organized well, but not as much detail or organization is expressed as in a score of 4.

2—A few parts of the story are developed somewhat. Organization and language usage need improvement.

1—Parts of the story are addressed without attention to detail or organization.

Here is an example of an analytic rubric:[4]

ANALYTIC RUBRIC FOR MAKING A BROCHURE

Teacher Name:

Student Name: _____

Category	4	3	2	1
Writing and Organization	Each section in the brochure has a clear beginning, middle, and end.	Almost all sections of the brochure have a clear beginning, middle, and end.	Most sections of the brochure have a clear beginning, middle, and end.	Less than half of the sections of the brochure have a clear beginning, middle, and end.
Content and Accuracy	All facts in the brochure are accurate.	99–90% of the facts in the brochure are accurate.	89–80% of the facts in the brochure are accurate.	Fewer than 80% of the facts in the brochure are accurate.
Spelling and Proofreading	No spelling errors remain after one person other than the typist has read and corrected the brochure.	No more than one spelling error remains after one person other than the typist has read and corrected the brochure.	No more than three spelling errors remain after one person other than the typist has read and corrected the brochure.	Several spelling errors in the brochure.
Attractiveness and Organization	The brochure has exceptionally attractive formatting and well-organized information.	The brochure has attractive formatting and well-organized information.	The brochure has well-organized information.	The brochure's formatting and organization of material are confusing to the reader.

The Student Journal

The student journal contains notes kept by the student that can be shown to the teacher or referred to by the student during a conference. The notes are from free-writing exercises about learning, or responses to prompts by the teacher intended to help the student think about her learning.

Teacher Notes

Teacher notes are an "on-the-fly" record of what the teacher observes. For example, on an index card a teacher might record, "Observed Amelia leading the group through excellent analysis comments during… "

GUIDELINES FOR DECIDING IF STUDENT-DIRECTED INVESTIGATION IS APPROPRIATE

Weighing the advantages and disadvantages of student-directed investigation will be important as you determine if this is an appropriate strategy. Some of the advantages are that it is often motivating to students as they pursue topics that interest them. It can be stimulating to perhaps explore outside of the traditional classroom, especially in a venue that allows you to serve another person or the community. This approach encourages autonomy and initiative, while giving students an opportunity to think deeply about issues. Some of these advantages may be similar to what you have in mind in your objectives.

You should also consider some of the unique challenges in student-directed investigation when deciding if you should use it. It can take considerably more time to complete than other approaches. Remember, you will need to balance a need to "cover" material with an opportunity to learn through exploration and experience. You will need to have the appropriate resources, such as community experts, informational media (can you get access to the computer lab or go to the library?), and materials necessary for student to be successful. You should determine if you feel comfortable acting as a facilitator, often being pulled in many directions at one time. How is your energy level? This is not a study hall approach. Are you prepared to engage with students in an environment that at times can look like controlled chaos?

MAKING IT WORK IN YOUR CONTENT AREA

Student-Directed Investigations for Differentiated Learning

Tomlinson (2003) offers criteria for what she calls a *high-quality curriculum*. This is a curriculum that promotes learning for all students by being engaging and promoting understanding. Obviously, no teacher would be able to achieve all of these in one lesson or probably in one unit. However, these indicators will help you evaluate your instructional direction. After you have created a unit of instruction that includes student-directed investigation, assess your unit using the following check-list. Indicating a check, plus, or minus for each criterion may be helpful before you write self-evaluative comments about your work.

Engagement:
  Is fresh and surprising to the students
  Seems "real" and purposeful to the students
  Connects with the students' lives
  Allows choice
  Requires active learning
  Is pleasurable—or at least satisfying—for the students
  Is focused on products that matter to the students
  Taps personal interest
  Allows students to make a contribution to something greater than themselves
  Challenges students and provides support for success
Promotes Understanding:
  Is clearly focused on the essential knowledge, understanding, and skills a professional in the field would value
  Is coherent (organized, unified, sensible) to students
  Attends to student misconceptions
  Deals with profound ideas that endure across years of learning
  Enables students to use what they learn in important ways
  Requires cognition and metacognition
  Causes students to grapple with significant problems
  Causes students to raise useful questions
  Necessitates that students generate (vs. reproduce) knowledge

Comments: _____

CHAPTER REVIEW

Student-directed instruction is a means by which differentiated learning can take place in your classroom. It promotes learning through experience in an environment that involves the "real world" and offers meaningful, personally interesting challenges; requires active learning; provides opportunities to solve problems, answer questions, or address real needs; allows for student owner-ship, responsibility, and choices; and offers students an opportunity to perform as experts or professionals.

NOTES

1. These criteria are copyright 1997–2005, The Write Place. Reproduction is granted for educational purposes.

2. This checklist was created with the assistance of 4teachers.org (http://pblchecklist.4teachers.org); retrieved September 2, 2006.

3. This holistic rubric was adapted from Pearson Education's TeacherVision (http://www.teachervision.fen.com); retrieved June 1, 2006.

4. This analytic rubric was created with the assistance of Rubistar (http://rubistar.4teachers.org); retrieved September 4, 2006).

REFERENCES

Boekaerts, M. (1997). Self-regulated learning: a new concept embraced by researchers, policy makers, educators, teachers, and students. *Learning and Instruction, 7*, 161–186.

Bransford, J. D., Brown, A. L., & Cocking, R. R. (Eds.). (2000). *How people learn: Brain, mind, experience, and school.* Washington, DC: National Academy Press.

Brooks, J. G., & Brooks, M. B. (1993). *The case for constructivist classrooms.* Alexandria, VA: Association for Supervision and Curriculum Development.

Brown, A. L. (1997). Transforming schools into communities of thinking and learning about serious matters. *American Psychologist, 54*(4), 399–413.

Brown, H. (2004). Walking into the unknown: Inquiry-based learning transforms the English classroom. *English Journal, 94*(2), 43.

Brown, J. S., Collins, A., & Duguid, P. (1989). Situated cognition and the culture of learning. *Educational Researcher, 18*(1), 32–42.

Bruce, B. C., & Davidson, J. (1996). An inquiry model for literacy across the curriculum. *Journal of Curriculum Studies, 28*, 281–300.

Cognition and Technology Group at Vanderbilt (1990). Anchored instruction and its relationship to situated cognition. *Educational Researcher, 19*(5), 2–10.

Collins, A., Brown, J. S., & Newman, S. E. (1994). Cognitive apprenticeship. In L. B. Resnick (Ed.), *Knowing, learning, and instruction* (pp. 453–494). Hillsdale, NJ: Lawrence Erlbaum Associates.

Duffy, T., & Jonassen, D. (Eds.). (1992). *Constructivism and the technology of instruction: A conversation.* Hillsdale, NJ: Lawrence Erlbaum Associates.

Exline, J. (2004). Inquiry-based learning. Retrieved February 1, 2006 from http://www.thirteen.org/edonline/concept2class/inquiry/.

Fosnot, C. T. (1989). *Inquiring teachers, enquiring learners.* New York: Teachers College Press.

Gallagher, S., Sher, B., Stepien, W., & Workman, D. (1995). Implementing problem-based learning in science classrooms. *School Science and Mathematics, 95*(3), 136–146.

Harris, K., Marcus, R., McLaren, K., & Fey, J. (2001). Curriculum materials supporting problem-based teaching. *School Science and Mathematics, 101*(6), 310–318.

McGrath, D. (2003). Developing a community of learners: What will it look like and how will it work? *Learning and Leading with Technology, 30*(7), 42–45.

Newmann, F., Bryk, A., & Nagaoka, J. (2001). *Authentic intellectual work and standardized tests: Conflicts or coexistence?* Chicago: Consortium on Chicago School Research. Retrieved February 15, 2006 from http://www.consortium-chicago.org/publications/p0001.html.

Pithers, R. T., & Soden, R. (2000). Critical thinking in education: A review. *Educational Research, 42*(3), 237–249.

Saye, J. W., & Brush, T. (1999). Student engagement with social issues in a multimedia-supported learning environment. *Theory and Research in Social Education, 27*(4), 472–504.

Scheurman, G. (1998). From behaviorist to constructivist teaching. *Social Education, 62,* 6–9.

Scheurman, G., & Newmann, F. M. (1998). Authentic intellectual work in social studies: Putting performance before pedagogy. *Social Education, 4*(3), 150–153.

Skinner, B. F. (1968). *The technology of teaching.* New York: Appelton.

Struthers, K. (2005). Assessing the credibility of online sources. Retrieved February 1, 2006 from http://leo.stcloudstate.edu/research/credibility1.html.

Tomlinson, C. (2003). *Fulfilling the promise of differentiated classrooms: Strategies and tools for responsive teaching.* Alexandria, VA: Association for Supervision and Curriculum Development.

West, S. A. (1992). Problem-based learning—A viable addition for secondary school science. *School Science Review, 73*(265), 47–55.

Wilke, R., & Straits, W. (2005). Practical advice for teaching inquiry-based science process skills in the biological sciences. *American Biology Teacher, 67*(9), 534–540.

Wisker, G., & Brown, S. (Eds.). (1996). *Enabling student learning.* London: Kogan Page/Staff and Educational Development Association.

APPENDIX A
Glossary of Key Terms

504 plan: A program of instructional services to assist a student with a physical or emotional disability, an impairment that restricts one or more major life activities (e.g., caring for one's self, performing manual tasks, walking, seeing, hearing, speaking, breathing, working, and learning), or who is recovering from a chemical dependency.

Action research: Purposeful ways a teacher identifies a phenomenon in the classroom, determines an approach for gaining insight into this phenomenon, and assesses if the approach was effective.

Affective domain: Learning that is tied to feelings or emotions. Learning in this domain does not require students to develop particular feelings or emotions, but it helps students use their emotions and feelings to learn.

Analysis: Breaking down whole entities into their component parts to identify relationships, make comparisons and contrasts, and look for patterns. Level four on Bloom's taxonomy.

Anticipatory set: Some refer to this metaphorically as the "hook" by which a teacher catches students' attention, or the manner by which a teacher helps students anticipate what will be happening for the day. This could be a question, a poster, music, or even a short activity.

Application: Students' practical use of skills, concepts, and information in new situations. Level three on Bloom's taxonomy.

Assessment: A plan that allows teachers and students to monitor their progress toward meeting specified goals and objectives.

Authentic assessment: Assessments that resemble tasks that might occur outside of the school as well as in the classroom. Both the material and the assessment tasks look as natural as possible. Authentic assessment values the thinking behind the work, or the process, as much as the finished product.

Authentic task: An activity where students need to use information and skills learned in school to complete a complex task that is realistic and might occur outside of school.

Backward design: Wiggins and McTighe (2000) describe backward design as follows: "One starts with the end—the desired results—and then derives the curriculum from the evidence of learning called for by the standard (learning objective) and the teaching needed to equip students to perform" (p. 8).

Behaviorism: A long-established approach for thinking about learning, where learning occurs when the overt behavior changes.

BICS: An abbreviation for Basic Interpersonal Communicative Skills. This is best thought of as conversational language.

Bilingual: An ability to speak two languages.

Bilingual education: An approach to instruction that includes the continued development of the student's native language, the learning of a second language, and the use of both languages to teach academic content.

Biliteracy: The ability to read and write in two languages.

Bodily-kinesthetic intelligence: One of Howard Gardner's multiple intelligences. This involves the potential of using one's whole body or parts of the body to solve problems. It is the ability to coordinate bodily movements.

Biological development: Considers the influence of the body's physical changes on the adolescent. This applies to learning and teaching because physical changes impact adolescent body size and shape, nutritional needs, mood swings, and the many other changes that are occurring in the body.

Bloom's taxonomy: This is a hierarchy of thinking proposed by Benjamin Bloom. At the lowest level, thinking is comprised of simple knowledge. As one moves along the taxonomy, thinking becomes more complex as it moves to comprehension, application, analysis, synthesis, and finally evaluation.

CALP: An abbreviation for Cognitive Academic Language Proficiency, or the ability to communicate beyond conversation and engage in academic learning through the language.

Canter's Assertive Discipline Model: Provides a set of clear cut expectations for the classroom. Students can expect teachers to provide a safe learning environment, and teachers can expect students to pay attention and not disrupt the class.

Classroom management: Proactive approaches for helping students learn. It includes all of the aspects of the classroom that will promote student learning.

Cognitive domain: The thinking skills and academic content to be learned in the classroom.

Comprehension: Demonstrating understanding by being able to explain ideas.

Concept: An idea.

Concept formation: An instructional strategy that uses an inductive approach for helping students learn the critical attributes of a given concept. Students look at examples of a concept, then generalize their conclusions to incorporate all examples of this concept.

Concept label: The word or phrase that a group of people have agreed to use when referring to a concept.

Concept telling: The critical attributes of a concept are told to students, and students do not have opportunities to think deeply about the concept. Often concepts are reduced to vocabulary words.

Constructivism: An approach based on the idea that learners construct, or build, meaning and understanding as they learn. It usually implies hands-on activities where students spend a good amount of time processing the information so they understand it in depth.

Content: Facts, concepts, skills, and attitudes that students learn in a class. While teachers will "teach content," it is more important for teachers to know what content students are learning.

Convergent questions: Questions that allow for only one or a few correct responses. These questions tend to be lower-order questions on Bloom's Taxonomy.

Cooperative learning: Students work in groups to help them learn content. The five "essential elements" of cooperative learning are: 1) positive interdependence; 2) face-to-face interactions; 3) group goals and individual accountability; 4) interpersonal and small-group skills; and 5) group processing.

Criterion-referencing: Assessment against fixed criteria. Potentially everyone can pass a criterion-referenced assessment—or everyone can fail.

Critical attributes: The traits or characteristics that every example of a particular concept will have.

Curriculum: The expected learning outcomes of the classroom, the content students will learn, and the lesson plans that provide detailed description for each class period. The curriculum has five parts: 1) the formal curriculum; 2) the delivered curriculum; 3) the learned curriculum; 4) the hidden curriculum; and 5) the null curriculum.

Delivered curriculum: Also known as the taught curriculum, and can be thought of as the instructional processes or methods used to communicate the formal curriculum.

Diagnostic assessment: Assessment techniques that usually occur prior to instruction, and attempt to determine students' strengths, weaknesses, knowledge, and skills. Identifying these helps teachers differentiate the curriculum to meet each student's unique needs.

Direct instruction: A label for a prescribed approach to teaching. Often direct instruction is referred to as "big D.I." and as "little d.i." The first is the label for a scripted and sequential approach for helping students learn, and the latter a general description of teacher-led instruction.

Discipline: A reaction to student misbehavior that refers to how the teacher effectively controls students so their behaviors maintain a positive learning environment in the classroom.

Discussion: An instructional strategy that engages students in a conversation with one another about a specific topic. Discussion takes many forms in the classroom, and serves many purposes. Generally, discussion helps students understand a topic or issue more clearly, and it helps students learn how to communicate effectively.

Divergent questions: Questions that require deliberation and encourage broad responses. A number of appropriate responses are possible to this type of question and they typically require higher-order thought processes.

Dramatization: Students act in a given role, during a scene, and often with a script. Usually, this technique is used to help students empathize with a particular viewpoint or better understand an event, but it can also be effectively used to help improve student communication skills.

Dreikurs/Albert model: A classroom management model that is based on the idea that classrooms needs to be democratic. This has implications for classroom rules, classroom management, and the instructional strategies used by the teacher.

Dynamic concepts: Concepts that do not have an easily agreed upon set of critical attributes.

Electronic threaded discussions: A type of discussion where students "talk" with one another electronically and asynchronously via a computer. Discussions are typically referred to as "forums," and comments made by students are called "posts."

ELL: An abbreviation for English Language Learners/students who are not proficient in English.

Epistemology: The study of knowledge that seeks to explain how we know—literally how we obtain, use, and think about knowledge of the world around us.

ESL: An abbreviation for English as a Second Language. A program or system of instruction designed to teach English to those that speak other languages. This system typically will use academic content and is usually thought of as a component of bilingual education.

ESOL: An abbreviation for English Speakers of Other Languages. Some prefer this to ESL because it recognizes that English could be the third or fourth language of the student and that this should be acknowledged. For example, a student from Mexico may speak Mixteco (a Native language) as his first language and Spanish as his second language.

Essential questions: Questions about the big ideas or fundamental concepts that teachers want students to think about and learn during the span of a unit. By posing questions, students and the teacher are able to focus their attention on content that will help answer the questions. Essential questions, thus, provide a focus for the unit.

Established concepts: Concepts that have a widely agreed upon set of critical attributes.

Evaluation: The highest level of Bloom's taxonomy. Activities and questions encourage students to take their own points of view or to express their ideas on issues. At the evaluation level, divergent thinking is encouraged and differences of opinion are to be expected. Evaluation is also a term associated with measuring student achievement. See "Assessment."

Examples of a concept: An example contains all of the critical attributes of a concept.

Exit card: A formative assessment technique where students briefly write a response to a teacher's request on a card or slip of paper, and hand this in at the end of the period/day. The teacher uses the students' responses to help determine if they understood a key point in the lesson.

Explicit teaching: A synonym for "direct instruction." Both terms imply that the teacher explicitly/directly provides information or step-by-step skills.

Extrinsic motivation: People are motivated to do something by outside, or external, factors that they believe will provide desirable results.

Fact: A phenomenon that can be verified through observing, experiencing, reading, or listening. Facts are necessary for building conceptual knowledge and generalizations.

Fishbowl discussion: A discussion technique where participants learn about the topic of discussion, and receive explicit direction for developing the requisite skills and attitudes needed to listen and talk during a discussion.

Flow: A theory of intrinsic motivation suggesting that we have a sense of calm and increased engagement in a task when we perceive that our ability matches the requirements for completing a challenging task. Developed by Mihalyi Csikszentmihalyi.

Formal cooperative learning: Student groups "are actively involved in the intellectual work of organizing material, explaining it, summarizing it, and integrating it into existing conceptual structures" (Johnson, Johnson, & Holubec, 1998, p. 7).

Formal curriculum: Consists of all that educators purposefully intend to teach students. This is also referred to by some as the intended, planned, explicit, or official curriculum. This is the part of the curriculum that most think of first, and it includes syllabi, unit plans, lesson plans, national and state standards, or textbooks.

Formative assessment: Assessment that occurs continually during each school day so the teacher is able to monitor student learning. Formative assessment provides information on how students are "forming" their understanding.

Futures wheel discussion: A discussion technique that focuses classroom discussions in a way that leads to decision-making. Students think through the implications of potential outcomes on any issue, and begin to think about the future, and the implications of decisions on future decisions, actions and policies.

Generalization: A descriptive statement of a relationship between two or more concepts.

Ginott's model: A classroom management model built around the key term of congruent communication, or communication that is about situations rather than student character or personality.

Glasser's model: A classroom management model predicated on the idea that the teacher expects all students to produce quality work.

Goal: A broad general statement that allows a teacher to focus the content, skills, and dispositions that students need to learn. Goals are usually written for the entire course as well as for segmented sections of the course called units of instruction.

Group investigation: A six-step cooperative learning strategy that provides students with a significant amount of choice and control. Groups are mixed, but they are additionally formed to match students who share an interest about the same topic. Group members help plan how they will research a topic, how they will present it, and how they will divide the work among themselves.

Guided inquiry: One of three types of inquiry learning. Here students are given a research direction and materials but need to determine the research method themselves.

Hidden curriculum: The knowledge, skills, and attitudes students learn at school that are not part of the formal curriculum. It is often not explicitly taught, but "picked up" or informally learned in the process of being at school.

Heterogeneous groups: Student groups with some combination of mixed ability, mixed ethnicity, and mixed gender. Placing students in heterogeneous groups is a requirement of cooperative learning.

Homogenous groups: Groups that are comprised of students who are more similar than different.

IDS approach: An alternative approach for considering the domains of learning where the teacher writes objectives that focus on Information, Disposition, and Skill (IDS).

Ill-structured: An authentic assessment that requires students to demonstrate learning by determining the structure and organization of their solution to a problem or task.

Immersion: A term associated with teaching students with English as a second language. Technically immersion is a bilingual program developed in Canada where 90% of the early elementary school student's day is in the minority language (the non-mainstream language). Many times, however, this term is used in school to refer to placing a student in a mainstream classroom (not necessarily as part of a well-thought-out program).

Individualized Education Program (IEP): An individualized program that specifies educational supports and services that will help a child with a disability receive appropriate instruction. An IEP may specify instructional strategies, strategies for managing behavior, motivational techniques, and other insights about how to best help the student learn.

Informal cooperative learning: Students work in groups that are formed quickly and/or spontaneously for a few minutes to an entire class period.

Inquiry learning: Problem-based learning that is initiated with a problem, uses student investigation and/or research, and has the teacher serve as a facilitator to the student or student group.

Interdisciplinary unit plan: Unit plans that integrate topics from more than one course around a common theme or idea.

Interpersonal intelligence: One of eight intelligences from Howard Gardner's Multiple Intelligence Theory. Interpersonal intelligence is the capacity to understand the intentions, motivations, and desires of other people. With this intelligence a person works effectively with others.

Intrapersonal intelligence: One of eight intelligences from Howard Gardner's Multiple Intelligence Theory. Intrapersonal intelligence is the capacity to understand one's own feelings and emotions. With this intelligence a person has an useful understanding of him/herself and is able to use this information to regulate his/her life.

Intrinsic motivation: People are motivated to engage in an activity because of the satisfaction derived from the activity itself.

Issues/values continuum: A discussion technique that allows the teacher and students to assess the diversity of opinions in the classroom, while requiring students to think about their own positions on issues.

Jigsaw: A cooperative learning strategy where students are in two groups: an expert group where they learn with others about specific information, and a home group where they share their newly formed expertise. Students work interdependently in both groups.

Jones's model: A classroom management model emphasizing the importance of a teacher's non-verbal communication such as body language, expressions, gestures, proximity. This model also suggests that teachers provide incentives for students that are genuine, and that teachers should provide efficient and limited help to students.

Knowledge: This is the first and most basic of Bloom's taxonomy. It addresses recall of information and whether students remember what they have read, were told, or saw. Knowledge is also referred to by some as synonymous with key facts and skills. In this use, student learning refers to knowledge, skills, and dispositions.

Kounin's model: A classroom management model that emphasizes the importance of teachers engaging students in the classroom lessons. This model suggests that misbehavior rarely occurs when students are actively learning.

Learned curriculum: A representation of all that a student learns in school. Some refer to this as the "realized" curriculum and it comes into play when assessing the students and the curriculum itself.

Learning: A "relatively permanent change, due to experience, either in behavior or in mental representations or associations" (Ormrod, 2006, p. 184).

Learning objective: Statements that help teachers, students, and others involved in education answer three basic questions related to teaching and student learning: What content do students need to learn? How will student learning be assessed? What activities will students engage in to promote learning?

Lecture: An instructional strategy where the teacher presents a specified set of information to students. These presentations take a variety of forms.

LEP: An abbreviation for Limited English Proficient. Some prefer not to use this term because it focuses on what a student cannot do.

Lesson plan: A document used by a teacher that provides the structure, instructional strategies, and plan of action for each day.

Linguistic/verbal intelligence: One of eight intelligences from Howard Gardner's Multiple Intelligence Theory. Linguistic/verbal intelligence involves abilities with spoken and written language, the ability to learn languages, and the capacity to use language to accomplish certain goals.

Logical-mathematic intelligence: One of eight intelligences from Howard Gardner's Multiple Intelligence Theory. Logical-mathematic intelligence consists of the capacity to think logically, carry out mathematical operations, and investigate issues with a systematic/scientific approach. This intelligence includes the ability to detect patterns, reason deductively, and think logically.

Long-term objective: Learning objectives that are met during a longer unit, semester, or even an entire course. These tend to be more general than short-term objectives and more specific than goals.

Metacognition: Thinking about one's own thinking. Teachers use metacognitive strategies to assist students with this process.

Momentum: A characteristic of a well-designed lesson that shows smoothness, good transitions, and pacing during a lesson.

Multicultural education: "A field of study and an emerging discipline whose major aim is to create equal educational opportunities for students from diverse racial, ethnic, social-class, and cultural groups. One of its important goals is to help all students to acquire the knowledge, attitudes, and skills needed to function effectively in a pluralistic democratic society and to interact, negotiate, and communicate with peoples from diverse groups in order to create a civic and moral community that works for the common good" (Banks & Banks, 1995, pp. xi–xii).

Multiple intelligences: Howard Gardner's theory suggesting that there are eight different intelligences and that these account for a broader conception of what we think about human potential.

Musical intelligence: One of eight intelligences from Howard Gardner's Multiple Intelligence Theory. Musical intelligence involves skill in the performance, composition, and appreciation of musical patterns.

Naturalist intelligence: One of eight intelligences from Howard Gardner's Multiple Intelligence Theory. Naturalist intelligence involves abilities for sensing patterns in and making connections to elements in nature.

Non-examples of a concept: Non-examples are lacking one or more critical attributes of a concept.

Norm-referencing: Assessing students based upon how their scores rank in comparison with other students. This could be at the class, district, state, or national level.

Null curriculum: The content that students do not learn.

Open inquiry: A type of inquiry learning in which students determine the research question, methods, and necessary resources.

Overlapping: Kounin's term for multi-tasking. Having the ability to attend to two or three tasks at the same time.

Peer coaching model: A type of reflective teaching through peer teacher observations. A critical friend model.

Performance assessment: The process of assessing student learning while the students are performing an authentic task.

Planning: The process of organizing the curriculum into long- and short-term plans.

Positive interdependence: A synonym of cooperation, this is an essential element of any cooperative learning strategy.

Prior knowledge: Knowledge about a topic that students have before a lesson.

Problem-based learning: A type of student-directed investigation that focuses on the process of solving a problem.

Progress monitoring: Formative assessment.

Psychological/cognitive development: Ideas about mental development that help teachers understand how the age of the student impacts psychological responses and cognitive ability.

Psychomotor domain: Learning with or about the coordinated use of the body's muscular system.

Questioning: A teacher-centered strategy used to encourage deeper thinking through the use of a series of questions. This is sometimes referred to as a Socratic seminar.

Recitation: A teaching activity in which students "repeat orally or explain material learned by individual study or previously presented by the teacher and in response to questions raised by the teacher" (Good, 1983, p. 478).

Reflection: A process of thinking that focuses on learning from experiences. Typically used by students to consider their learning or by teachers to improve the quality of their teaching.

Reflection-for-action: Focusing reflective thinking on improving future actions.

Reflection-in-action: The process of monitoring students work and progress during the class meeting.

Reflection-on-action: Thinking critically about a lesson and one's actions after the lesson is completed.

Relational teaching: A way of thinking about teaching that places a high value on the relationship the teacher has with the whole class as well as with each student.

Reliability: The degree of confidence that an assessment tool will produce the same results over time.

Ripple effect: A phrase used by Kounin to refer to when the teacher's words or actions are directed at one student but affect behavior of other students.

Role-play: A theatric strategy that allows a student to assume another role including a change in values and attitudes. This may or may or may not involve a change in environment but would probably not involve the use of a script.

Rubric: A type of scoring guide typically used for a student project or performance. This guide is used to help teachers evaluate student work and for students to understand expectations.

Satiation: Kounin's term for when students are done thinking about a topic and the teacher needs to change his/her approach.

Schwab's four commonplaces: Four interrelated aspects of the classroom that affect teaching and learning. These include the teacher, the students, the subject matter that is to be learned, and the milieu.

Scope: The breadth of content and skills students will be expected to learn.

Self-efficacy: Our self expectation or belief about what we can accomplish as a result of our efforts.

Self-referencing: An assessment by the student against his/her self or more particularly against previous best performances. This is used to help gauge improvement.

Sequence: The order in which students will be expected to learn content and skills.

Short-term objective: Objectives that are met during an activity or after a few class sessions.

Simulation: A theatric strategy that allows for a "scene change" while students maintain their own sense of self (their own values and attitudes).

Sociological/cultural development: An individual's development of ideas related to their self-concept. Usually associated with an adolescent's thoughts about who he or she is while considering the many aspects of human identity.

Socratic seminar: A teacher-directed questioning session that encourages students to think deeply about issues.

Spatial intelligence: One of eight intelligences from Howard Gardner's Multiple Intelligence Theory. Spatial intelligence involves the potential to recognize and use the patterns of wide space and more confined areas.

Structured academic controversy: A type of cooperative learning strategy that uses small group discussions to explore controversial issues.

Structured debate: A teaching strategy that is competitive and helps encourage wide participation in the classroom. It serves a different purpose than classroom discussions. It is used when there are two dominant positions on an issue.

Structured inquiry: A type of inquiry lesson in which students are given a research question or direction, a method, and materials, but not expected outcomes.

Student accountability: Kounin uses this phrase to refer to a teacher's efforts to keep students alert and involved in the lessons. This may involve calling on students to answer questions, or other requests that require students to be attentive.

Student teams achievement divisions (STAD): A formal cooperative learning strategy that involves cooperation within groups and competition among groups to help them review information.

Student-directed investigation: A learning strategy in which students are encouraged to pursue personal interests or questions that would include inquiry learning, discovery learning, problem-based learning, project-based learning, experiential learning, and service learning.

Summative assessment: The attempt to summarize student learning usually at the end of a unit, term, or course.

Synthesis: The level of Bloom's taxonomy that deals with combining ideas.

T-chart: Charts that have two columns and are shaped like the letter "T." These charts can help students identify behavioral expectations for specific cooperation skills.

Take a stand discussion: A form of discussion used when teachers want students to consider opposing viewpoints around a controversial issue.

TESOL: An abbreviation for Teaching English to Speakers of Other Languages.

Think-pair-share: A discussion or cooperative learning activity in which students are asked to think about a topic, tell a partner about their reflections, and share ideas with the entire class.

Unit plan: A teacher's plan for students to learn a selected topic or portion of their intended curriculum. This usually is a plan for several weeks of the course.

Usability: The degree to which an assessment tool is difficult or easy to administer.

Valence and challenge arousal: Kounin's term for how teachers might make activities more enjoyable/challenging.

Validity: The degree to which an assessment is an accurate and appropriate measurement of student learning.

Wait time: The time a teacher waits for a student response or before a teacher responds to a student.

Webquest: An inquiry-oriented online project developed by San Diego State University (webquest.org)

With-it-ness: The ability of a teacher to show awareness of student behavior throughout the classroom even while working with other students or in another part of the room.

Zone of Proximal Development: Vygotsky theorized that this "zone" exists between our current level of understanding and deeper understanding.

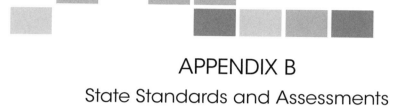

APPENDIX B
State Standards and Assessments

State	Name of Standards	High-Stakes Test	Consequences
Alabama "http://www. alsde.edu/html/home. asp"	Alabama Course of Study (ACS) by discipline	Alabama High School Graduation Exam (AHSGE)	Must pass to graduate from high school; No Child Left Behind (NCLB) consequences
Alaska "http://www. eed.state.ak.us/"	Alaska Content Standards (ACS) and Alaska Performance Standards and Grade Level Expectations (PSGLE)	High School Graduation Qualifying Examinations (HSGQE)	Must pass to graduate from high school; NCLB consequences
Arizona "http://www. ade.state.az.us/"	Arizona Academic Content Standards (AACS)	Arizona's Instrument to Measure Standards (AIMS)	Must pass to graduate from high school; NCLB consequences
Arkansas "http:// arkedu.state.ar.us/"	Arkansas Curriculum Frameworks (ACF)	Arkansas Comprehensive Testing Assessment and Accountability Program (ACTAAP)	NCLB consequences
California "http:// www.cde.ca.gov/"	California Education Standards	High School Exit Exam (HSEE)and Standardized Testing and Reporting (STAR)	Must pass HSEE to graduate from high school; NCLB consequences
Colorado "http://www. cde.state.co.us/"	Colorado Model Content Standards (CMCS)	Colorado Student Assessment Program (CSAP)	NCLB consequences; consistently low-scoring schools converted to charter schools

(continued)

State	Name of Standards	High-Stakes Test	Consequences
Connecticut "http://www.state.ct.us/sde/"	Connecticut Framework K–12 Curricular Goals and Standards	Connecticut Academic Performance Test (CAPT)	CAPT not sole measure for graduation, but can be part of it; state currently rejects NCLB
Delaware "http://www.doestate.de.us/info/sbe/"	Delaware Content and Framework Standards	Delaware Student Testing Program (DSTP)	NCLB consequences
District of Columbia "http://www.k12.dc.us/dcps/"	Learning Standards	Testing program exists, but name not available on website	NCLB consequences
Florida "http://www.fldoe.org"	Sunshine State Standards (SSS)	Florida Comprehensive Assessment Test (FCAT)	Must pass to graduate; NCLB consequences
Georgia "http://public.doe.k12.ga.us/"	Georgia Performance Standards (GPS)	Criterion Referenced Competency Tests (CRCT), End of Course Tests (EOCT), and Georgia High School Graduation Tests (GHSGT)	Must pass EOCT to pass class (high school); must pass five kinds of GHSGT to graduate; NCLB consequences (linked to CRCT)
Hawaii "http://doe.k12.hi.us/"	Hawaii Content and Performance Standards (HCPS)	Hawaii State Assessment (HSA)	NCLB consequences
Idaho "http://www.boardofed.idaho.gov/"	Idaho Achievement Standards (IAS)	Idaho Standards Achievement Test (ISAT)	Must pass ISAT to graduate; NCLB consequences
Illinois "http://www.isbe.state.il.us/"	Illinois Learning Standards (ILS)	Illinois Standards Achievement Test (ISAT)	NCLB consequences
Indiana "http://www.doe.state.in.us/"	Indiana's Academic Standards (IAS)	End of Course Assessments (ECAs), Indiana Statewide Testing for Educational Progress (ISTEP), and Graduation Qualifying Exam (GQE)	Must pass GQE to graduate; ECAs determine passing for Algebra I and English 11; NCLB consequences (linked to ISTEP)
Iowa "http://www.state.ia.us/educate/ecese"	Core Content Standards and Benchmarks	Iowa Tests of Basic Skills (ITBS) or Iowa Tests of Educational Development (ITED)	NCLB consequences

(continued)

State	Name of Standards	High-Stakes Test	Consequences
Kansas "http://www.ksbe.state.ks.us"	Kansas Curricular Standards (KCS)	Kansas Assessment of Multiple Measures (KAMM)	NCLB consequences
Kentucky "http://www.education.ky.gov"	Kentucky's Learning Goals and Academic Expectations (KLGAE) of Kentucky's Academic Expectations (KAE) and Kentucky's Student Performance Standards (KSPS)	Kentucky Core Content Test (KCCT)	NCLB consequences
Louisiana "http://www.doe.state.la.us/lde/index.html"	Louisiana Content Standards (LCS)	Louisiana Educational Assessment Program (LEAP 21) and Graduate Exit Examination (GEE 21)	Must pass English and math sections of LEAP 21 to be promoted in fourth and eighth grades; must pass GEE to graduate; NCLB consequences
Maine "http://www.state.me.us/education/"	Maine Learning Results (MLR)	Maine Educational Assessment (MEA)	NCLB consequences
Maryland "http://www.marylandpublicschools.org/msde"	Maryland Content Standards (MCS) and Voluntary State Curriculum (VSC)	Maryland School Assessment (MSA) and Maryland High School Assessments (MHSA)	Must pass MHSA in algebra, biology, English, and government to graduate in or after 2009; NCLB consequences (linked to MSA)
Massachusetts "http://www.doe.mass.edu/"	Massachusetts Curriculum Frameworks (MCF)	Massachusetts Comprehensive Assessment System (MCAS)	Must pass to graduate; NCLB consequences
Michigan "http://www.michigan.gov/mde"	Michigan Content Standards and Grade Level Content Expectations (GLCE)	Michigan Educational Assessment Program (MEAP)	NCLB consequences
Minnesota "http://education.state.mn.us/mde/index.html"	Minnesota Academic Standards (MAS)	Minnesota Comprehensive Assessments (MCA-II) and Basic Skills Test of Written Composition	Must pass MCA-II (in math and reading) and Basic Skills Test of Written Composition to graduate; NCLB consequences

(continued)

State	Name of Standards	High-Stakes Test	Consequences
Mississippi "http://www.mde.k12.ms.us/"	Mississippi Curriculum Frameworks (MCF)	Mississippi Assessment and Accountability Reporting System (MAARS) and End of Course Exams (ECEs) in, algebra, biology, English, and history	Must pass ECEs to graduate; NCLB consequences (linked to MAARS)
Missouri "http://dese.mo.gov/"	The Show-Me Standards	Missouri Assessment Program (MAP)	NCLB consequences
Montana "http://www.bpe.state.mt.us/"	Montana Content and Performance Standards (MCPS)	Montana Comprehensive Assessment System (MontCas)	NCLB consequences
Nebraska "http://www.nde.state.ne.us/"	Nebraska Leading Educational Achievement through Rigorous Nebraska Standards (LEARNS)	School-based Teacher-led Assessment and Reporting System (STARS)	NCLB consequences
Nevada "http://www.doe.nv.gov/"	Nevada Academic Standards (NAS)	High School Proficiency Examination (HSPE), Writing Assessment, andCriterion Referenced Tests (CRTs)	Must pass HSPE to graduate; NCLB consequences (linked to all three)
New Hampshire "http://www.ed.state.nh.us"	Grade Level Expectations (GSEs)	New Hampshire Educational Improvement and Assessment Program (NHEIAP); New England Common Assessment Program (NECAP)	NCLB consequences
New Jersey "http://www.state.nj.us/education/"	New Jersey Core Curriculum Content Standards	New Jersey Assessment of Knowledge and Skills (NJAKS), Grade 8 Proficiency, and High School Proficiency (HSP)	Must pass HSP exam to graduate; NCLB consequences (linked to NJAKS)

(continued)

State	Name of Standards	High-Stakes Test	Consequences
New Mexico "http://www.ped.state.nm.us/"	New Mexico Content Standards and Benchmarks	New Mexico Standards Based Assessment (NMSBA) and New Mexico High School Standards Assessment (NMHSSA)	Must pass MNHSSA to graduate; NCLB consequences (linked to NMSBA)
New York "http://www.nysed.gov/"	Core Subjects/Learning Standards	Regents Examinations	Must pass the Regents Examinations to graduate; NCLB consequences
North Carolina "http://www.ncpublicschools.org/"	North Carolina Standard Course of Study	Pretest-grade 3, End-of-Grade Assessments (EOGs) in grades 3-8; North Carolina Writing Assessment (NCWA) in grades 4, 7, and 10; North Carolina Tests of Computer Skills (NCTC) in grade 8, North Carolina End-of-Course Tests (EOCs) in 10 different high school courses	NCLB consequences
North Dakota "http://www.dpi.state.nd.us/index.shtm"	Content Standards and Achievement Standards in many subjects	North Dakota State Assessment	NCLB consequences
Ohio "http://www.ode.state.oh.us/"	Academic Content Standards	Ohio Graduation Tests (OGTs), Ninth Grade Proficiency Tests, Achievement Tests (grades 3–8)	Must pass OGTs to graduate; NCLB consequences (website does not specify which tests are linked)
Oklahoma "http://www.sde.state.ok.us"	Oklahoma Priority Academic Student Skills (PASS)	Oklahoma Core Curriculum Tests (OCCT's) in grades 3–8; End-of-Instruction Tests (EOIs) in high school for algebra 1, biology 1, English 2, and U.S. history	Must pass EOIs to graduate; NCLB consequences (website does not specify which tests are linked)
Oregon "http://www.ode.state.or.us/"	Academic Content Standards and Benchmark Standards	Oregon Statewide Assessment	NCLB consequences

(continued)

State	Name of Standards	High-Stakes Test	Consequences
Pennsylvania "http://www.pde.state.pa.us"	Content and Achievement Standards	Pennsylvania System of School Assessment (PSSA)	NCLB consequences
Rhode Island "http://www.ridoe.net/standards"	Content and Performance Standards	New England Common Assessment Program (NECAP); New Standards Reference Exams (NSREs)	Information not available on website
South Carolina "http://www.myscschools.com/"	South Carolina Academic Standards	Palmetto Achievement Challenge Tests (PACT)	Schools must develop individual Academic Plans for Students (APSs) for those who score below basic level; NCLB consequences
South Dakota "http://doe.sd.gov/"	South Dakota State Content Standards	Dakota Assessment of Content Standards (DACS); South Dakota State Test of Educational Progress (STEP)	NCLB consequences (linked to STEP)
Tennessee "http://www.state.tn.us/education/"	Curriculum Standards	Tennessee Comprehensive Assessment Program (TCAP)	Must score "proficient" on the Gateway portion of the TCAP to graduate; NCLB consequences
Texas "http://www.tea.state.tx.us/"	Texas Essential Knowledge and Skills (TEKS)	Texas Assessment of Knowledge and Skills (TAKS)	Must score "Satisfactory" on the grade 11 TAKS to graduate; NCLB consequences
Utah "http://www.usoe.k12.ut.us/"	Utah State Core Curriculum	Utah Basic Skills Competency Test (UBSCT); Utah Performance Assessment System for Students (U-PASS)	Must pass UBSCT to graduate; NCLB consequences (linked to U-PASS)
Vermont "http://www.state.vt.us/educ/"	Vermont's Framework of Standards and Learning Opportunities	Vermont Developmental Reading Assessment (DRA), New Standards Reference Exams (NSRE), New England Common Assessment Plan (NECAP)	NCLB consequences (website does not specify which tests are linked)

(continued)

State	Name of Standards	High-Stakes Test	Consequences
Virginia "http://www.pen.k12.va.us/"	Standards of Learning for Virginia Public Schools	Standards of Learning (SOL) Test	NCLB consequences
Washington "http://www.k12.wa.us/"	Essential Academic Learning Requirements (EALRs)	Washington Assessment of Student Learning (WASL)	Must pass to graduate from high school; NCLB consequences
West Virginia "http://osa.k12.wv.us/"	West Virginia Content Standards and Objectives (CSOs)	West Virginia Educational Standards Test (WESTEST)	NCLB consequences
Wisconsin "http://www.dpi.state.wi.us/"	Wisconsin's Model Academic Standards	Wisconsin Knowledge and Concepts Examination– Criterion Referenced Test (WKCE–CRT)	Must pass WKCE–CRT to advance from fourth to fifth and eighth to ninth grades; NCLB consequences
Wyoming "http://www.k12.wy.us/index.asp"	Wyoming State Standards	Proficiency Assessment for Wyoming Students (PAWS)	NCLB consequences

REFERENCES

Cummins, J. (1979). Cognitive/academic language proficiency, linguistic interdependence, the optimum age question and some other matters. *Working Papers on Bilingualism, 19*, 121–129.

Freire, P. (1978). *Pedagogy of the oppressed.* New York: Continuum.

APPENDIX C

Verbs to Help Identify Student Behaviors at Each Level of Bloom's Cognitive Taxonomy

Knowledge		Application	Analysis	Synthesis	Evaluation
cite	arrange	adapt	analyze	arrange	appraise
choose	associate	apply	appraise	assemble	approve
define	clarify	catalog	audit	build	assess
label	classify	chart	break	combine	choose
list	convert	compute	calculate	compile	conclude
locate	describe	consolidate	categorize	compose	confirm
match	diagram	demonstrate	certify	conceive	criticize
name	draw	develop	compare	construct	critique
recall	discuss	employ	contrast	create	diagnose
recognize	estimate	extend	correlate	design	evaluate
record	explain	extrapolate	criticize	devise	judge
repeat	express	generalize	deduce	discover	justify
select	identify	illustrate	defend	draft	prioritize
state	locate	infer	detect	formulate	prove
write	outline	interpolate	diagram	generate	rank
	paraphrase	interpret	differentiate	integrate	rate
	report	manipulate	discriminate	make	recommend
	restate	modify	distinguish	manage	research
	review	order	examine	organize	resolve
	sort	predict	infer	plan	revise
	summarize	prepare	inspect	predict	rule on
	transfer	produce	investigate	prepare	select
	translate	relate	question	propose	support
		sketch	reason	reorder	validate
		submit	separate	reorganize	
		tabulate	solve	set up	
		transcribe	survey	structure	
		use	test	synthesize	
		utilize	uncover		
			verify		

Source: Adapted from work by Kathy V. Waller, PhD, CLS (NCA), National Accrediting Agency for Clinical Laboratory Sciences (NAACLS) Board of Directors (http://www.naacls.org/docs/announcement/writing-objectives.pdf; retrieved November 2004).

APPENDIX D

Verbs to Help Identify Student Behaviors at Each Level of Krathwohl's Affective Taxonomy

Receiving	Responding	Valuing	Organization	Characterizing by Value
accept	agree	adopt	anticipate	act
acknowledge	allow	aid	collaborate	administer
attend (to)	answer	care (for)	confer	advance
follow	ask	complete	consider	advocate
listen	assist	compliment	consult	aid
meet	attempt	contribute	coordinate	challenge
observe	choose	delay	design	change
receive	communicate	encourage	direct	commit
	conform	enforce	establish	counsel
	cooperate	foster	facilitate	criticize
	demonstrate	guide	follow through	debate
	describe	initiate	investigate	defend
	discuss	interact	judge	disagree
	display	join	lead	dispute
	exhibit	justify	manage	empathize
	follow	maintain	modify	enhance
	give	monitor	organize	excuse
	help	praise	oversee	forgive
	identify	preserve	plan	influence
	locate	propose	qualify	motivate
	notify	query	recommend	negotiate
	obey	react	revise	object
	offer	respect	simplify	persevere
	participate	seek	specify	persist
	practice	share	submit	praise
	present	study	synthesize	promote
	read	subscribe	test	question
	relay	suggest	vary	reject
	reply	support	weigh	resolve
	report	thank		seek
	respond	uphold		serve
	select			solve
	try			tolerate

Source: Adapted from work by Kathy V. Waller, Ph.D., C.L.S. (NCA), National Accrediting Agency for Clinical Laboratory Sciences Board of Directors (http://www.naacls.org/docs/announcement/writing-objectives.pdf; retrieved November 2004).

APPENDIX E
Overview of Instructional Strategies

Lecture Usage

Purpose
Present a specific amount of information quickly and efficiently.
Transfer your passion and enthusiasm about a topic to your students.

Benefits
Enable you to present important content that students may not be able to learn on their own.
Provide students with content that is particularly important or difficult to learn directly through books, the Internet, or other project-based activities.
Highlight keys points that best meet your students' interests and needs.

Obstacles
Students are often passive observers during lectures, and may not recall all the information from your lecture.
Attention span of the students.
Boredom.
Students may not understand the content in the manner you have organized it.

Management Logistics/Issues
Focus on the key ideas, skills, facts, and/or principles that your students will use after the lecture.
Provide notes or a graphic organizer that will help students follow along with your lecture.
Move the lesson along at a pace that keeps the students engaged, continually monitor your students' level of engagement, and show enthusiasm and excitement about the topic.

Valid Assessments

Exit cards.

Facts and feelings journal.

Think/pair/share.

Recall of specific information during Q/A or quizzes/tests.

Differentiating Instruction

If an issue is controversial, or multifaceted, represent multiple perspectives during your lecture.

When students' primary language is not the same as the language used for the lecture, and when students have learning difficulties related to listening skills, lecture may not be appropriate. It also becomes critical to teach note-taking skills, speak clearly, and build from graphic organizers.

Technology Enhancements

PowerPoint or other presentation software.

Dynamic visual aids (such as live cameras, video clips, and primary source documents accessed from the Internet).

Question Usage

Purpose

Quickly and efficiently lead students to think about content.

Prod students into thinking more deeply or considering other points of view.

Formatively assess or use for classroom management.

Benefits

Provide guidance for students to think more critically.

Do not take as much time as some other strategies.

Obstacles

Teacher-centered strategy that may be overused.

Include all the students rather than a favored few.

Management Logistics/Issues

Consider appropriate wait time.

Planning question prompts will help assure student practice of higher order thinking.

Quality seminars require a positive and safe learning environment.

Valid Assessments

Questioning itself can be a formative assessment strategy.

Exit cards.

Journals.

Differentiating Instruction

The questions should be adjusted for the needs of individual students.

Technology Enhancements

Student questions can be encouraged through computer lab activities.

Hypertext documents can be used to help students obtain information from websites that help answer questions or encourage consideration of another point of view.

Concept Formation

Purpose

Helps students form a robust understanding of significant concepts in your content area.

Benefits

Provide a structure for students to think through the critical attributes of a concept.

Rather than you telling students about a concept, they form their own understanding.

Students follow a step-by-step process for examining several examples of a given concept in light of the critical attributes, and then draw conclusions about the similarities and differences among these examples.

Obstacles

Preparation by the teacher is extensive.

This works best for examples that possess critical attributes that are established and not dynamic.

Management Logistics/Issues

Concept formation requires teachers to facilitate students' independent work and whole-class interactions. Independent work occurs when students gather data, write their synthesized definitions, develop labels, and engage in the classifying tasks. Whole-class interactions occur when students report their findings, consider differences and similarities, share their labels, and explain their classifying decisions.

Encourage students to think of answers to focus questions and not merely try to guess. Emphasize thinking.

Valid Assessments
   Three classifying tasks:
      Type 1: distinguishing examples from nonexamples.
      Type 2: producing examples
      Type 3: correcting nonexamples
   Quizzes.

Differentiating Instruction
   The structure of the concept formation lesson allows for students to work
      independently.
   During this time you are able to work with students one-on-one or in
      small groups.

Technology Enhancements
   The Internet may allow students to explore examples of concepts in
      depth.
   You are not limited to completing a worksheet, but can have students go
      online to access photos, essays, streaming video, and the like.

Cooperative Learning Usage

Purpose
   Teach new information and broaden current levels of understanding.
   Develop social interaction skills.
   Teach students to work interdependently with classmates.

Benefits
   Academic achievement increases for low- and high-ability students.
   Students learn how to set group goals and structure interdependent
      tasks.
   Increases in classmates' acceptance of others.

Obstacles
   Requires significant amount of class time to allow for group processing.
   May reinforce stereotypes and status of students if the teacher is not care-
      fully monitoring interactions.

Management Logistics/Issues
   Actively monitor each group's progress to assess it both collectively and
      individually.
   Reposition desks and chair to allow for face-to-face group interactions.
   Establish group norms and expectations to keep students on task and to
      help students hold each other accountable.

Consider using a T-chart for social skill development.
Be aware of the progress each group is making.

Valid Assessments

Self assessment.
Peer assessment.
Components of the task need to allow for individual accountability.
T-charts allow for assessment of social skills.
STAD has assessment built into its design.
Rubrics for final projects and/or performances.
Quizzes.

Differentiating Instruction

Differentiation is the key component of cooperative learning. Students
 work together to help differentiate learning uniquely for each member.
 The teacher needs to be sure the group has established goals for interdependent work, and ensure that interactions encourage all members
 to participate, contribute, and succeed.

Technology Enhancements

Research using digital technologies allow for in-depth explorations.
Student/group presentations can be dynamic, interactive, and use
 multimedia.
Projects may be posted to a class website.
Software that encourages collaborative writing.

Simulations, Role-Play, and Dramatization Usage

Purpose

Help students move into the affective and psychomotor domains.
Provide variety.
Have students consider the intricacies and difficulties of real-world
 problems.
Help students understand a new perspective.
Help students develop communication skills.

Benefits

Can be motivating.
Can involve students who may not otherwise participate.
Can be provocative and uniquely interesting.
Encourage creativity.

Obstacles

Can be intimidating or make some students feel uncomfortable.

Can take a large amount of class time.

May not be appropriate for sensitive issues.

Teacher comfort level.

Management Logistics/Issues

Consider ways to help move students from passive to active learning.

Establish a climate that is energized, fun, and supports risk taking.

Be certain students are aware of appropriate behaviors and expectations during unusual classroom activities.

Consider effective group formation activities.

Valid Assessments

Well-designed rubrics that include both process and lesson objective expectations.

Differentiating Instruction

Consider roles appropriate for individual learners.

Physical involvement enhances learning a second language.

The nature of the strategy allows a teacher to work individually with students or in small groups.

Technology Enhancements

Simulation software is available (through, e.g., Tom Snyder Productions).

Discussionsns

Purpose

Teach new information by having students interact with the teacher and each other about class content.

Teach students to think critically (and use other higher-order thinking skills) about a topic.

Teach students to develop the democratic citizenship skill of interacting civilly about controversial issues.

Benefits

Explore an issue in depth.

Develop interaction and social skills.

Develop insight into multiple perspectives around an issue.

Obstacles

Require a significant amount of class time (both for the discussion and
for the preparation).

Depend on students being in control of the interactions.

Management Logistic/Issues

Establish classroom expectations.

Provide adequate time for student preparation.

Help students learn "how to discuss" as well as learn about the topic of
discussion.

Recognize that most issues are multifaceted and have more than a point
and a counterpoint.

Valid Assessments

Dialogical essay.

Exit cards.

Rubrics for determining students' understanding of content and for their
discussion skills.

Differentiating Instruction

Help students understand nonverbal communication.

Require students to critique ideas and not people.

Assign roles to discussants.

Allow students who are shy, not comfortable speaking, or non-English
speakers opportunities to write about what they learned during a
discussion.

Small groups may be better than whole-class discussions because they
promote more talk (the smallest being a group of two during a think/
pair/share activity).

Technology Enhancements

Threaded discussions using the Internet.

Research with digital technologies helps students gain insight into multiple points of view. This includes e-mail and visiting websites for
information.

Posting opinions and policy recommendations to a class website or to an
approved blog.

Student-Directed Investigations

Purpose

Confront students with real world problems and challenges.

Provide an opportunity for active learning.

Benefits

Provide students with choice and allow them to explore issues of personal relevance.

Independent learning while pursing a personal interest.

Gives students an opportunity to perform as experts or professionals.

Can give students an opportunity to take action or volunteer and help meet a need.

Obstacles

Take a large amount of time.

Classroom can be somewhat chaotic as students move in different directions.

Management Logistics/Issues

Development of a community of learners.

Create a work plan together.

Monitor students' schedule.

Valid Assessments

Checklists.

Conferencing.

Portfolios.

Rubrics.

Journals.

Teacher notes.

Differentiating Instruction

Students encouraged to pursue personal interests.

Technology Enhancements

Spreadsheets.

Databases.

Presentation software.

Internet resources.

INDEX